Intellectual Property and Theories of Justice

Also by the editors

Axel Gosseries

PENSER LA JUSTICE ENTRE LES GENERATIONS. DE L'AFFAIRE PERRUCHE A LA REFORME DES RETRAITES

Alain Marciano

POSNER. L'ANALYSE ECONOMIQUE DU DROIT (*with Sophie Harnay*)

DEMOCRACY, FREEDOM AND COERCION. A LAW AND ECONOMICS APPROACH (*edited with Jean-Michel Josselin*)

LAW AND THE STATE. A POLITICAL ECONOMY APPROACH (*edited with Jean-Michel Josselin*)

ELGAR COMPANION TO ECONOMICS AND PHILOSOPHY (*edited with John Davis and Jochen Runde*)

FROM ECONOMIC TO LEGAL COMPETITION. NEW PERSPECTIVES ON LAW AND INSTITUTIONS IN EUROPE (*edited with Jean-Michel Josselin*)

Alain Strowel

DROIT D'AUTEUR ET COPYRIGHT, DIVERGENCES ET CONVERGENCES

DROIT D'AUTEUR ET NUMÉRIQUE: Logiciels, Bases De Données, Multimédia, (*with Est. Derclaye*)

OF AUTHORS AND ORIGINS, ESSAYS ON COPYRIGHT LAW (*edited with B. Sherman*)

PRÉVENTION ET RÉPARATION DES DOMMAGES CAUSÉS PAR LES MÉDIAS (*edited with Fr. Tulkens*)

DROIT D'AUTEUR ET LIBERTÉ D'EXPRESSION. REGARDS FRANCOPHONES, D'EUROPE ET D'AILLEURS (*edited with Fr. Tulkens*)

NOUVEAUTÉS EN MATIÈRE D'EXPERTISE ET DE PROPRIÉTÉ INTELLECTUELLE (*edited with P. Jadoul*)

Intellectual Property and Theories of Justice

Edited by

Axel Gosseries
Fonds de la Recherche Scientifique
and Université catholique de Louvain, Belgium

Alain Marciano
Université de Reims, France

and

Alain Strowel
Facultés Universitaires Saint-Louis, Belgium

palgrave
macmillan

First published 2008 by
PALGRAVE MACMILLAN

Palgrave Macmillan in the UK is an imprint of Macmillan Publishers Limited, registered in England, company number 785998, of Houndmills, Basingstoke, Hampshire RG21 6XS.

Palgrave Macmillan in the US is a division of St Martin's Press LLC, 175 Fifth Avenue, New York, NY 10010.

Palgrave Macmillan is the global academic imprint of the above companies and has companies and representatives throughout the world.

Palgrave® and Macmillan® are registered trademarks in the United States, the United Kingdom, Europe and other countries.

ISBN-13: 978–0–230–00709–3 hardback
ISBN-10: 0–230–00709–0 hardback

This book is printed on paper suitable for recycling and made from fully managed and sustained forest sources. Logging, pulping and manufacturing processes are expected to conform to the environmental regulations of the country of origin.

A catalogue record for this book is available from the British Library.

Library of Congress Cataloging-in-Publication Data
Intellectual property and theories of justice / edited By Axel Gosseries, Alain Marciano, Alain Strowel.
p. cm.
Includes bibliographical references and index.
ISBN 978–0–230–00709–3
1. Intellectual property. 2. Intellectual property—Moral and ethical aspects. I. Gosseries, Axel. II. Marciano, Alain. III. Strowel, Alain.
K1401.I581 2008
346.04′8—dc22 2008021224

10 9 8 7 6 5 4 3 2 1
17 16 15 14 13 12 11 10 09 08

Printed and bound in Great Britain by
CPI Antony Rowe, Chippenham and Eastbourne

Contents

Acknowledgements

The editors would like to thank the Centre for Innovation and Intellectual Property (CIPI) of the Facultés universités St-Louis for organizing, together with the Chaire Hoover d'éthique économique et sociale (Louvain, Belgium), the 2005 international workshop in Brussels, which initiated this editorial project (later joined by more contributors). They also want to warmly thank the anonymous referees who kindly accepted to assess each of the papers at an early stage of their development. Such a book is definitely a collective achievement and it would not have been possible to bring it to existence without them.

Notes on the Editors and Contributors

The editors

Axel Gosseries is a Permanent Research Fellow at the Belgian Fund for Scientific Research National, based at the Chaire Hoover in economic and social ethics, University of Louvain, Belgium. His work in moral and political philosophy focuses specifically on theories of intergenerational justice, tradable quota schemes and the idea of workplace democracy. He is the author of *Penser la justice entre les générations* (2004) and of articles in books and journals including the *Oxford Handbook of Practical Ethics, Economics & Philosophy, Canadian Journal of Philosophy, Politics, Philosophy & Economics, Stanford Encyclopedia of Philosophy, Loyola of Los Angeles Law Review* and *International Economic Review* (forth.).

Alain Marciano is an Associate Professor at the University of Reims Champagne-Ardenne, France. He is the author of *La Philosophie économique* and *Éthiques de l'économie*, a co-editor of the *Elgar Companion to Economics and Philosophy* and one of the main editors of the *Review of Economic Philosophy*. He has published many book chapters and articles in academic journals, including *Constitutional Political Economy*, the *European Journal of the history of Economic Thought*, the *European Journal of Law and Economics, History of Political Economy*, the *International Review in Law and Economics, Journal of History of Economic Thought* and *Public Choice*.

Alain Strowel is a Professor at Saint-Louis University (FUSL, Brussels), the University of Liège and the Catholic University of Brussels-Leuven, where he teaches copyright, design and media law. He is the author of *Droit d'auteur et copyright* (1993) and *Droit d'auteur et numérique: logiciels, bases de données, multimédia* (2001). He also edited *Of Authors and Origins* (with Brad Sherman, 1994), *Prévention et réparation des dommages causés par les médias* (with Fr. Tulkens, 1998) and *Droit d'auteur et liberté d'expression* (with Fr. Tulkens, 2006). A member of the Brussels Bar since 1988, his practice focuses on intellectual property issues in relation to ICT.

The contributors

Daniel Attas is Senior Lecturer in Philosophy and director of the Integrative Programme: Philosophy, Economics, Political Science at the Hebrew University of Jerusalem. His research interests include distributive justice, egalitarianism, libertarianism and property rights. He is the author of *Liberty, Property and Markets: a Critique of Libertarianism* (2005) and has published papers in journals such as *Philosophical Quarterly, Law and Philosophy* and *Politics, Philosophy, and Economics.*

Paul Belleflamme is Professor of Economics at Université catholique de Louvain. He holds an MA in economics from Columbia University (1992) and a PhD in economics from the University of Namur (1997) and was formerly a lecturer in economics at Queen Mary, University of London. He is associate editor of *Information Economics & Policy* and of *e-conomics*, and has published in leading economics journals. His research includes work on the economics of information goods and technologies, coalitions and networks, on collusion, multi-sided markets and the economics of intellectual property.

Alexandra Couto is currently working on her doctorate at Oxford University. She previously completed an MPhil at Oxford and a BA in Geneva. Her research is in political philosophy and moral philosophy, with a particular focus on impartiality. She has published on privacy in *Res Publica.*

Geert Demuijnck is Professor of Ethics and Political Philosophy at the Catholic University of Lille, France. He holds an MA in economics and a PhD in philosophy from the University of Leuven. He has been a Fullbright scholar at the University of Wisconsin-Madison. His interests include issues of distributive justice and the ethical foundations of the welfare state. His papers have appeared in *Imprints, Raisons Politiques* and *Ethical Perspectives.*

Peter Dietsch is assistant professor in the Philosophy Department, Université de Montréal. He holds a PhD in philosophy from the London School of Economics (2004). His research interests centre on questions of distributive justice and issues in the philosophy of economics. He is currently working on a normative evaluation of tax competition. His publications include articles in the *Journal of Social Philosophy* and the *Journal of Moral Philosophy.*

Speranta Dumitru is a post-doctoral research fellow at the CERSES (CNRS and Université Paris-Descartes). She holds a PhD from the Ecole des Hautes Etudes en Sciences Sociales (2004). She taught in the field of political philosophy and ethics at the Universities of Bucharest and Louvain. She published a number of articles on Rawlsian and luck egalitarian matters, including in the *Revue de philosophie économique, Raisons politiques* and *Diogenes*.

Gilles Falquet is Professor of Informatics at the University of Geneva. His research interests include representation, management and access to knowledge through computerised systems. He works on problems related to semantic digital libraries, multilingual knowledge representation and retrieval, and spatialised hypertexts and documents. He is the author of *Java de l'esprit à la méthode* (1999) as well as contributions to *Semantic Digital Libraries. Bringing Digital Libraries to the Next Generation of Internet* (ed. S. Kruk and B. McDaniel, forthcoming), *Ontologies for Urban Development, Studies in Computational Intelligence* (ed. J. Teller, 2007) and *Knowledge Management and Organizational Memories* (ed. R. Dieng and N. Matta, 2002).

Shubha Ghosh is currently Professor of Law at the University of Wisconsin Law School having been Professor of Law at SUNY, Buffalo, Law School for six years. He holds a PhD in Economics from the University of Michigan and a JD from Stanford. He writes on intellectual property as well as legal and market theory.

François Grin is Professor of Economics at the University of Geneva and a visiting professor at the University of Lugano, where he teaches the management of ethnic, linguistic and cultural diversity. He has worked at various universities in Switzerland, Canada and the United States. His research focuses on language economics, education economics and policy evaluation in those areas. His publications include *Language Policy Evaluation and the European Charter for Regional or Minority Languages* (2003), and contributions to *Language Policy: Theory and Method* (ed. T. Ricento, Blackwell, 2006) and the *Encyclopedia of Language and Education* (ed. S. May and N. Hornberger, 2008).

Annabelle Lever is a Fellow in the Philosophy Department, London School of Economics and Political Science. She holds a PhD in Political Science from the MIT (1997). Her book, *On Privacy*, is forthcoming, and she is currently writing *Contemporary Democratic Theory: A Critical Introduction*. She has published articles on privacy and democracy, the secret ballot, compulsory voting, women and rights, and racial profiling, as well as on the ethics of patenting human genes.

Giovanni Battista Ramello is Associate Professor of Industrial Economics at the Università del Piemonte Orientale, Italy, and he chairs the International PhD Programme in Institutions, Economics and Law at Collegio Carlo Alberto (Torino). His research interests include industrial economics, anti-trust and regulation, economic analysis of law and institutions, intellectual property, information goods and knowledge production. He is managing editor of the *European Journal of Comparative Economics*, and has recently published *Property Rights Dynamics: A Law and Economics Perspective* (2007) and *Class Actions for Europe* (2008).

Seana Valentine Shiffrin is Professor of Law and Professor of Philosophy at the University of California, LA. Her research addresses issues concerning autonomy and equality in the foundations of substantive legal areas and in ethics and political philosophy, including distributive justice and accommodation, intellectual property, promising, contracts, freedom of speech, freedom of association and due process. She has published in journals such as *Philosophy and Public Affairs, Philosophical Review* and *Ethics*.

Jonathan Trerise is a Lecturer at Florida International University (Miami). He received his PhD in philosophy from the University of Missouri-Columbia (2007). His current work involves two aspects of intellectual property rights: the implications of their role as incentives and possible solutions to the dispute among various libertarian thinkers on IP rights. He has a paper forthcoming in the *Southwest Philosophy Review*.

Introduction

How (Un)fair is Intellectual Property?

*Axel Gosseries**

Intellectual property (IP) affects many dimensions of our daily lives. It covers four types of rights: patents, copyright (or '*droit d'auteur*'), trade marks and trade secrets. Here, we focus on copyright and patents only. As Varian (2005, pp. 124–5) puts it, IP rights can be analysed through three of the key variables constitutive of their scope. The first is *height*, which is the standard of novelty required to be eligible for protection. The patent regime is more demanding than the copyright regime in this respect, for it requires 'novelty', 'inventiveness' ('non-obviousness' in the US) and the possibility of an industrial application ('usefulness' in the US). The second dimension is *width*, that is, 'the breadth of coverage that the protection offers' (Varian, 2005, p. 125). Copyright offers less protection than patent since it applies to the expression only – not to the use of the ideas – and even allows for some 'fair use' (e.g. 'quotes' or 'parody'). Finally, there is the *duration* of protection. For patents, it is in principle 20 years. For copyright, it was initially 14 years (renewable once) in the 1790 US Copyright Act, but since 1993 (Europe) and 1998 (US) it is granted to the copyright owner for a period extending to 70 years beyond the creator's death (Varian, 2005, p. 122).

Why analyse IP rights through the prism of theories of justice? This concern is not new. Immanuel Kant, for example, wrote in the eighteenth century on moral questions related to the reproduction of books (see Kant, 1995); and we are still in the middle of what Boyle (2003) calls the 'second enclosure' (the first enclosure consisting of gradually fencing off the arable commons starting in the fifteenth century). For what we are facing today is the gradual proprietarisation of our informational commons. Consider the current debates as to whether we should grant patents on living organisms such as the Leder's onco-mouse (Kevles, 2002), on surgical procedures (Garris, 1996; Wear et al., 1998) or on sports methods (such as some athletic moves) (see Kunstadt et al., 1996; Bambauer, 2005). In the same vein, should copyright protection apply to software or choreographic works (Van Camp, 1994)? Coincidental to this gradual informational enclosure, there is the 'free' software movement which is moving in the opposite direction.[1] Clearly, the simultaneous development of these two trends – the second enclosure and free software – calls for a normative analysis. And besides these practical reasons, the very object of IP, with its non-rivalry and non-excludability dimensions, presents theoretical challenges of its own.

We thus need to address questions such as: Is the exclusion of the poor from access to patented drugs not in clear violation of basic human rights? Does peer-to-peer file exchange amount to an unacceptable form of free riding? This requires a good command of the technicalities of IP tools and their legal and economic dimensions, as well as a full grasp of philosophical theories of justice. Let us not misunderstand, however, what is meant here by concerns of justice. Changes in IP status raise two broad types of concern, associated with worries fed respectively by a given conception of the *good life* and a specific theory of *justice*. Consider by analogy an extension of the market by decriminalising prostitution. Some people will be worried that it will affect the way in which we see our affective and sexual relationships. Others will wonder whether women who engage in such activities are not being unjustly treated by those who either hire their services or are their so-called 'protectors'. There is, of course, room for disagreement at both levels (see Sandel, 1998; Boyle, 2003, p. 35). What matters is that 'good life' and 'justice' are both features in the IP debate. We will focus only on the latter in this book. This does not imply, however, that the former is of little importance when it comes to looking at, for example, the ethics of hackers, the flourishing of a culture specific to free software developers or the way in which readers conceive of the nature of collective knowledge.

Theories of justice

Philosophical theories of justice come in many varieties and differ along various dimensions in the ways in which they justify the existence of and how they define the nature of our obligations. Let us consider here a few key elements for those unfamiliar with these theories.[2]

Mutual advantage?

First, how do we justify the very existence of moral obligations and the need for people to comply with them? One of the answers consists in trying to derive the existence (and content) of such obligations from the self-interest of a so-called 'rational' agent. This, of course, raises the question: Why should we be rational? (Kolodny, 2005). Roughly, the 'mutual advantage', or 'contractarian', strategy amounts to showing that it is in each individual's interest to abide by certain social rules, the latter being required to generate a cooperative surplus that will make everyone better off. Gauthier's work (1986) is paradigmatic of such neo-Hobbesianism.

In contrast, other approaches do not try to derive justice from well-understood self-interest. Consider John Locke, who like Thomas Hobbes was a social contract thinker. Unlike the latter, he clearly defended the idea of 'natural' rights pre-existing (rather than derived from) the social contract (see Morris 1999). Hence, Lockean thinkers (referred to as 'libertarians'), among whom Robert Nozick is exemplary, defend such rights independently of any idea of mutual advantage (Nozick, 1974; Vallentyne and Steiner, 2000). Attas' chapter in this volume looks at IP issues from a Lockean perspective. Note that theories such as utilitarianism and egalitarianism are generally also among approaches that do not rely on the concept of mutual advantage.[3]

John Rawls – discussed more specifically in Dumitru and Shiffrin's chapters in this volume – is emblematic of the fact that theories of justice often remain undecided as to whether or not to rely on the idea of mutual advantage (Barry, 1989). In the use of his hypothetical contractual device (the 'original position'), agents are mutually disinterested, not altruistic. With the idea of a veil of ignorance hypothetically concealing some of one's features, ideal agents in the original position are asked to derive principles of justice applicable to all, including themselves. A neo-Hobbesian would ask real agents: 'Look at whether you actually suffer from such and such a congenital handicap and ask yourself which principle of justice would drive your policy on handicap benefits.' In contrast, a Rawlsian would ask a hypothetical agent: 'Imagine that you *could* actually suffer from such and such a congenital handicap (without knowing anything about the probabilities) and ask yourself which principles of justice would drive your policy on handicap benefits'. The two questions are of course quite different. But the original position device still invites us to conceive of justice as having to do with fear for oneself rather than impartiality. Moreover, Rawls' insistence on the idea of *social cooperation* at times brings him close to the neo-Hobbesians (Barry, 1989).

Aggregation vs. distribution

A second key distinction is that between distributivists and aggregativists, which has to do with a dimension separable from the issue of 'metrics' or 'currency' of justice (welfare, opportunity for welfare, capabilities, primary goods, etc). Aggregativism has been well represented by the utilitarians since the time of Jeremy Bentham and John Stuart Mill. Yet, one does not need to be a utilitarian to be an aggregativist, as Trerise illustrates in this volume. Utilitarians are concerned with setting up social institutions in order to maximise the total amount of well-being in society as a whole. Too often 'utilitarianism' is caricatured as 'instrumentalism'. Two of its features are central. First, its metrics: 'utilitas' (i.e. well-being), understood today in most cases as 'preference satisfaction'; second, its aggregativism. Utilitarianism is not primarily concerned about the *distribution* of well-being in society. It cares about its *total amount*, internationally and inter-generationally. In contrast, a typical egalitarian will primarily care about inequalities. For example, welfare egalitarianism will be concerned about reducing inequalities in well-being among people, even if this comes at the cost of reducing the *total* amount of well-being in society.

Fully worked-out theories admittedly turn out to be more complex. Two sources of complexity are worth emphasising. First, one variety of egalitarianism *lato sensu* – referred to as prioritarianism or maximin egalitarianism – does not primarily care about inequalities. Rather, it is concerned with maximising the absolute level of the least well off (Parfit, 1997; Van Parijs, 2003). This means that increasing inequalities may sometimes be judged to be acceptable, not because of a vague trade-off between distributive and aggregative concerns, but if we can show that increasing inequalities is *necessary* to 'improve' the situation of the least well off.

In many cases, reducing inequalities will automatically improve the level of the least well off. However, this is not the case when incentive issues are at stake. The best example here is determining a fair rate of taxation for the highest wage tranches. Under some conditions, the fiscal authorities may have to choose between, on the one hand, a more progressive taxation scheme – reducing the inequalities in disposable income – and, on the other, the concern that a more progressive taxation regime will create a disincentive to work for the most productive workers. This disincentive may be so great that, in the end, the total amount of money raised will be less than what would have been raised had the taxation regime been less progressive, and may in turn mean that less money is available to the least well off. Hence, a choice may have to be made between reducing inequalities and adopting a fiscal regime such that the least well off end up better off than under alternative schemes. This only arises under certain conditions (e.g. in terms of elasticity of productivity to taxation) and it raises moral issues to which we return below.[4] What matters is that the maximin egalitarian version, which amounts to an aggregativo-distributive view, takes seriously the issue of (dis-)incentives to production, crucial in the case of IP.

There is a second qualification to a strict separation of distributivists and aggregativists. Not only do some distributive theories take into account in their principles the reality of incentives. Conversely, aggregative theories are concerned in some circumstances about distributive issues for strictly aggregative reasons. Consider, for example, diminishing marginal utility: that is, the more you have of a given good, the less an additional unit of it will bring you additional well-being. It follows that in order to maximise the return in terms of *aggregate* well-being of a given allocation, it will often be more welfare-maximising to give more to the *poor*. Hence, even strict aggregativists may be concerned about the way in which existing IP rights distribute access to goods such as patented drugs – an issue to which we return in Belleflamme's chapter.

Property and freedom

Finally, there are two dimensions that can be combined in various ways with the previous ones, leading to theories of justice that frame the nature of issues in very different ways. Consider first libertarian approaches that rely more than other theories on the idea of ownership. Such Lockean theories typically begin with an account of who owned the world before any human intervention. It was either owned in common by everyone, or owned by no one, and so up for grabs. Add to this the concept of self-ownership, i.e. that before we engage in any intervention in the world, we own ourselves. The theory then tells us under which conditions appropriating external objects can be fair. The different libertarian views on fair appropriation range from first come, first served – central in patent law – to demanding versions of the Lockean proviso requiring that we leave to others 'as much as is good'. This variety within libertarianism is clearly of significance for libertarian accounts of fair IP.

There may, however, be a strong temptation to focus exclusively on theories of justice for which the concept of property is more central. Hegelian and Lockean accounts of property tend to come first to mind (Hugues, 1988; Drahos, 1996, chs. 3 and 4; Menell, 2000, pp. 157–9; Schroeder 2004). Yet, the concept of property is nothing but a way of accounting for the justification and content of rights and obligations. While the preferred term in the eighteenth century was 'monopoly', it is only since the second world war that the expression 'intellectual property' has become common (Fischer, 1999; see, however, Mossoff, 2007). Similarly, trade mark law was initially part of tort law, not of property law (Fischer, 1999, sect. II-D). We should thus keep a twofold idea in mind when engaging in a normative assessment of IP rights, which is also what Ghosh's chapter invites us to do. On the one hand, as Attas' chapter demonstrates, while theories in which the concept of property seems more at home will look like a natural candidate for such a normative assessment, these very theories may have difficulty justifying strong IP rights. On the other hand, it is both necessary and possible to establish what other theories of justice, which rely more centrally on other concepts such as 'fundamental rights', 'equality' or 'liberty', have to say about IP rights. In short, it is not certain that libertarians will be most sympathetic to IP rights, nor is it true that only libertarians have something to say about IP rights.

In the same vein, we should also look with a critical eye at debates that may appear descriptive while actually pertaining to a normative agenda. Pierre-Joseph Proudhon's critique of the 'land ownership/intellectual property' analogy is emblematic in this respect, as is Ghosh's chapter in this volume. One of Proudhon's claims is that owning what you harvest from your land presupposes that you own the land in the first place. He claims that in order for creators to own the product of their intellectual efforts, they would first need to own some intellectual equivalent of 'the land', which is not the case. As he writes: 'Insofar as a writer is concerned I can see the product. But where is the property? Where could it be? On which *fonds* could it be grounded?'[5] Interestingly enough, Proudhon's conceptual arguments are mixed with (separable) concerns for the fairness of contracts between author and publisher, or risks associated with the reduction of competition (see e.g. 1862, pp. 34–5, 127). His central worry is with copyright held in perpetuity (ibid., pp. 32–5, 63, 70).

Finally, besides the centrality of 'property', the dimension not captured above is *freedom,* which is central to Trerise's chapter. Merely invoking the latter without looking at whose and which freedom we are concerned with is insufficient. Freedom is key to claims for *free* access. IP rights such as moral rights are also aimed at preserving other dimensions of the freedom of creators. What should be stressed here is again that it is not only libertarians who care about freedom. For example, egalitarians (whether of the strict or maximin type) also care about freedom. First, they can endorse the view that the protection of some *basic freedoms* should have priority over the goal of socio-economic equalisation. This is typical of so-called 'liberal egalitarian' views and in particular of Rawls' lexical priority of his principle of 'equal liberty' (see Barry, 1973; Taylor, 2003). Second, many egalitarians also design a metrics (i.e. an account of 'equality *of what*?') such that room is left for individual freedom. This is how Dworkin's choice/circumstance distinction can be read. A Dworkinian will typically claim that disadvantages resulting from people's circumstances (e.g. a congenital handicap) should be fully compensated by society, whereas disadvantages resulting from people's choices (e.g. handicap resulting from a hazardous sporting accident) should not.[6] This is also one way of preserving some freedom for taxpayers while remaining egalitarians. The same holds for *sufficientarian* views on the metrics, limiting the (maximin) egalitarian demands to the provision of resources sufficient to cover people's *basic needs*.[7] Third, egalitarians, as distributivists, will insist that their concern actually amounts to a concern for *redistributing freedom*. They will generally claim that the *means* of exercising freedoms should be a central concern to those who really care about freedom. Not having enough money to buy non-generic drugs clearly raises problems of both equality and freedom. Therefore, redistributing resources, even at the cost of taxing people, amounts to redistributing real freedom.[8]

Non-rivalry and exclusion

Having sketched some of the key dimensions of theories of justice, let us focus on the specifics of IP. Various conceptual and epistemological questions of significant normative and practical consequences arise: Who can be said to be a 'creator' or 'author'? What is the difference between an invention and a discovery? To what extent does an invention/discovery result from individual effort as opposed to being a joint product of a given culture? (see Attas on this). How far is an idea separable from its expression? Does the concept of property really fit with the specifics of patents or copyright? Crucial in understanding the nature of the issues of justice at stake, conceptual issues also potentially enrich the pool of solutions available to address these challenges. By way of introduction, we focus here on the two key characteristics and their implications for the normative assessment of IP.

Non-rivalry

Consider a legal entitlement to a plot of land in comparison to a patent. The total amount of land is limited. Its use by one individual limits the extent to which others can use it. In other words, my neighbours have something to lose from my appropriation, and I have something to lose from relinquishing my property right. In contrast, IP applies to man-made immaterial goods that are by nature non-rival. Non-rivalry in consumption refers to the fact that, for such a good (e.g. an invention made two centuries ago), my use of it does not reduce the degree to which my neighbour can use it.

Exclusive rights on non-rival goods are harder to *justify* than for rival goods. Why? Consider simultaneously a person in desperate need of a life-saving drug and a foreigner 'simply' dying of hunger miles from here. In the IP example, the poor may challenge the alleged unfairness of not giving anything to fund a patented drug formula without a licence. She would ask: 'Whom am I harming since I'm not depriving anyone else from using the drug formula?' In the hunger case, it is the rich who may challenge the unfairness development aid. They will ask: 'Why do I owe these people anything as I'm not responsible for their destitution?' Interestingly enough, challenges invite similar strategies. When confronted with non-rival goods and with one's doubts regarding the unfairness of using other people's inventions, we can either show that we *do* deprive the authors and others of something, and hence justify our moral obligation to contribute on such grounds. Or we may try to show that other grounds for an obligation to contribute obtain. Similarly, in the world poverty and foreign aid debate, we can either try to show that we are *causally* responsible for such poverty and justify part of our obligations to contribute on such grounds (see Pogge, 2002), or we can argue that even if we are not causally responsible for the poorest people's plight, we are nevertheless obliged to them on the grounds of distributive justice. This comparison helps us understand one way in which non-rivalry matters to theories of justice. It jeopardises the grounds of obligations that rely on the assumption that others could be deprived of something by the alleged duty holders.[9] It conveys the idea that there is no scarcity at stake.

Are theories of justice well equipped to identify injustices in the absence of rivalry? Karl Marx's concept of 'exploitation', David Gauthier's treatment of free riding and John Rawls' 'principle of fairness' all offer possible resources; and these are discussed in Dumitru and Demuijnck's chapters. Consider the case of free riding. Gauthier distinguishes parasitism from free riding. While a parasite imposes negative externalities on others, a free rider merely benefits from positive externalities without contributing to the costs of their production. In a non-rival goods context, we thus have to assess whether we find ourselves in a situation of free riding, whether the form of free riding one faces is *unfair* and whether the means set up to prevent it – such as the requirements set in copyleft licences – are not unfair themselves.

One should not underestimate the difficulties involved in accounting for the nature of the unfairness involved in an unfair form of free riding. Consider the following:

> [Piracy of copyrighted operating system software] is conventionally though imprecisely referred to as a form of 'theft'.... While a theft of physical property deprives the property's owner of its use, the 'theft' of intellectual property does not. Indeed if the software pirate, or those who purchase the pirated software from him, could not or would not pay the price charged by the owner of the patented or copyrighted software (this assumes that the owner's ability to price discriminate is limited, so that the owner cannot snag the poorest customers by reducing the price to them to just a shade above the owner's marginal cost), then piracy does not cost the owner any lost sales.
>
> (Posner, 2005, p. 64)

Analysing this is quite complex. First, we need to ask ourselves to what extent it is morally defensible to break the law if the law is considered unjust (see Shiffrin, 2007). Second, even if we leave this dimension aside, what would be unfair if pirates were so poor that they could not buy the good anyway and would not sell it to others? This requires determining whether there is anything wrong if the counterfactual is not better at all for the producer than the piracy case (because the pirates *could not* buy it anyway). Of course, as Posner points out, such a situation results in part from the difficulties involved in price differentiation. We also need to ask ourselves how far poverty can justify breaking the law, even to gain access to what may not be subsistence goods.

Third, imagine that the pirate could (but would not *want to*) buy the good. Here, free riding could be unfair. Reference to the idea of 'theft' obliges us to consider whether piracy really deprives the producer and other consumers of anything. It does in this case. For the non-indigent pirate deprives the producer of the fee he would otherwise earn, and other consumers from benefiting from a lower fee. Non-rivalry means that my *use* of a good does not prevent the use by another of the same good. Yet, we may want to extend the word 'use' beyond mere 'consumption use' to include 'commercial use'. One of the problems is then how to provide separate normative treatment of losses in use value and losses in exchange value (see Attas's chapter in this volume). In short, while piracy by indigents does not impose losses on others in use or exchange value, does it follow that there is nothing unfair in it? Conversely, when pirates are not poor, and when free riding on positive externalities in that case imposes some form of loss on producers and other consumers who do pay, what is the nature of the unfairness at play?[10]

(Un)fair exclusion

Besides being non-rival, the goods to which IP applies will often tend to be *non-excludable*.[11] Non-excludability refers to the fact that enforcing rules of exclusive use may be, if not impossible, at least difficult or costly. In the era of copyists, it took months or even years, not only to get a manuscript sent to a copyist, but also to get it copied by hand. It was also much easier to keep the book under lock and key. Nowadays, quality adjusted copying costs still remain high (e.g. for works of art) (Posner, 2005, p. 66). In contrast, downloading a music file is not only cheap, it is also very difficult to prevent, notwithstanding the development of technological remedies falling under the heading of 'digital rights management'. In short, transmission and copying costs are falling and enforcement costs are rising, partly as a result, the latter making many goods practically non-excludable. If restrictions on downloading commercial music without paying for it are hard to enforce, it is all the more important to rely on potential users' ethos to prevent them as far as possible from acting unfairly. This requires a clear account of why potential downloaders should not take advantage of the work produced by some, and downloaded on payment by others. While the non-excludability of some of the objects of IP makes it *more necessary* to come up with justifications, we have seen that the non-rivalry of such goods makes such justifications *more difficult*. The conjunction of these two facts is thus especially challenging.

Moreover, whenever exclusion is *possible* – IP being in fact premised on such a possibility – we still need to ask ourselves to what extent such exclusion is fair. Interestingly enough, while non-rivalry makes it more difficult to account for what people are *deprived of* by someone's use of an idea, the very same idea of 'absence of deprivation' is also deployed to *defend* IP rights rather than to criticise them. As Nozick (1974, p. 182) writes, 'An inventor's patent does not deprive others of an object which would not exist if not for the inventor.' This pro-IP argument, rather than derived from the non-rival nature of immaterial goods, rests on the idea that an inventor brings to the world an object that *did not exist* before its invention. To address the 'non-rivalry-based' anti-IP challenge, one may want to show that non-rivalry does not prevent the possibility of deprivation (e.g. by insisting on losses in exchange value) or rely on accounts of injustice that are not deprivation-based. To address Nozick's pro-IP argument, one can challenge the individualistic concept of 'invention' underlying his claim and/or show that under a more relevant baseline, others are in fact being deprived of something by the monopoly right granted to the inventor. Attas's discussion illustrates how Lockeans may want to do just that. In particular, they will tend to debate the proper content and scope of so-called Lockean provisos, show that exclusion actually obtains and identify the conditions under which it is unfair.

Yet, the problem of fair exclusion can be analysed by non-Lockean theories as well. For example, in the case of copyright, such exclusion could generate tensions with some *basic freedoms*, such as freedom of expression – an issue to which Couto devotes her chapter. Similarly, Van Houweling (2005) provides us with tools that an *egalitarian* could use to assess the fairness of copyright (see also Rakowski, 1991, pp. 83–7; Menell, 2000, pp. 160–1). Considering creators only, there are three interesting distributive dimensions:

> First, the rights granted by copyright indirectly subsidize some would-be creators by facilitating financing of their work. Copyright thus ensures that creative opportunities are not available solely to the independently wealthy. Second, copyright's limits, including the fair use doctrine, serve the needs of some poorly financed creators by letting them build upon existing copyrighted works without paying for permission. Third, copyright has not, until recently, been enforced

> frequently against those infringers who are unlikely to be able to pay for their uses of copyrighted works.
>
> (Van Houweling, 2005, p. 1540)

On each of these dimensions, Van Houweling examines whether recent technological and legal developments affect the degree to which copyright disadvantages poor creators who creatively incorporate copyrighted material. For example, while disseminating creative work has become much cheaper for poorly financed creators thanks to technological developments, the latter, while possibly increasing the number of copyright violations, also makes copyright enforcement more likely (2005, p. 1564). Similarly, the content of the doctrine of fair use in the US may be evolving adversely for such poor creators (2005, pp. 1565–6).

As Van Houweling acknowledges (2005, p. 1572), merely focusing on financially disadvantaged creators falls short of a comprehensive distributive impact assessment. The publishers–creators relationship also requires close scrutiny. Egalitarians should turn their attention to (poor) readers or listeners, a concern present as far back as in the 1710 Statute of Anne.[12] In this respect, all options have to be considered, including making books available in public libraries, or the possibility of improving the situation of poor potential creators or readers through taxation and transfers more generally (2005, pp. 1576–7). Once completed, a full distributive impact analysis would need to be plugged into the normative apparatus of a given egalitarian theory. For some of these theories, the incentive dimension will also have to be considered (2005, p. 1575), as well as the choice/circumstance aspect.

In the realm of patents, a distributive impact analysis is probably even more crucial, considering e.g. pharmaceutical patents, an issue dealt with by Ghosh, Belleflamme and Dietsch in this volume. Pogge (2008, ch. 9) offers one illustration of how an egalitarian, of a sufficientarian type or not, could proceed. His distributive analysis of various patent regimes looks at four types of affected groups (Pogge, 2008, sect. 9.2). Focusing on what he calls 'essential' medicines, he considers two avenues. The first is poverty-sensitive price differentiation, which includes compulsory licensing. It raises enforcement difficulties when the differential is large (smuggling) and does not seem sufficient to address the problem of drugs to cure so-called orphan diseases (diseases not adopted by the pharmaceutical industry because they offer little financial incentive). The other, which he supports, mixes open access and alternative 'pull' funding (Pogge, 2008, sect. 9.5ff.).[13] Funding takes the form of a specific patent regime (referred to as patent-2) 'that entitles the patent holder, during the life of the patent, to be rewarded out of public funds in proportion to the impact of the invention on the [global burden of disease]' (Pogge, 2008, sect. 9.6). How would it differ from a standard patent and why should it be referred to as a patent rather than as a mere prize? The proposal – a 'median way' proposal in Belleflamme's terminology – amounts to an option for patentees:

> This option is to renounce any veto powers over the manufacture of the patented medicine worldwide in exchange for title to a stream of reward payments proportioned to this medicine's global health impact. By thus converting... its patent-1 into a patent–2, the owner chooses to turn the centerpiece of its patented knowledge into a public good by making the new medicine available for free generic production worldwide. The owner retains all other proprietary rights to its invention.
>
> (Pogge, 2008, sect. 9.6)[14]

Incentives and justice

The incentives dimension is crucial in both justifying and questioning the legitimacy of intellectual property. This is not of interest only for IP issues, since problems of under-investment (in production, commercialisation, etc.) also occur in the case of tangible property. Yet, due to the absence of the *overuse* issue, it becomes much more salient in the case of non-tangible informational goods. This may explain why the incentives dimension is present – admittedly in a particular manner – as far back as the third century BC, in the practice of the inhabitants of the Greek city-state of Sibaris, as reported by Athenaeus in his *Deipnosophists*:

> If any caterer or cook invented a dish of his own which was especially 'choice', it was his privilege that no one else but the inventor himself should adopt the use of it before the lapse of a year, in order that the first man to invent a dish might possess the right of manufacture during that period, so as to encourage others to excel in eager competition with similar inventions.
>
> (Athenaeus, V, pp. 348–9)[15]

Two sets of questions, factual and normative, are to be addressed in examining issues of incentives in relation with IP. Let us briefly introduce each of them in turn. First, at the factual level, we need to ask whether IP rights are efficient (see Nordhaus, 1969). One argument for IP is that in the absence of excludability, creators would neither be able to cover the costs of their investments, nor profit from their work. IP tools therefore constitute one of the means used to preserve such incentives (see Landes and Posner 2003). In the case of patents, other means exist, such as (*ex-ante*) grants and (*ex-post*) prizes.[16] There are, of course, significant differences between monopoly rights and rewards (see e.g. Shavell and Van Ypersele 2001). Prizes will be funded differently from patents. The criteria on the basis of which they are granted may also differ. One should not underestimate the controversy here. While at the normative level readers will discover that the various theories of justice are far from providing us with a straightforward defence of the fairness of IP, it is crucial to keep in mind that, at the factual level, the economic literature is equally far from concluding in a clear-cut manner that IP rights are efficient in promoting innovation. For while IP generates incentives, it simultaneously erects barriers to access or to further production by others.

Even for tangible property, the extent of the productivity gains resulting from the first enclosure (i.e. of land) is a contested matter (Boyle, 2003, p. 36, n. 9). In the case of IP, one interesting challenge is the flourishing of free software initiatives. Economists are trying to understand why actors invest in collaborative projects from which they cannot expect any exclusive property rights. Of course, free or open source software does not mean that *no* intellectual property rights are relied upon. Yet, they are tools that prevent private appropriation rather than guarantee such private appropriation. More generally, Belleflamme reviews some of the economic literature in this respect in the case of patents. And the issue is also central to Ramello, Shiffrin and Dietsch's chapters too. In the end, what is at stake is probably not whether we should abandon IP rights altogether, which not even free software does. Rather, it is about finding out what are the most efficient ways of designing them.

Moreover, efficiency concerns are not the end of the matter. They need to be plugged into theories of justice. Let me make a few remarks in this respect. First, one may be tempted to consider that taking efficiency concerns seriously necessarily commits us to a utilitarian approach. This is not the case. Maximin egalitarianism – which is neither utilitarian nor a natural rights theory – typically takes efficiency concerns seriously, in ways that go beyond merely defending a trade-off or convergence (see Ramello's chapter on the latter). Even Lockean theories could have their own way of incorporating efficiency concerns (see Attas on separating invention from proprietarisation). In the end, the challenge is to identify to what extent and how each theory of justice characterises in its own language *underproduction* as such as a problem of justice.

Consider maximin egalitarianism ('prioritarianism') again. From a regulator's perspective, it is crucial to decide on the extent to which inequalities in access to inventions (and inequalities in opportunity for welfare more generally) are more worrying than the possibility that the least well off will end up not being as well off as they possibly could, especially in the long term. One could, for example, envisage a case in which granting a patent for a limited period will simultaneously increase inequalities between those having access during that period and those who do not, while improving the situation of the worst off in the long term, beyond the patent's life. This shows that it is not only a matter of deciding whether we agree to increase inequalities in order to improve the situation of the least well off. It is also about whether it is fair to sacrifice the least well off today in order to improve the situation of the least well off in the future. This illustrates one way in which distributive theories of justice could incorporate a concern for productivity, i.e. for the quantity and quality of inventions and literary production.

However, there is a second key normative issue relevant to maximin egalitarians. It is one thing to consider what IP regulators should decide, taking the elasticity of economic actors as given. It is another to decide whether economic actors – pharmaceutical researchers, writers, etc. – are fair in stipulating the conditions under which they are willing to engage in creative activity (see Cohen, 1992; Van Parijs 2003). This is the focus of Shiffrin's chapter. Both the regulator's choices and the investor's demands can be assessed from a normative perspective, and to some extent independently. Moreover, one should not think that the only problem with a fair price is one of access to information as to the true costs an investor incurs. It is admittedly hard for an outsider to know what the costs really are. Yet, it is also normatively difficult to define, assuming full information, what a fair demand would be. For patent demands are no different from price demands. They raise classic problems of fair wage and fair price. Consider the following two possible counterfactual tests of fair price. One tells us that the fair price is the one that obtains if the market is operating under perfect competition conditions. Alternatively, a fair price is one that the parties would be willing to accept if the initial background conditions are fair. Such a 'fair price' (translated into fair scope, fair breadth and fair length of the IP protection) will have to be compared with existing proposals and properly located within the whole theory of justice at play.

The chapters

Having set the stage, let us turn to the chapters. They are presented in two parts. The first, General Approaches, deals with a full account from one theory of justice or with core issues in principle applicable to the whole IP realm. Part II, Specific Issues, focuses on dimensions more specifically relevant to copyright or to patent.

General approaches

In the first chapter, Attas asks whether IP can be justified on Lockean grounds. He shows that the idea of self-preservation is central for Locke to justify the need for property. Understanding Locke's justification of property in this 'sufficientarian' way is not without implications. Attas then asks how IP rights – if any – could be allocated among people, relying on a positive and a negative principle of appropriation, the latter consisting in a set of so-called Lockean provisos. As to the former principle, regarding the allegedly special relationship between intellectual products and self-ownership (defended by Ayan Rand among others), Attas insists on the implications of finding out whether and what a solitary individual could possibly invent or discover in the absence of a surrounding culture. As to the negative principle, he stresses the importance of the 'non-waste' proviso, given the fact that IP rights are monopoly rights and that price differentiation may be difficult to achieve. Finally, he discusses the difficulties involved in identifying who invented (the problem of origination) and what was invented (the problem of individuation). For Attas, IP rights are better justified on non-Lockean than Lockean grounds.

One candidate is Rawls' theory, which is the focus of Dumitru's chapter. One entry point relevant to IP is Rawls' 'thin theory' of the good and its Aristotelian principle. For Dumitru, the satisfaction of this principle, for which the performance of complex activities matters, calls for an extensive right to copy. A second Rawlsian entry point is the fact that non-rivalry seems to leave us outside the 'circumstances of justice'. Dumitru shows that at the interconnection of the ideas of circumstances of justice and free riding, as envisaged by Rawls in his 'principle of fairness', there is a real dilemma at work. Finally, she insists on the fact that if monopoly rights can be assessed through the lens of the ability of their impact to satisfy the second Rawlsian principle, we too often forget that monopoly rights also entail *inequalities of rights per se*. This calls for a separate analysis, Dumitru argues, that cannot be reduced to a concern for incentives and distributive impact, the case of independent inventors (also central to Trerise's chapter) being an ideal test in this respect.

It is essential to look at the various resources in Locke or Rawls, as well as the shortcomings of these theories. We can also do things the other way round – start from efficiency and then bridge them with concerns of social justice. One way of doing so consists in focusing on the incentive argument for IP, which is central to Ramello's chapter. He insists on a set of specific features of 'knowledge' as a good. For example, it is both an output ready for consumption and an input for further knowledge production. It requires sharing. It is hard to divide into discrete units. Such features help us to understand that efficiency concerns should go beyond a mere focus on 'incentives to create'. The latter requires exclusion, which in turn generates its own inefficiencies. Ramello claims that, in the end, optimal efficiency may require only *weak* IP rights. This explains why *convergence* between efficiency concerns and social justice may not be out of reach.

Shiffrin also discusses incentives, illustrating her argument with derivative works protection, which is ideal in considering knowledge as an input for further production. Her chapter deals with two concerns. The first is in line with Ramello's: does strong IP protection of derivative works encourage outputs from primary creators that are superior to the work that would have been produced in the absence of strong IP rights? Insisting on the uncertainties involved, Shriffin shows what taking the right to free speech seriously entails in such a context. The second part of her argument brings us back to Rawls. Shiffrin focuses on the extent to which one should regard demands for incentives as fair, following the work of G. A. Cohen. Among five possible motives underlying demands for incentives, she argues that only one could ground justified demands.

Ghosh's chapter looks at the issue more strictly from the angle of legal theory. He stresses the relevance of conceptual work to a normative approach. As Proudhon did in the case of copyright, Ghosh points to disanalogies between IP and real property. In US patent law, the interpretation of what 'prior art' is, the idea of the 'one sale bar' and rules applicable to patent infringement suits do not fit with the characteristics of real property. The same holds, Ghosh claims, for rules on infringement, the doctrine of fair use or the possibility of compulsory licensing in the case of copyright. This invites considering IP law as the regulation of creative activity rather than simply recognising rights on objects, which according to Ghosh has normative implications. The latter are fleshed our through four models (expertise, civic participation, market failure and management) each of them constituting possible rationales for IP regulation. The relevance of Ghosh's approach is illustrated with respect to the 'experimental use' exception in US patent law as it applies to pharmaceutical products.

The final chapter in Part I examines the significance of Pierce's type/token distinction. It translates as a distinction between strong (type-protecting) and weak (token-protecting) IP rights. It also provides us with an extra tool to contrast real property and IP, complementary to Proudhon or Ghosh. Trerise not only explains what *weak* IP rights might consist in. He also offers a defence of such weak rights, relying on two possible liberty-focused conceptions: total liberty consequentialism and what he refers to as libertarianism. Each of these views has its own ways of balancing losses and gains of liberties consecutive to weak or strong IP rights.

Specific issues

We then move on to chapters that focus on specific issues – three on copyright and three on patents. In Demuijnck's chapter, peer-to-peer file-sharing is taken as an example of how theories of justice deal with the issue of free riding – an issue also discussed by Dumitru. Starting from Gauthier's 'parasitism/free riding' distinction and building on Cullity's work, Demuijnck spells out three conditions under which free riding can be said to be unfair. He proceeds with a close examination of the reasons why and cases in which these conditions are *not* met in the case of peer-to-peer MP3 file-sharing. Demuijnck shows that two paradigmatic cases of free riding should not be seen as unfair: when music is downloaded from a creator who is a winner of what turns out to be an unfair 'winner-takes-it-all' music market, or when the downloader has no purchasing power due to poverty. Special attention is devoted in this respect to the doctrine of fair use.

Couto's angle is quite different since she aims at mapping through a conceptual tree the various ways in which one can articulate copyright and freedom of speech, the latter being often invoked as a reason to restrict copyright. Among the various options, let us highlight a few of her points. First, she insists on the need to take seriously the possibility that, in most cases, copyright and freedom of expression may actually not conflict, especially if we consider the doctrine of fair use. Second, she looks at different ways of handling cases in which the two rights do nevertheless conflict – some of which are related to the strategies envisaged in Trerise's chapter. In particular, if there are no reasons to rank the value of one of the rights above the other, one way of addressing conflicts of rights is qualitative analysis. This draws on Waldron's concept of 'internal connection' and on Rawls' considerations on free speech.

In the third chapter on copyright-related issues, Falquet and Grin look at a very specific problem: the choice between free/open source and proprietary software, from the perspective of linguistic justice, i.e. a concern for the distribution of resources between native speakers of different *natural* languages. More specifically, they are concerned with risks of linguistic hegemony, stressing four advantages it gives its native speakers. Is free/open source software less or more prone to generate such hegemony than proprietary software? There seems to be no overriding reason to believe that one or the other is more likely to preserve/generate more diversity in natural languages. Falquet and Grin identify other aspects of software products that may affect language dynamics. Moreover, reasons other than linguistic justice may justify a case for free/open source software.

Three chapters on patents follow. In the first, Belleflamme asks – in ways complementary to Ramello – whether patents are efficient. He presents the essential tension facing any IP design between avoiding underproduction and preventing underutilisation. There is a 'patent paradox': we observe a very significant development in patent counts while innovators keep saying that patents are not that important. The 'patent portfolio theory', an explanation for it, insists on the importance for firms to file collections of related patents rather than individual ones. Does the strengthening and development in patent counts encourage more innovation? The empirical literature is at best sketchy, Belleflamme concludes. He then focuses on pharmaceutical patents. They can be regarded as more efficient in fostering innovation than in other sectors. At the same time, the aggregate loss in disability-adjusted life years following from patents on drugs is much more significant than from patents on other products. These two facts make things especially challenging and call for properly designed IP rules, in particular when it comes to drugs for diseases that are endemic in the developing world. Special attention is devoted to the 'disease burden incentive system', the 'transferable patent exclusivity right' and the 'priority-review voucher' proposals, i.e. median way proposals that try to align private return with social return.

Dietsch's chapter also looks at patents on drugs. It starts from a needs principle, indicates what is special about health needs and defends a cosmopolitan scope for this principle. Dietsch argues that the needs principle should have priority over the justice-based or consequence-based justifications of patents. In the latter case, this has to do with what he refers to as production failure and access failure. As in Belleflamme, this entails the need to compare alternative policy options, which Dietsch does in the last section of his chapter.

The third and final chapter on patents turns to a different issue, i.e. whether patenting human genes should be allowed. Lever develops three main theses. One is that the gap between owning and patenting should not be overestimated, which contrasts with Proudhon, Ghosh and Trerise above. Second, she explains that, while patents on human genes do not threaten people's bodily integrity, they do threaten their jobs and careers as well as their health and well-being. Finally, she shows why objections to patents on human genes based on the idea of human dignity do not need to be treated as 'unreasonable' and are no more controversial than the justifications usually invoked to defend the need for patents.

Acknowledgement

I wish to thank S. Dumitru, A. Marciano, Y. Ménière, A. Strowel, P. Van Parijs and P. Waelbroeck for their help in the preparation of this introduction.

Notes

1. On open source/free software, see Evans et al. (2001); Stallman (2002).
2. For a standard presentation, see Kymlicka (2002).
3. See Heath (2006) for an example of a mutual advantage egalitarian.
4. On the moral dimension, see Cohen (1992). Note that the argument from incentives differs from a mere trickle-down argument. For a discussion of trickle-down in the copyright context, see Van Houweling (2005, p. 1575).
5. Proudhon (1862, p. 19) 'Je vois bien, en ce qui concerne l'écrivain, le produit; mais où est la propriété? Où peut-elle être? Sur quels fonds allons-nous l'établir?' (our translation).
6. On choice and circumstance, see Dworkin (2000).
7. On sufficientarianism, see Casal (2007).
8. On the concept of 'real freedom', see Van Parijs (1995).
9. There is another way in which the importance of non-rivalry can be expressed. The first enclosure movement (the privatisation of common land) could be justified through reference to the risks of overuse and of underinvestment. In the case of the second enclosure (fencing off ideas), the non-rivalry of the goods at stake is such that only the problem of underinvestment may arise in its absence, not the problem of overuse. See Boyle (2003).

10. Interestingly enough, both Stallman (2002) and Posner (2005) use the term 'piracy'. The word has been used for long in the IP context (see Mossoff, 2007, n. 193). While Martin Luther used the term in the sixteenth century to refer to unauthorised printers of his bible (Tallmo, 2005), Stallman uses it to point to developers breaching the rules set up in a free software scheme, and Posner uses it to refer to mere users (or intermediaries) of copyrighted software. It is also used in the field of traditional medicinal knowledge as bio-piracy. The key for theories of justice is to translate the word into the language of the relevant theory of justice. For example, a Gauthier defender will have to decide whether what is referred to as piracy in a given context belongs to the realm of parasitism or free riding, and in the latter case, whether it is fair or not.
11. Jefferson (1813), in his famous letter to Isaac McPherson, emphasised and distinguished non-excludability ('but the moment it is divulged, it forces itself into the possession of every one') and non-rivalry ('its peculiar character, too, is that no one possesses the less, because every other possesses the whole of it').
12. See www.copyrighthistory.com/anne.html.
13. On open source bio-technology, see Hope (2004).
14. See www.patent2.org.
15. See Jefferson: 'Inventions then cannot, in nature, be a subject of property. Society may give an exclusive right to the profits arising from them, as an encouragement to men to pursue ideas which may produce utility, but this may or may not be done, according to the will and convenience of the society, without claim or complaint from anybody.' Thomas Jefferson (1813) to Isaac McPherson. See, however, Mossoff (2007).
16. See also Pogge's distinction between 'push' and 'pull' strategies (2008, sect. 9.5).

References

Athenaeus (1927–41), *The Deipnosophists*, 7 vols, trans. C. Burton Gulick. London, New York and Cambridge, MA: Harvard University Press.

Bambauer, D. (2005) Legal Responses to the Challenges of Sports Patents, *Harvard J. of Law & Technology*, 18(2): 401–33.

Barry, B. (1973) John Rawls and the Priority of Liberty, *Philosophy and Public Affairs*, 2(3): 274–90.

Barry, B. (1989), *A Treatise on Social Justice. 1: Theories of Justice*, Berkeley, CA: University of California Press.

Beitz, C. (2005) The Moral Rights of Creators of Artistic and Literary Work, *Journal of Political Philosophy*, 13(3): 330–58.

Boyle, J. (2003) The Second Enclosure Movement and the Construction of the Public Domain, *Law and Contemporary Problems*, 66: 33–74.

Casal, P. (2007) 'Why Sufficiency is not Enough', *Ethics*, 117: 296–326.

Cohen, G. A. (1992) Incentives, Inequality and Community, *The Tanner Lectures on Human Values*. Salt Lake City: University of Utah Press, pp. 261–329.

Drahos, P. (1996), *A Philosophy of Intellectual Property*. Aldershot: Ashgate.

Dworkin, R. (2000) *Sovereign Virtue. The Theory and Practice of Equality.* Cambridge, MA and London: Harvard University Press.
Epstein, R. (2005) Liberty versus Property? Cracks in the Foundations of Copyright Law, *San Diego Law Review*, 42(1): 1–28.
Evans, D. S., Reddy, B., Layne-Farrar B. and A. (2001) Open Source Software, 32pp. (manuscript on file with the author)
Fisher, W. W. III (1999) The Growth of Intellectual Property: A History of the Ownership of Ideas in the United States, cyber.law.harvard.edu/property99/history.html.
Garris, J. (1996) The Case for Patenting Medical Procedures, *American Journal of Law and Medicine*, 22(1): 85–108.
Gauthier, D. (1986) *Morals by Agreement.* Oxford: Clarendon Press.
Ghosh, R. A. (ed.) (2005) *CODE. Collaborative Ownership of the Digital Economy.* Cambridge, MA: MIT Press.
Heath, J. (2006) On the Scope of Egalitarian Justice, *Les Ateliers de l'éthique*, 1(1): 21–41.
Hettinger, E. (1989) Justifying Intellectual Property, *Philosophy & Public Affairs*, 18: 31–52.
Hope, J. (2004) Open Source Biotechnology. PhD Thesis, Australian National University: Canberra, RSSS & Faculty of Law, 266pp. available at: opensource.mit.edu/papers/hope.pdf.
Hugues, J. (1988) The Philosophy of Intellectual Property, *Georgetown Law Journal*, 77, 287.
Jefferson, T. (1903) Letter from Thomas Jefferson to Isaac McPherson (13 August 1813), in A. Lipscomb (ed.) *The Writings of Thomas Jefferson.* Washington, DC: Thomas Jefferson Memorial Association, pp. 333–5.
Kant, E. (1995) *Qu'est-ce qu'un livre?* Paris: Presses universitaires de France.
Kevles, D. (2002) Of Mice and Money. The Story of the World's First Animal Patent, *Daedalus*, Spring: 78–88.
Kirzner, I. (1981) Entrepreneurship, Entitlement, and Economic Justice, in J. Paul (ed.) *Reading Nozick. Essays on Anarchy, State and Utopia.* Totowa, NJ: Rowman & Littlefield, pp. 383–411.
Kolodny, N. (2005) Why Be Rational? *Mind*, 114 (455): 509–63.
Kunstadt, R., Kieff, S. and Kramer, F. and R. (1996) Are Sports Moves Next on IP Law? *National Law Journal*, 20 May, C1.
Kymlicka, W. (2002) *Contemporary Political Philosophy: An Introduction*, 2nd edn. Oxford: Oxford University Press.
Landes, W. and Posner, R. (2003) *The Economic Structure of Intellectual Property Law.* Cambridge, MA: Harvard University Press.
Menell, P. (2000) Intellectual Property: General Theories, in B. Bouckaert and G. de Geest (eds), *Encyclopedia of Law & Economics*, II. Cheltenham: Edward Elgar, pp. 129–72. Available at: encyclo.findlaw.com/1600book.pdf.
Moore, A. (1997) A Lockean Theory of Intellectual Property, *Hamline Law Review*, 21: 65–108.
Morris, C. (ed.) (1999) *The Social Contract Theorists. Critical Essays on Hobbes, Locke, and Rousseau.* Lanham, MD: Rowman & Littlefield.
Mossoff, A. (2007) Who Cares What Thomas Jefferson Thought about Patents? Re-evaluating the Patent 'Privilege' in Historical Context, *Cornell Law Review*, 92, 953–1012.

Nordhaus, W. (1969) *Invention, Growth and Welfare: A Theoretical Treatment of Technological Change*. Cambridge, MA: MIT Press.

Nozick, R. (1974), *Anarchy, State and Utopia*. Oxford and Cambridge, MA: Blackwell.

Outterson, K. (2006) Patent Buy-outs for Global Disease Innovations for Low- and Middle-income Countries, *American Journal of Law and Medicine*, 32: 159–73. Available at: ssrn.com/abstract=873402.

Parfit, D. (1997) Equality and Priority, *Ratio*, 10(3): 202–21.

Pogge, T. (2008) *World Poverty and Human Rights. Cosmopolitan Responsibilities and Reforms*, 2nd edn. Cambridge: Polity Press.

Posner, R. (2005) Intellectual Property: The Law and Economics Approach, *Journal of Economic Perspectives*, 19(2): 57–73.

Proudhon, P. -J. (1862), *Les Majorats littéraires. Examen d'un projet de loi ayant pour but de créer au profit des auteurs, inventeurs et artistes, un monopole perpétuel*. Brussels: Office de la publicité.

Rakowski E. (1991), *Equal Justice*. Oxford: Clarendon Press.

Samuelson, P., Davis, R., Kapor, M. and Reichman, J. (1994) A Manifesto Concerning the Legal Protection of Computer Programs, *Columbia Law Review*, 94: 2308–431.

Sandel, M. (1998) What Money Can't Buy: The Moral Limits of Markets, *The Tanner Lectures on Human Values*. Salt Lake City: University of Utah Press, pp. 87–122.

Shavell, S. and Van Ypersele, T. (2001) Rewards versus Intellectual Property Rights, *Journal of Law and Economics*, 44(2), 525–47.

Shiffrin, S. (2001) Lockean Arguments for Private Intellectual Property, in S. Munzer (ed.) *New Essays in the Legal and Political Theory of Property*. Cambridge: Cambridge University Press, pp. 38–167.

Shiffrin S. (2007) Intellectual Property Theory, in R. Goodin and P. Pettit (eds.) *The Blackwell Companion to Contemporary Political Philosophy*. Oxford: Blackwell, pp. 653–68.

Shroeder, J. (2004) Unnatural Rights: Hegel and Intellectual Property, *Cardozo School of Law, Working paper*, 80, 48pp. Available at: papers.ssrn.com/sol3/papers.cfm?abstract_id=518182.

Stallman, R. (2002) *Free Software, Free Society. The Selected Essays of Richard M. Stallman*, ed. J. Gay. Boston, MA: Free Software Foundation.

Tallmö, K.-E. (2005) The Misunderstood Idea of Copyright, www.nisus.se/archive/050902e.html.

Taylor, R. (2003) Rawls's Defense of the Priority of Liberty: A Kantian Reconstruction, *Philosophy and Public Affairs*, 31(3): 246–71.

Vallentyne, P. and Steiner, H. (eds.) (2000) *Left-libertarianism and its Critics: The Contemporary Debate*. New York: Palgrave Macmillan.

Van Camp, J. (1994) Copyright of Choreographic Works, in S. F. Breimer, R. Thorne and J. D. Vieira (eds.) *1994–95 Entertainment, Publishing and the Arts Handbook*. New York: Clark, Boardman & Callaghan, pp. 59–92.

Van Houweling, M. S. (2005) Distributive Values in Copyright, *Texas Law Review*, 83(6): 1535–79.

Van Parijs, P. (1995) *Real Freedom for All. What (if Anything) Can Justify Capitalism?* Oxford: Oxford University Press.

Van Parijs, P. (2003) Difference Principles, in S. Freeman (ed.) *The Cambridge Companion to John Rawls*. Cambrige, Cambridge University Press, pp. 200–40.
Varian, H. (2005) Copying and Copyright, *Journal of Economic Perspectives*, 19(2): 121–38.
Waelbroeck, P. (2006) Evolution du marché de la musique préenrégistrée à l'ère numérique, *Reflets et Perspectives de la vie économique*, XLV(4): 83–92.
Wear, S., Coles, W., Szcygiel, A., McEvoy, C. and Pegels, C. (1998) Patenting Medical and Surgical Techniques: An Ethical-Legal Analysis, *Journal of Medicine and Philosophy*, 23(1): 75–97.

Part I
General Approaches

1

Lockean Justifications of Intellectual Property

Daniel Attas

Locke's theory of property is one of the more influential readily available accounts. In *Two Treatises of Government* he discusses only tangible property, and it would be somewhat anachronistic to think that he had given any systematic thought to the matter of ownership of ideas.[1] Nonetheless, as information increasingly becomes a central aspect of the economy, and with it the increasing legal protection afforded by intellectual property, the need for a theoretical justification arises. Going back to Locke's theory in search of such a justification is one obvious option.

The main purpose of this chapter is to explore the possibility of extending Locke's theory with respect to tangible property so that it might offer a feasible theoretical basis for intellectual property too. The main conclusion is that such an attempt must fail.

Locke's theory comes in three parts: first, a general justification of property which serves to explain why assets ought to be under the exclusive control of individuals; second, a positive method of private appropriation whereby an individual acquires a *prima facie* exclusive claim to previously commonly held natural resources; and third, a negative requirement that other individuals' crucial interests are not harmed by such an appropriation whereby it receives its final approval.

This chapter follows Locke's threefold structure. For each part I present the basic Lockean argument, pointing out the main problems of the theory as it applies to material objects. I then discuss the difficulties involved in applying that part of the theory to the sphere of ideas. Finally, I focus on what I take to be a central aspect of intellectual property that raises the problems of application for each part of the theory.

Two preliminary points are warranted.

First, to qualify as Lockean (or neo-Lockean), the kind of right a theory of property must argue for is a *natural* right, based on a notion of entitlement rather than on desert or on incentive, both of which allow degrees and fine-tuning to adjust the reward to its justification. It follows that it is a *direct* right to the thing, not a contractual right, i.e. not a consequence of agreeing to certain conditions attached to the selling of a material object that embodies the idea. It also follows that it is a right in perpetuity; therefore we would expect that, if we are able to justify ownership of ideas from a Lockean perspective, these will be at odds with the most common forms of institutionalised intellectual property, such as patents and copyrights that are limited in time.

That brings me to the second point I want to emphasise. My question is this: can a Lockean (or neo-Lockean) theory of property justify private ownership of ideas? I am not asking if such a theory can justify the kind of IP regimes institutionalised today. It is evident that certain aspects of these regimes – such as fair use, limited duration, and so forth – make it impossible to justify them on Lockean grounds. My argument seeks to show that any kind of regime that recognises ownership of ideas, whatever its specifics, cannot find its grounds in Lockean theory.

General justification of property

Lockean theory with respect to tangible property

Locke begins his account with a general justification property: an explanation of why property is necessary or justified at all. Property is introduced as a solution to a practical problem. Were there no special need to divide the world into bundles of exclusive control the very notion of property would make no justificatory sense. For Locke, the problem is the need to enable persons to provide for their own subsistence:

> men, being once born, have a right to their preservation, and consequently to meat and drink, and such other things, as nature affords for their subsistence
>
> ...yet being given for the use of men, there must of necessity be a means to appropriate them some way or other before they can be of any use, or at all beneficial to any particular man
>
> (Locke, 1960/1698, pp. 285, 286f)

In order to survive, people must eat and drink, perhaps wear protective clothing and inhabit a dwelling. To do this they must take natural resources, initially not owned, and make them their exclusive property. This is a crucial background supposition that gives the subsequent discussion its urgency and ultimate justification. It also situates the basic notion of self-preservation as the dominant principle within the theory so that any consequences of the theory that might come into conflict with it would be checked or overridden.

Though it seems reasonable that food and drink must exclude others in the process of their consumption, it is far from clear that this implies a property right in any interesting sense. For a property right includes not merely use, but also control, management and the right to transfer. Yet these incidents do not apply in the case of a chewed, swallowed and digested apple, for example. If what I am permitted to take from nature is what I need to eat and drink, then I may do just that. Of course, in a slightly more advanced economy I may want to specialise in apples, say, and trade them for your eggs. Exclusive property rights are certainly required to allow a division of labour to develop and for the possibility of trade, but it does not follow that these are necessary for subsistence.[2]

Rights to clothing and shelter, in so far as they are justified as necessary means of subsistence, may not be used in any way other than that. This allows such little discretion regarding how these assets may be used that it is hardly plausible to call whatever rights one may have in respect of these property rights. Nevertheless, whatever rights these are they would need to be exclusive if even a minimal degree of privacy is to be secured.

We may need exclusive rights over agricultural land, but then again, only over the amount necessary to produce our subsistence needs, that is to say, the produce that we are likely to consume. Other raw material, such as timber or metal required to produce tools and machinery for the production of subsistence needs, does not necessarily need to be our exclusive property. These can sometimes be used more efficiently when shared rather than privately owned. It is even less plausible that land for recreation requires exclusivity for its effective use, though it might need a rationing mechanism for its most efficient use. For example, public parks and beaches might have opening and closing hours and a restriction on the number of people on the premises at any one time. The same goes for some material consumption goods such as books or DVDs. Sharing through public libraries might be a more efficient system than private possession.[3]

So subsistence may be very weak grounds to establish a general justification of property. It can justify only use (consumption) and then only with respect to a narrow range of objects. Contemporary Lockeans typically demote the idea of subsistence, but they must appeal to some other value instead. They must explain why property is important at all, what fundamental interest it satisfies, prior to the particular justification of who rightly owns what. They might appeal to the value of freedom: I cannot really be free unless I have a material domain within my exclusive control.

Another possible basis for the general justification of exclusive property might be as a means to welfare or the pursuit of long-term life plans. According to Loren Lomasky, persons 'have a natural interest in having things'. That interest amounts to the ability to employ the object in the furtherance of one's project. Since control of such objects is a necessary condition of being able to pursue one's projects, there is an interest not merely in having objects but also in being accorded property rights with respect to them (Lomasky, 1987, pp. 120–1). Such a basis seems a more promising avenue for a general justification of property. It allows for more elaborate goods and for a wider range. Land or diamonds, food or mansions, can be part of a project. After all, at least in so far as we are considering material objects as a means to the pursuit of happiness, anything can be such that necessitates exclusive control.

One more justification for exclusive property is to avoid what is known as the tragedy of the commons (Hardin, 1968). When land and other resources are not privately owned there appears to be a robust internal logic for individuals to overuse the asset and to under-maintain it. A common grazing ground provides the paradigmatic example where for each individual farmer it seems rational to add one more animal to the common, for he will gain the full benefits of adding that animal yet the cost will be equally distributed among all users. Privatisation of the land will internalise the costs and prompt owners to invest in the asset and guard against its degradation due to excessive use. Thus exclusive private property is a necessary means for the efficient use of natural resources.[4]

One problem with this influential account is that it is inconsistent with historical experience (see Levine 1980; Rose 1986). The commons were a system that operated efficiently for several hundred years in Europe and even longer in other parts of the world. Their demise was less a result of inefficiencies and more the outcome of an avaricious campaign of enclosure led by the growing number of capitalist farmers. Moreover, the argument seems to conflate collective control with no control of an asset. The fact that the commons are not owned does not mean that they cannot be regulated by the community, as indeed they were in various ways (Levine, 1980, pp. 86–8).

Application to intellectual property

Further difficulties are encountered in the application of the different proposed bases for a general justification of property to intellectual products. We saw that even for material goods exclusivity is not necessary in order to secure the basic interest that might be thought to ground a general justification of property in the first place. It appears to be even more tenuous to require exclusivity with respect to ideas.

Though exclusive use of material goods might be necessary for their consumption, it does not seem to be so in the case of ideas. Ideas are not literally consumed. Unlike food, drink and, at a slower rate, clothing and housing, ideas are not destroyed in the process of their use; they suffer no wear and tear. Of course, they might depreciate in value, but that is only because of the appearance of more useful and advanced technological innovation, or because they are replaced by other styles. In any case, ideas lose their value only when they are succeeded by other ideas. Moreover, the same ideas can be used simultaneously by an unlimited number of people. Use by one does not hinder use by another. This point has been raised countless times.

Seana Shiffrin, though she makes the same point about ideas in general, thinks that at least some intellectual works do require exclusive control for their effective use (Shiffrin, 2001, p.157). She cites two examples. The first relates to the products of creative processes that need, at key stages of their development, a certain degree of isolation or protection from too much interference. Forced publication might prove so disruptive as to inhibit the full effective use of these ideas. Her second example is intimate intellectual products, such as diaries, revealing personal letters, and so forth. Public display and scrutiny would 'disrupt the pure full expression of the author's personality'. No doubt, public exposure can be debilitating and might kill some ideas before they reach fruition. But to think that exclusive property rights might follow from this is to confuse property with much lesser rights of use. For example, secrecy, as the right not to disclose an idea in my mind, is not sufficient for a full-blown notion of property. Likewise, privacy as the protection of an intimate domain is also insufficient for property. These protect against the forced publication of what is under my control. Property, on the other hand, effectively enters only after an idea is publicised. It guarantees the continued exclusive use and control of an idea that others might get to know about since it is not kept secret. This is not to maintain that privacy in one's own diary or secrecy in the ideas one is in the process of developing is unjustified. What I am denying is that property in ideas is necessary to provide such secrecy or privacy. So I think Shiffrin's examples do not present an exception to the thought that ideas, unlike some material objects, do not require for their effective use the kind of exclusive control that property affords.

Similar considerations apply to freedom as the basis of a general justification of property. The free use of an idea by one person does not exclude the possibility of another to use the same idea freely. There seems to be no reason grounded on freedom for granting exclusive rights to control ideas. Moreover, exclusive rights to ideas arguably restrict freedom in ways more severe than those by which material property restricts freedom. If exclusive rights to material objects restrict everyone other than the owner to use those objects freely; exclusive rights to ideas restrict everyone from using objects they fully own or their own bodies in ways specified by the owned idea. If a certain way of performing an action, such as a productive process or a dance, is patented, non-owners are to that extent unfree. Tom Palmer insists that 'property rights in tangible objects do not restrict liberty at all – they simply restrain action. Intellectual property rights, on the other hand, do restrict liberty' (Palmer, 1990, p. 831;. cf. Moore's response, 1997, p. 84). This may be taking the contrast a little too far. Whatever the supposed difference between restraining action and restricting freedom, tangible property certainly restricts freedom in so far as it prohibits the use of material objects owned by another. Nevertheless, there is a real contrast in the sense that tangible property and intellectual property restrict liberty in different ways. IP restricts freedom in the same way that a law against smoking, for example, might restrict people from this activity. It is a restriction that is not conditional on your lack of access to the material conditions for performing the action. You may have the space, time and tobacco, but you will still be prohibited from using them in the specified ways. Yet the legitimacy of law stems from the idea of political authority or sovereignty from which follows a moral obligation of compliance. Property, on the other hand, does not imply a right to control people. Palmer is correct if his point is that there is something qualitatively different between the restriction of freedom by control of ideas and that by control of tangible objects, though, at least in theory, they may be extensionally equivalent. Substantial ownership of tangible objects might become as restrictive. If all land is privately owned, dwellers are bound to accept any conditions the owner might impose within his dominion. It is hard to see how this kind of unfreedom might be any better.

Ideas can certainly be made use of in the various projects one chooses to pursue. But there seems to be no necessity for these ideas to be exclusively owned. We can all use the same ideas simultaneously and none will be worse-off for it. No doubt, the market value of these ideas will decrease significantly the more widely available they become. If my project is an entrepreneurial venture, it may indeed be frustrated. Making money is the only project I can conceive of that might necessitate exclusive control of ideas. To be sure, money can be instrumental in the realisation of our projects. The more money we have, the more of our projects we will be able to fulfil. Why is this not a plausible interest for grounding property rights within a Lockean justification? As a preliminary reply I can only reiterate the point that whatever advantages may be obtained from the *use* of an idea can be secured without excluding anyone from a comparable use. Whereas excluding others appears to be a regrettable though necessary condition of obtaining *any* advantage from material resources, in the case of ideas most advantages are available without exclusion. I am not suggesting that profit is an illegitimate purpose or activity, nor that money cannot contribute to an autonomous life. Only that if this is the basis, it robs the general justification of property of the moral urgency that is associated with subsistence or an autonomous life.

Nor, it seems, could avoiding the tragedy of the commons justify the private ownership of ideas. Ideas cannot be overexploited or undermaintained since they are not subject to physical deterioration. Perhaps the contrary – a free flow of ideas might enable and encourage more creativity and innovation, which would enhance rather than impoverish the commons.

Ideas are non-rival

Before asking 'who owns what?' we should answer the question 'why should anybody own anything at all?' The kind of answers proposed by Lockean theories simply do not apply to ideas and intellectual products. The crucial problem of applying a Lockean general justification of property to the realm of ideas is in the often cited fact that ideas are non-rival. They can be used simultaneously by everyone without their use-value being diminished.

My insistence on the non-rivalry of use-value, ignoring the losses in exchange-value, might appear to some as unwarranted. Though use-value is not reduced by simultaneous access to ideas, the value these ideas carry in a market most certainly is (or so the objection goes). Why could this competitive interest in excluding others from the use of ideas not justify a property right in them? I have already hinted at a deep disanalogy between intellectual products and tangible products as well as between rivalry in use and rivalry in exchange. I now want to present the case more explicitly and cogently. The problem of tangible goods is that, generally speaking, greater use reduces both their use-value and their exchange-value. For example, a swimming pool will be less valuable for the bathers the more crowded it is, and consequently they will be willing to pay less and the owner will probably charge more to restrain usage. Control of these goods, as provided by rights of ownership, is necessary to check or ration use and to protect their value in use. The use-value of intellectual goods, on the other hand, does not decrease with greater use. *Nor does their exchange-value*. Indeed, in certain cases, their use- and exchange-value are likely to *increase* with increased use. If millions use Microsoft Windows (even if many do so illegally) it does not affect the use-value of the software or the exchange-value (roughly speaking) as long as permission to use is restricted and payment may be obtained. The value of Windows may increase with wider use due to compatibility and network effects. Control of intellectual products, as provided by rights of ownership, is not necessary to check, use and protect their value in use. Its only purpose is to secure the extraction of an increased pay for use. But note that this is not an integral aspect of the concept of ownership. If someone were to set up a lemonade stall next to mine, thereby reducing the market value of my lemonade and my stall, I would have no legitimate complaint – or at least not a complaint based on property. But it is this sort of interest that intellectual property is designed to protect. Moreover, it is the only interest that might require property rights to intellectual products in the first place, since interests in use are in any case safe even without such protection.

One final point is that in the context of a Lockean general justification of property the concern with exchange-value makes little sense. In a state of nature, where we are considering the recognition of rudimentary property rights prior to any sort of society-wide contractual arrangement, we can understand the kind of interests in use a prospective owner might have. But the sorts of interest in exchange-value, which already presuppose a more elaborate social context and developed economy, seem conceptually premature.

The non-rivalrous nature of ideas casts serious doubt on the notion of a natural property right in intellectual products. Lacking any basis of the sort that provides a general justification of property, it is not clear why there should be property rights in ideas at all, even before we begin allocating the various objects to different individuals. Some neo-Lockeans deny the need for a general justification of property. The rest of this chapter, dealing with a particular justification of property, goes along with them to some extent.

Positive principle of appropriation

Appropriation of material resources

The second part of a Lockean theory of property is a particular justification of property. It must explain why a particular individual should own a specific asset. When distributions are regulated by rules of property, people own whatever they do because they received it from the previous owners either as a gift or as part of an exchange. Even so, long as it might be, this regressive chain of transfers must reach a point where something unowned becomes the private property of an individual. A theory of property such as this must advance a positive principle of original acquisition. Some action on the part of the individual must make it the case that certain parts of the natural world become his property and must be recognised as such. In Locke's account, self-ownership and labour fill this role. In virtue of these, a person can take something out of the common and mark it in such a way that it becomes his private property.

> every man has a property in his own person.... The labour of his body, and the work of his hands, we may say are properly his. Whatsoever then he removes out of the state that nature hath provided, and left it in, he hath mixed his labour with, and joined to it something that is his own, and thereby makes it his property.
>
> (1960/1698, p. 288)

The principle of self-ownership states that every individual owns his own body, in the same way he might own an animal. Thus, he enjoys all the rights of control, income and transfer with respect to his own body. Hence, he would also own each of his body organs taken separately. By the same token he would own any of his body products (hair, fingernails, blood, etc.), as well as the activity of his body. At least for Locke and most of his successors this principle is taken as self-evident.

Arguably, there are better ways to capture the intuitive moral status of our bodies that do not rely on such a proprietorial view of our relation to our own bodies (Attas, 2000; 2005, pp. 49–79). Setting aside this concern, were there a way to extend the kind of privileged status one has with respect to one's body so that it might also encompass parts of the natural world, we could see how one might come to own not only one's body and its products, but also some external resources. For Locke, labour provides such a means.

By labouring on the natural world one mixes one's labour, in Locke's notorious phrase, with some unowned resources. If private property in the newly created object is not respected, in so far as that object contains some self-owned labour, one's self-ownership is violated. Thus one can come to acquire private property in natural resources by infusing them with self-owned substance. It is difficult to view this argument in any way other than metaphorical. On a literal reading there seems to be no end to the problems it raises. Labour in this argument has to be owned and mixed, but depending on its meaning, it cannot be both (see Day, 1966, p. 212; Waldron, 1988, p. 181). Even if labour can be owned and mixed in objects, why would that be a reason for a person to gain ownership over the unowned resource rather than to lose her ownership over her labour? (Nozick, 1974, p. 174f).

Labour could be considered either as a sign of virtue, such as industriousness, or as adding value to the thing laboured on, or of somehow benefiting everyone. As such, it might be thought, labour's deserved reward is a property right in the thing laboured on (see Becker, 1977, pp. 48–56; Gaus and Lomasky, 1990, p. 498; Munzer, 1990, ch. 10; Annis and Bohanon, 1992, pp. 538–43; Spinello, 2003). One problem with a desert argument for appropriation is that appropriation, by its nature, applies only to the first person to act in the relevant way. But if ownership is a fitting reward for the value-adding, general benefiting virtue of labour, it should apply to *all* consequent labouring, not just the first instance (Miller, 1980, p. 9; Waldron, 1988, pp. 203–4; Thomson, 1990, p. 326). Another problem with the desert argument is that if adding value or benefit by labouring on an unowned resource justifies the appropriation of the thing laboured on as a deserved reward, then, by the same principle, subtracting value or harming by labouring on your own property would justify the expropriation of the thing laboured on. And it is not clear what could be an appropriate penalty for subtracting value from an unowned resource. Moreover, even if one deserves a reward for labour, why is the *whole* thing laboured on a proper reward rather than just a part of it? And why is *ownership* of the thing (including management, income and power of transfer) a fitting reward rather than its consumption, a priority in use or any other lesser interest? (Becker, 1977, p. 51; Waldron, 1988, p. 205).

Though labour as a basis for appropriation is intuitively strong, it raises many problems. Another path taken by neo-Lockeans is the idea of material incorporated in one's ongoing project. If the world is originally unowned and I designate some material resource publicising my intention of integrating it into my project, this might be seen as sufficient grounds for appropriation.

One thought common to both this line of argument and to the argument based on labour is the idea that the world is originally unowned, that neither anyone in particular, nor humanity collectively has any innate claim of ownership on natural resources. There are things to be said in favour of this assumption as well as in favour of the contrary assumption. I shall merely note here that the argument crucially depends on this controversial premise (see Attas, 2003; 2005, pp. 113–18). If the world was jointly owned, no unilateral act lacking agreement could possibly justify the privatisation of collectively owned resources.

Though appropriation by labour does appear to have some initial plausibility, I have identified several complexities it needs to overcome. Whatever the merits of this approach for tangible property, the case of intellectual property raises further insurmountable difficulties, to which we now turn.

Application to intellectual property

On a very simple notion of intellectual creativity, ideas are simply extensions of the self. That is to say, mental products such as ideas, inventions, works of art, and so on, come into being as parts of the mind, in the same way as body products, such as hair or blood, come into being as parts of the body. Since we own our body, we also own its products; if we similarly own our mind, we also own our mind's products. Were Locke to have given any thought to the idea of intellectual property when he was writing *Of Civil Government*, he might have said not only that 'The labour of his body, and the work of his hands', but also that the *ideas of his mind*, 'we may say are properly his'. There is no real need to 'appropriate' anything in the genuine sense, since these things come into the world already attached to persons having foundational rights of self-ownership with respect to them.

In the same vein, Adam Moore asserts that 'while all matter, owned or unowned, already exists, the same is not true of intellectual property... it seems that many intellectual works are created *ex nihilo* – from nothing' (1997, p. 76). What follows from this seems to him so self-evident that he adds: 'If we have rights to control anything, it is the contents of our minds' (ibid., p. 78). But such a statement, if true, can hardly be the basis of intellectual property. In fact, it seems inconsistent with intellectual property. Controlling the contents of our minds is not equivalent to controlling ideas *originating* in our minds when they are *outside* our minds. And that is the crux of IP. Controlling ideas originating in our minds when they are in other minds violates the principle of others' right to control the contents of *their* minds. Anyway, this statement makes the idea of original acquisition, by labour or any other way, irrelevant. We 'own' it because it is there – that is to say, in our minds.

Shiffrin objects to this line of reasoning on similar grounds.

> completion and publication of a work seems to effect a separation from the private self. It is not clear that the values animating self-ownership can sensibly be extended to protect individuals' ability to disperse aspects of themselves into the public domain while simultaneously retaining complete control over them.
>
> (2001, p. 165)

She asks us to imagine a person who cuts her hair and throws it around in public. Does she continue to have the right to exclude others from its use? Shiffrin suggests that such control cannot be based on the values of autonomy or physical security that underlie the right of self-ownership. Analogously, once publicised, ideas must lose whatever protection self-ownership affords them while they were held in the privacy of one's mind. I agree that if these are the values we care about, it would be hard to see how we could justify control of dispersed body products. But it would also be unclear how we could justify self-ownership in the first place. Taking the idea of ownership of one's body seriously, rather than referring to some extensive set of personal freedoms, separation of body parts from the body does not imply a loss of title. If I own a tree I also own the fruits and I continue owning them even after they drop or are picked. Deliberately throwing my hair on the ground in public view might be conventionally considered relinquishing title to my hair. But publishing my ideas can hardly be considered so. In sum, if some ideas emanate from our minds alone and we own our minds in the same way that we own our bodies, then we continue to own the ideas once they are publicised.

If this is the basis of rights to intellectual products, then there is no parallel to material property and the elaborate framework for original appropriation turns out to be unnecessary. The structure of a Lockean theory of appropriation includes an unowned common and a means by which individuals can privatise parts of that common. This structure, developed within a material conception of assets, seems unsuited to the sphere of ideas. What would be the unowned intellectual common? Perhaps it is the kind of historical basic knowledge available to all, and by working on this infrastructure and making use of that knowledge one may come to develop new ideas, innovations and artistic creations. Now, in the simple material framework of Lockean appropriation, by working on the common one appropriates bits of that common. But in the intellectual analogue, no one would seriously suggest that by developing certain ideas one comes to own the previously unowned foundational knowledge at the basis of these new ideas. The disanalogy gets deeper still. We come to own things previously unowned because labour imbued them with our selves, so that denying from us exclusive control over them would compromise our self-ownership. Or refusing to grant exclusive control of a material object incorporated in a project will defy our attempts to pursue that project. But the non-rivalrous nature of ideas casts its long shadow here too. Control of a non-rivalrous asset such as ideas by their very nature is not necessary for controlling our selves or for pursuing our projects.

On the simple material model we recognise, on some commonsensical notion, that a product may embody the labour of an individual person alone as well as some unworked natural substance. This might justify ownership of the complete object. In the realm of ideas there is no 'natural substance'. One way or another, all ideas are mental products. Facts may be just out there, but knowledge, methods and imagination all ultimately emanate from a mind. If we begin questioning the origination of ideas we come to doubt not only the plausibility of owning the underlying knowledge to a new idea, but also the individual ownership of whatever is new about that idea.

I now turn to explore in more detail the problem of origination.

The problem of origination

We can classify ideas for our purposes in a rough and ready manner as discoveries, inventions and creations. The first concern a set of facts that exist independently of human perception. The task of science is to bring these facts to light. The second are the technological innovations that put to some use the underlying ideas of science. The third are ideas that are apparently created *ex nihilo* – they are the work of novelists and artists.

It is very difficult to view scientific discoveries as the product of individuals emanating from their minds alone, and using no resources in the process other than the internal resources of the individual. Surely, they exist independently, even if labour is required to bring them to light. The fact itself (a law of physics, the make-up of a molecule, the correlation between a gene and a behavioural trait, and so on) is not the product of human labour. The effort expended in revealing it and bringing the idea to light might deserve some compensation, but there seems to be no Lockean basis for granting ownership over the idea itself.

Moreover, not all discoveries are the result of a conscious attempt and focused effort to search for and ascertain a fact. Occasionally, scientists stumble on a discovery. In such cases the match between the labour expended and the serendipitous outcome becomes even vaguer and the prize of ownership more difficult to justify. When a conscious effort is made, it is done within the framework of an existing – dominant or emerging – paradigm which includes the kind of questions asked, the theory assumed and the methodology used.

A salient aspect of both scientific discoveries and technological inventions is how often they appear to occur to different people at roughly the same time. As long ago as 1922, William Ogburn and Dorothy Thomas documented almost 150 independent and more or less simultaneous major discoveries and inventions. Classic cases include the development of calculus by both Newton and Leibniz; the proposal of evolutionary theory by both Darwin and Wallace; and the invention of the telephone by both Bell and Gray.

The more technologically advanced a society, the more likely are multiple independent discoveries and inventions. To be granted a patent in the United States the applicant must be considered the 'first to invent' and not merely the first to file an application. Sometimes two or more applications for the same invention are received within a short time of each other. In cases such as these the Patent and Trademark Office must investigate to determine which is the first. Some 200 cases of this kind are filed each year (Kingston, 2004, pp. 209–20).

Some (e.g. Merton, 1961) have taken this as confirmation of a social deterministic theory of invention. Rather than a heroic account, these are seen as the inevitable outcome of historical social circumstances that make them ripe for the taking.[5] I am making the much weaker, almost trivial claim that the phenomena of multiple inventions support the idea that inventions and discoveries cannot be considered the product of a lone inventor. Much of their substance is owed to circumstances, common knowledge, a social problem awaiting a solution, a methodology of technological innovation based primarily on imitation and piecemeal improvement, and chance.

Literary and artistic creations seem the best candidates for the notion of products of an individual mind. The odds that two writers will write virtually the same book, or two composers the same musical score, are infinitesimally small. But even artistic works cannot be considered as created in a social vacuum. Story plots and artistic themes are often borrowed from real life. The artist presents an impression of something that exists independently.[6] At other times the artist or writer take their cue from earlier works – plays adapted from novels, paintings that reinterpret old masters.[7] Even abstract expressionists, who allegedly use only internal resources and their individuality to express themselves on canvas, make use of a style, develop within a school, and so on. They make a statement that can only be comprehensible within a context of a social practice of creative art (Friedland, 2001, pp. 185–99).[8]

Richard Spinello deridingly identifies the problem of origination, or what he calls authorship, as a postmodern concern. While offering a Lockean justification of intellectual property, he raises three objections to 'radically revising the concept of authorship and disengaging the concept of property from intellectual and creative endeavors' (Spinello, 2003, pp. 7–8). His first concern is that if the thought that we cannot easily identify an originator of an idea were to become generally accepted, 'we will end up diluting intellectual property laws to the detriment of innovation'. Now, this is not the sort of argument a Lockean can make. We can indeed solve the origination problem conventionally and construct a notion of authorship for the sake of putting into place a system of incentives. But we cannot then take this notion as metaphysically fundamental and employ it in a Lockean justification of property. Second, Spinello is worried that 'if the post-modern deconstruction of the author is taken to its logical conclusion ... if all creation is communal, how do we hold anyone accountable for egregious acts of plagiarism or for a tract full of defamatory remarks?' He seems to believe that ownership and accountability stand or fall together; that if we cannot attribute authorship as a basis for ownership, we will not be able to attribute agency as a basis for accountability. But there is no obstacle to ascribing responsibility to individual acts such as plagiarism and defamation without considering the results of these acts as original or owned. There is no question when expressing some harmful or fallacious idea of who it is that is putting across the idea and who may be held accountable for the performance of that act. What we are questioning is the originality of the content of that idea. Third, Spinello believes that challenging the idea of authorship entails a rejection of the common-sense idea of originality. We do, it is true, distinguish genuine original art from copy-cats, imitations and strong influences. This is a common-sense idea of which we would not be easily willing to dispose. A valid account of Mozart composing *Don Giovanni* 'does not suggest that there were no influences or tendencies outside the composer, but those influences do not fully explain his creative activity'. This is all that is required to raise the problem of origination with credibility. External influences do not *fully* explain the creative activity but, Spinello agrees, they do explain some. The question is how we disentangle the real contribution of the author from the contribution of a wider culture within which the author works. Even if there were a natural right to property, it would apply only to that part of the product that we can attribute to the 'author', not to the whole product. Hence, the product cannot be wholly attributed to an author, and there is nothing especially postmodernist about that claim.

The non-rivalrous nature of ideas robs a Lockean theory of property from its general justification. But even if ideas were not non-rival, and their effective use required exclusivity, it would be difficult even in theory to pinpoint the individual to whom we could attribute the production of the idea. Although we could imagine a first and solitary human being gathering and hunting to satisfy his needs, it is more difficult to form a coherent image of a person inventing or making discoveries in a social-scientific vacuum. A theory of appropriation that depends on a one-to-one relation between producer and product is useless in the case of intellectual products.

Negative principle of appropriation

The proviso with respect to material resources

The third and final part of a Lockean theory of property posits a negative condition on appropriations. It is a condition that, out of concern for the interest of others, limits the kind or amount of resources that may be privatised in this way. Thus, a resource laboured upon or incorporated in one's project will only become one's property if it complies with the stated condition. The *prima facie* claim generated by the positive aspect of the principle of original acquisition is finalised only if it meets the terms set by the Lockean proviso.

Locke proposes two such provisos. The first is the *non-spoilage proviso* and it appears to follow from the same rationale of the general justification of property, namely, subsistence or self-preservation:

> The same law of nature that does by this give us property, does also bound that property too ... As much as any one can make use of to any advantage of life before it spoils; so much he may by his labour fix a property in.
>
> (Locke, 1960/1698, p. 290)

This can be interpreted quite literally in the sense that spoiled food is an offence against the provider of all food and His intentions. Or perhaps an expression of greed, taking more than one could hope to make use of, as a vice one ought to suppress. Indeed, the proviso appears to apply primarily to gathered fruit and hunted game. Concerning these Locke says:

> But if they perished, in his possession, without their due use; if the fruits rotted, or the venison putrified, before he could spend it, he offended against the common law of nature, and was liable to be punished; he invaded his neighbour's share, for he had *no right, farther than his use* called for any of them, and they might serve to afford him conveniences of life.
>
> (ibid., p.295; emphasis in the original).

Here it appears that violating the non-spoilage proviso is an offence against others, an invasion of a neighbour's share. The problem with letting food rot is not so much the vice of greed or acting against God's purposes, but the waste involved when others who could make use of it are denied access to it. Similar considerations concern ownership of land:

> if either the grass of his inclosure rotted on the ground, or the fruit of his planting perished without gathering, and laying up, this part of the earth, notwithstanding his inclosure, was still to be looked on as waste, and might be the possession of any other.
>
> (ibid.)

If a person encloses more land than he could usefully employ so that crops perish before they are gathered, the proviso is breached. Thus, not only does he lose his ownership of the fruits of the land, but also of the land itself. This is an important point: the non-spoilage proviso is motivated not by the aesthetic of rotting fruit or the insult to the Creator, but by what is denied other needy people. Thus it does not understand waste as the ruin or perishing of foodstuffs, but the non-use, abuse or misuse, that is to say, the criminally inefficient use, of resources.[9]

Now it is sometimes claimed that the introduction of money in Locke's scheme, without contract and prior to the formation of civil society, overcomes the non-spoilage proviso (Hughes, 1988/9, pp. 325f). For money, 'a lasting thing that men might keep without spoiling' (Locke, 1960/1698, p. 300), removed the limit to accumulation. Whereas before the introduction of money people could accumulate only as much as they could make use of, they can now accumulate durables indefinitely. But money does not eradicate the notion of non-waste itself. It allows the accumulation of wealth, and therefore enables great inequalities to which the tacit consent of all is allegedly given (ibid., p. 302). But it continues to prohibit the accumulation of perishables, and it should consistently still forbid the non-efficient use of land.

Neo-Lockeans usually ignore the non-waste proviso, either because they think it is transcended and no longer applicable in a money society, or, like Nozick, they think that it is redundant if Locke's other proviso – to leave enough and as good for others – is met (Nozick, 1974, pp. 175f). After asserting that labour sets apart the natural resource and makes it the labourer's property, Locke adds what sounds like an afterthought: 'at least where there is enough and as good left in common for others' (Locke, 1960/1698, p. 288).[10]

In a world where practically everything is owned, the idea of leaving anything, let alone enough and as good, seems hopelessly unrealistic. Nozick and others following in his footsteps think that the crucial point of the proviso is that no one's position is worsened. If that is the case, no one can reasonably complain. But this is exceptionally vague. The phrase 'worsening someone's position' can be interpreted more or less stringently in each of several dimensions. Nozick and other neo-Lockeans assume a very weak interpretation of the phrase in all possible dimensions. I have argued elsewhere that though this might be necessary to permit the creation of any property rights at all, it makes the proviso, whatever its rationale, highly unattractive. It is unlikely that a strong case could be made in favour of such a weak version (Attas, 2003; 2005, pp. 100–13).

Application to intellectual property

The non-spoilage proviso seems not to apply at all to intellectual products. Ideas do not rot or perish. If they become outdated it is only due to improvements through which more advanced or more fashionable ideas are made available. Thus a proviso that restricts appropriation to what can be made use of before it decays sets no limits on private property of ideas.

However, if we understand waste not as the ruin or rotting of perishables, but as the recklessly suboptimal use of resources, then the appropriation of intellectual products can definitely be checked by a non-waste proviso. Intellectual property widely and routinely denies use from all those who cannot or will not pay for it. Though in the case of tangible assets such a restriction is necessary for the enjoyment of most advantages, in the case of intellectual products it is not.

Consider the following. A commercial firm will typically adopt a pricing strategy that maximises their profits, not one that maximises their sales. Consequently, some technology will be made available only to the few who can afford it, even though more people could conceivably enjoy it with its production still viable. That is to say, in many cases the technology can be more widely shared without jeopardising the economic basis of its production. This is exacerbated by the monopolistic control held by the owners of intellectual property. Lacking any competition, their maximising strategy will tend to restrict even further the user base. In one intuitive sense, therefore, intellectual property can lead to waste.

How does Locke's other condition apply to intellectual products? According to contemporary understandings of the 'enough and as good' proviso, an original acquisition is permitted if it does not worsen anyone's material well-being. Our initial thought concerning intellectual products might be that since nothing that previously existed is now denied others, no one can be said to be harmed by private property in ideas. As Nozick put it: 'An inventor's patent does not deprive others of an object which would not exist if not for the inventor' (1974, p.182; see also Moore, 1997, pp. 80–2; Spinello, 2003, p. 10). Moreover, since ideas that did not previously exist are now made available to anyone willing to pay for them, it seems that the situation of at least some people other than the owner is improved by the appropriation. One might also argue, along with Hughes, that the proviso is satisfied since new ideas, even when privately owned, provide springboards for the generation of more ideas to everyone's benefit (1989/9, pp. 319, 322).

However, this line of reasoning appears to involve some sort of confusion. Though invention arguably harms no one, perhaps even benefits everyone, appropriation surely harms everyone other than the owner. The invention or discovery of an idea is not required to satisfy the condition of not worsening others' situation. It is the propertisation of an idea that must adhere to such a proviso. Whether an invention or discovery worsens or benefits people's situation, private ownership of an idea (even if that idea is new) restricts everyone in the use that would otherwise be freely available. In this sense, at any rate, all intellectual property violates the proviso. The fact that new ideas can contribute to the generation of even more ideas can only benefit those who would come up with the further developed ideas since under the regime we are considering these too will become the private property of their creators.

There is perhaps an implicit assumption that invention and propertisation stand and fall together. That without the promise of ownership there would not be an incentive to create, invent or discover. Though it seems reasonable to assume that there would be less of an incentive, there is ample empirical evidence that at least some intellectual work would continue nonetheless. Many of the most valued discoveries and works of art were produced and developed without the protection of intellectual property. To name the most obvious: the wheel, the alphabet, the Bible, the works of Homer, Archimedes, Shakespeare, Guttenberg, Bach, Leonardo, Newton, and so on. Much research that academics are engaged in is done without any concern for intellectual property protection. A significant number of contemporary inventions are developed with government funding, or as offshoots of military and space programme R&D. So at least for those ideas that would develop even without the incentive of appropriation, where the good of invention might be available without the bad of exclusive ownership, private property of ideas violates the proviso.[11]

Some inventions and discoveries, even when not privately owned, do more harm than good. Dangerous drugs or tobacco products are a case in point. Private ownership of these ideas, and the intensive marketing by the owner that often comes with it, might very well make things worse in so far as they encourage wider use of these products. For example, the high profits expected in the production and development of new drugs induces the pharmaceutical industry to engage in some practices of questionable value such as direct-to-consumer advertising. Most newly patented and marketed medications do not constitute an improvement on available generic drugs, thus promoting the use of less effective and more costly drugs (Lexchin and Mintzes, 2002). Other drugs offer a remedy to a condition that was not considered a 'medical problem' at all prior to their marketing, in effect fostering drug use by healthy people (Mintzes, 2002).

Certain useful and beneficial inventions can harm some people. When a newly introduced technology becomes so widespread that it engenders structural and environmental changes so that it becomes a social necessity, it harms those who cannot afford it. Take the motorcar – no harm was done when it is first introduced. But when it becomes the principal means of transportation, a network of roads is established, the city spreads out to the suburbs, walking to work or to the supermarket is no longer a reasonable option, public transport deteriorates, and one can hardly lead a normal life in such an environment without access to a motorcar. At that point individuals who cannot afford a motorcar are harmed in the sense that they would have been better off had society and urban living developed differently. Similarly, anyone who cannot afford the use and maintenance of a mobile phone is made worse off today by its invention compared to the time prior to its introduction. Moreover, the monopolistic position of the patent owner and the ability to extract rent only exacerbate the harm by increasing the number of individuals who cannot afford the new technology.

The simple view that invention and private property in new ideas harm no one and might even benefit some is simply false. Property and exclusive control always deprive those who are left out. In the case of intellectual property, appropriation unnecessarily denies others' use. The claim that property and invention stand and fall together, that we cannot have the good of invention without the bad of appropriation, is misleading. There is historical anecdotal evidence that at least some invention goes on without intellectual property. Moreover, not all invention is good, and the expected gains of intellectual property might spur owners to encourage use, thus aggravating the harm (for example, marketing new medications). Even good inventions might harm some people, and the number of people so harmed might increase by monopolistic power exerted by the owners (for example, mobile phones).

The problem of individuation

Prior to working out whether an appropriation of some intellectual product satisfies the conditions laid by the proviso in either its non-waste or its non-harm form, there must be a clear conception of what exactly the idea consists of. The problem is not altogether unique to the realm of ideas. Problems concerning the defined boundaries of a material object with which labour is mixed have also been raised. Nozick emphatically asks: 'If a private astronaut clears a place on Mars, has he mixed his labor with (so that he comes to own) the whole planet, the whole uninhabited universe, or just a particular plot?' (1974, p. 174). Does erecting a fence count as mixing one's labour with the enclosed land or just with the land immediately underneath the fence? These problems are real but not unmanageable. As Lawrence Becker points out, the fact that labour is purposive helps to define the extent of the object one labours on (Becker, 1977, pp. 33f).[12] The same cannot be said, however, about ideas. First, on many occasions discoveries are made accidentally. A scientist proceeding along a certain line of inquiry finds a solution quite by chance and not where he expected. One of the most famous cases is Fleming's discovery of penicillin. Sometimes in the search for one thing the researcher stumbles on another. Cases in point are x-rays and Teflon. With the inventor's focus and attention directed elsewhere, it becomes impossible to define the boundaries of an accidental invention or discovery on the basis of the inventor's purpose.

Second, individuating an idea seems a lot more baffling than individuating a material object. Say I am seeking a cure for cancer and I find a substance of type X that at a particular dosage successfully treats cancer of type Y. It is then discovered that X is also effective for the treatment of some other complaint; or that at a different dosage has some other desirable effect. Now, do I own any cure for cancer as I initially set out to find? Any cure for cancer of type Y? The substance X and any use to which it might be employed? Or only the use of X at a specified dosage for the treatment of Y?

Let me take a closer look at the problem of individuation. I can identify at least three such problems. First, the distinction between the idea in its first expression and the many secondary expressions it might stimulate. Does ownership of an idea include *imitation*? Microsoft Windows, for example, an independently developed graphical user interface for the PC, consciously set out to emulate the older Apple Mac operating system. Does Apple own the idea of double-clicking to open folders, files and applications, dragging and dropping them and so on; or only the particular way in which such operations are integrated into their machines? *Parody* is another tricky issue. Do the creators of the espionage movie genre back in the 1960s have any claim to Austin Powers' movies which, after all, would make no sense were it not for the object of their parody? Creations often *inspire* further creations, sometimes presented as homage, reinterpretation or development. Paul Gauguin's 1889 *Bonjour Monsieur Gauguin* was inspired by Gustave Courbet's *The Meeting*, or *Bonjour Monsieur Courbet*, painted in 1854 and depicting a meeting between the artist and an acquaintance in the countryside. Another homage to the famous nineteenth-century painting is *Have a Nice Day Mr. Hockney* (1981–83) by the pop-artist Peter Blake. Sometimes all that the secondary creations retain is the distinctive style of the source. Take, for example, the American Madeleine Peyroux singing like Billie Holiday, or debutants acting like Brando, or Miro-style paintings drawn in third-grade art classes. Do these cases in anyway transgress their predecessors' intellectual property?

A second problem lies in the distinction between a general and more abstract idea and the specific details that are required to put the idea to practice. Take for example the general idea of a light source produced by electrons travelling through a filament within a vacuum. Several elements that required much experimentation to determine remain unspecified such as the filament material, the kind of vacuum and the electrical charge. Using lower current electricity, a small carbonised filament and an improved vacuum inside the globe, Thomas Edison was able to produce a reliable, long-lasting source of light. In commercialising his improvements, was he transgressing an existing intellectual property right?

The third problem is the metaphysically most troubling. Does an idea I own extend to the ownership of a similar idea at which another arrived independently (the way that a legal patent does)? Or does ownership of an idea preclude independent discovery (the same way as trade secrets, in so far as they are considered intellectual property, fail to provide legal protection against independent invention)? The first possibility depends on a metaphysics of Platonic forms. The idea in an individual's mind is considered the same object as the idea in another's mind. Therefore, if I own that object I own its representation in any mind whatever way it got there. The second possibility follows an alternative metaphysics whereby the identity of an intellectual object depends on the ability to trace a continuous path back to a common precursor. If I learn from you that $2+2=4$, then the idea of that equation in my mind is identical with the same idea in your mind. But if I worked it out on my own, then that thought would not be identical with a similar thought in your mind. What is the 'idea' that one owns? Is it the substance of the idea, a Platonic object that transcends all particular mental representations? Or is it the form, the carrier of the substance, the identity of which is path-dependent?

The point is not that the law cannot handle these sorts of puzzles of individuation and come up with reasoned and principled justifications for recognising intellectual property in some cases and rejecting it in others. In doing so it might seek to balance competing values or to strive for an optimal solution in terms of scientific and cultural progress. The point is that a Lockean natural right justification is not available to determine whether intellectual property ought to be admitted in each of these cases. Moreover a Lockean justification cannot proceed prior to determination of the boundaries of the intellectual product to which there is no natural solution.

Even if it was not for the non-rivalrous nature of ideas and some general justification of property were available, and even if it was not for the problem of origination and a positive case could be made for the appropriation of intellectual products, there would still be the problem of individuation, of what it is exactly that one can lay a claim to and that must pass the negative test of the proviso in one version or another.

Conclusion

Lockean and neo-Lockean theories of property are often thought to furnish an adequate justification of intellectual property rights. Indeed, they are sometimes said to apply even better to the sphere of ideas than to the sphere of real assets. A tempting initial thought concerning intellectual products is that they are a product of our minds and that nothing that previously existed is denied from others when private property in ideas is recognised. Accordingly, ideas are merely an extension of our minds in the same way as hair is the product of our bodies, and both are similarly protected by the principle of self-ownership. Their ownership is justified simply by a full appreciation of the assumption of self-ownership without the need of genuine appropriation. Moreover, since no one can be harmed by an appropriation of something that would not otherwise exist, the appropriation of an idea by its originator necessarily conforms to the Lockean proviso.

It is this kind of thought that may have led Ayn Rand to proclaim that intellectual property is the first or paradigmatic sort of property: 'Patents and copyrights are the legal implementation of the base of all property rights: a man's right to the product of his mind' (1967, p. 130).

I have argued that rather than being a paradigmatic object of Lockean property rights, ideas are not susceptible to such justifications. Several relatively minor problems of application arise when attempting to extend Locke's theory beyond the material realm. These problems might be overcome by slight revisions to the theory. However, three major problems stemming from the nature of ideas make it ultimately impossible to justify natural property rights in ideas on Lockean grounds. First, the non-rivalrous nature of ideas, the fact that they can be used simultaneously by many individuals without their use-value diminishing in any way, robs such an attempt of any plausible grounds for a general justification of property. Whether the grounds be self-preservation, freedom or incorporation in a project, if there is no reason to allow exclusive control to an individual, and in so doing denying others control, all that follows is of no consequence. Second, a Lockean positive principle of appropriation assumes that we can unproblematically identify the producer of a material product. The problem of origination makes it impossible to make out the originator of an idea. Ideas, whether discoveries, inventions or artistic creations, develop within a social context that provides the major inputs for their cultivation as well as the social practice that gives them their meaning and significance. There is, therefore, no natural way to determine the individual originator of an idea who can claim ownership on the basis of such a status. If origination is *conventionally* determined, this opens the way for the kind of consequentialist reasoning that shifts intellectual property away from a theory of natural rights. Third, a Lockean proviso that approves or rejects particular appropriations on the basis of other people's interests assumes that the boundaries of the material resource appropriated can be straightforwardly determined. The problem of individuation is the mirror image of origination. If origination looks back to ask who else but the claimant of ownership is responsible for the intellectual product, individuation looks forward to ask what subsequent intellectual products will be considered as stemming from the present one and therefore included in its ownership. Similar to the problem of origination there is no natural way to draw the boundaries, to individuate, the intellectual product. Again, appealing to convention invites consequentialist reasoning and amounts to abandoning a natural rights account of intellectual property. The dual problems of origination and individuation pose a thorny problem even for a conventionalist account. For it appears that the more we are willing to recognise the owner as the originator of the idea, brushing aside inputs of preceding ideas, the less we are able consistently to recognise offshoots of the idea as included within it. That is to say, the narrower we individuate the intellectual product. For we cannot have it both ways: that the idea owes nothing to its predecessors yet its successors are wholly indebted to it.

All this leaves intact the plausible thought that ownership of ideas can be justified on non-Lockean grounds, that is to say, on consequentialist or other grounds not based on natural rights to intellectual property.[13]

Notes

1. Not that he had no thoughts at all on the matter. Ironically, for any one seeking Lockean support for strong natural rights to intellectual property, he wrote a letter in 1694 opposing the renewal of the Licensing, Act objecting to copyright 'in any book which has been in print fifty years' (Locker, 1997, quoted in Shiffrin, 2001, p. 154). Only *somewhat* anachronistic because *Two Treatises of Government* was published in 1698, whereas the origins of patents in Britain can be traced back to the fifteenth century.
2. Possibly, a structure of incentives created by the establishment of IP might contribute to some subsistence needs. This might form part of a consequentialist justification of IP, but not of a natural rights approach. I shall say more on a limited role that incentives might play in a Lockean account below.
3. I use the term 'efficient' in a very intuitive and non-technical sense: *sharing* is more efficient than *duplicating*.
4. This is different from a full-blown consequentialist argument of property. It is part of a justification of why there should be any property at all, rather than who should own what, and it is defensive, aimed at avoiding deterioration rather than inducing the creation of more value. Whereas consequentialists hold that the institution of property and its rules of allocation are the optimal system for creating value; the position being considered here maintains that unless we allow for some private property our natural resources would deteriorate beyond usefulness. Who should own what is justified on independent grounds.
5. Ogburn and Thomas claim that their analysis of multiple inventions 'indicates the great importance of the status of culture as a factor in the origin of inventions' (1922, p. 91).
6. Vincent van Gogh, perhaps one of the most original of the nineteenth-century artists, in a letter to his brother Theo (1888): 'I exaggerate. I sometimes change a motif, but in the end I don't invent the whole painting. Instead I find it ready-made in nature, though I still have to extract it.'
7. For example, Manet's *Le Déjeuner sur l'herbe* has been the subject of reinterpretations by several artists such as Monet and Picasso, and continues to inspire artists to this day.
8. If ideas really are the product of several, perhaps many, individuals, and even if we assume we know which individuals are responsible for each intellectual input, so that all these individuals would be the joint owners of an idea, this would raise the problem of joint products. The principles of property do not offer a solution to the question of the division of *joint* products. See Attas (2004; 2005, pp. 122–6).
9. John Steinbeck's unforgettable *The Grapes of Wrath* comes to mind: 'And a homeless hungry man, driving the roads with his wife beside him and his thin children in the back seat, could look at the fallow fields which might produce food but not profit, and that man could know how that fallow field

is a sin and the unused land a crime against the thin children. And such a man drove along the roads and knew temptation at every field, and knew the lust to take these fields and make them grow strength for his children and a little comfort for his wife' (p. 245).

10. Waldron interprets Locke as not intending to impose a proviso at all, but merely making explicit a factual assumption about the world when no one appropriates more than he can use without spoilage. (1988, pp. 210–11).
11. There is a crucial difference between the role incentives might play in consequentialist justifications and in natural rights (Lockean) justifications of (intellectual) property. On a consequentialist account we may ask about the structure of incentives *a system of IP* might generate, and whether the system as a whole might produce more good than harm. This is irrelevant for a proviso in a natural rights approach. To be sure, we may take into consideration the incentive effects without which the idea perhaps might not be developed at all. Nevertheless, we must focus on *each individual appropriation* and ask whether it produces more good than harm for others.
12. David Hume raised similar problems with respect to the extent of occupation. Disputes over such issues 'can be decided by no other faculty than the imagination' (Hume, 1978, p. 507). The extent of occupation, and similarly the extent of an object laboured upon, is a matter of human 'fancy', and must therefore be determined by convention.
13. I would like to thank David Enoch, Axel Gosseries, Alon Harel, Alain Marciano, Jonathan Trerise and an anonymous referee for their helpful written comments and valuable suggestions.

References

Annis, D. B. and Bohanon, C. E. (1992) Desert and Property Rights, *Journal of Value Inquiry*, 26: 537–46.

Attas, D. (2000) Freedom and Self-Ownership, *Social Theory and Practice*, 26(1): 1–23.

Attas, D. (2003) The Negative Principle of Just Appropriation, *Canadian Journal of Philosophy*, 33(3): 343–72.

Attas, D. (2004) Who Owns the Product? *The Philosophical Quarterly*, 54(217): 537–56.

Attas, D. (2005) *Liberty, Property and Markets*. Aldershot: Ashgate.

Becker, L. C. (1977), *Property Rights: Philosophic Foundations*. London: Routledge & Kegan Paul.

Day, J. P. (1966) Locke on Property, *Philosophical Quarterly*, 16: 207–20.

Friedland, J. (2001) Ideation and Appropriation: Wittgenstein on Intellectual Property, *Law and Critique*, 12: 185–99.

Gaus, G. F. and Lomasky, L. E. (1990) Are Property Rights Problematic? *The Monist*, 73: 483–503.

Hardin, G. (1968) The Tragedy of the Commons, *Science*, 166: 1103–7.

Hughes, J. (1989/9) The Philosophy of Intellectual Property, *The Georgetown Law Journal*: 77: 287–366.

Hume, D. (1978 [1739–40]) *A Treatise of Human Nature*, 2nd edn. Oxford: Clarendon Press.

Kingston, W. (2004) Light on Simultaneous Invention from US Patent Office 'Interference' Records, *World Patent Information*, 26: 209–20.
Levine, B. L. (1980) The Tragedy of the Commons and the Comedy of the Community: The Commons in History, *Journal of Community Psychology*, 14: 81–99.
Lexchin, J. and Mintzes, B. (2002) Direct-to-Consumer Advertising of Prescription Drugs: the Evidence Says No, *Journal of Public Policy and Marketing*, 21: 194–201.
Locke, J. (1960/1698) *Two Treatises of Government*. Cambridge: Cambridge University Press.
Lomasky, L. (1987) *Persons, Rights, and the Moral Community*. Oxford: Oxford University Press.
Merton, R. K. (1961) Singletons and Multiples in Scientific Discovery: a Chapter in the Sociology of Science, *Proceedings of the American Philosophical Society*, 105: 470–86.
Mintzes, B. (2002) Direct to Consumer Advertising is Medicalising Normal Human Practice, *British Medical Journal*, 324: 908–9.
Miller, D. (1980) Justice and Property, *Ratio*, 22: 1–14.
Moore, A. (1997) A Lockean Theory of Intellectual Property, *Hamline Law Review*, 21: 65–108.
Munzer S. R. (1990) *A Theory of Property*. Cambridge: Cambridge University Press.
Nozick, R. (1974) *Anarchy, State, and Utopia*. New York: Basic Books.
Ogburn, W. F. and Thomas, D. (1922) Are Inventions Inevitable? A Note on Social Evolution, *Political Science Quarterly*, 16: 83–98.
Palmer, T. G. (1990) Are Patents and Copyrights Morally Justified? The Philosophy of Property Rights and Ideal Objects, *Harvard Journal of Law and Public Policy*, 13: 817–65.
Rand, A. (1967) Patents and Copyrights, in *Capitalism: the Unknown Ideal*. New York: Signet
Rose, C. (1986) The Comedy of the Commons: Custom, Commerce, and Inherently Public Property, *The University of Chicago Law Review*, 53: 711–81.
Shiffrin, S. V. (2001) Lockean Arguments for Private Intellectual Property, in S. R. Munzer (ed.) *New Essays in the Legal and Political Theory of Property*. Cambridge: Cambridge University Press.
Spinello, R. A. (2003) The Future of Intellectual Property, *Ethics and Information Technology*, 5: 1–16.
Thomson, J. J. (1990) *The Realm of Rights*. Cambridge, MA: Harvard University Press.
Waldron, J. (1988) *The Right to Private Property*. Oxford: Clarendon Press.

2
Are Rawlsians Entitled to Monopoly Rights?

Speranta Dumitru[1]

Talented people are at the centre of Rawls' theory of justice. Of two principles, one is devoted to specifying what they are entitled to: equal opportunities for the equally talented, regardless of their social position; and unequal income for the unequally talented, provided that it benefits the least advantaged. Talented people are at the centre of the patent system, too. Within this system, some of the most talented people – those who are the first to invent and divulge a new device – are entitled not to a higher income, but to monopoly rights. They have a twenty-year right to prevent anyone from using, fabricating or selling the invention without their consent. How they manage this right determines the level of their income. Are monopoly rights for talented people justified by Rawls' criteria of justice?

In this chapter, I shall argue that Rawls' theory of justice is ill-equipped to answer this question. Tailored for rival goods and, as a result, centred on the distribution of benefits, it tends to restate questions of justice about unequal rights as questions about economic inequalities. Therefore, it lacks the tools necessary to distinguish among different forms of incentives for talented people. Once social and economic inequalities observe equality of opportunity and improve the least advantaged, the theory is indifferent as to whether talented people are allowed to compete for monopoly rights or for direct financial reward.

This chapter is divided into two sections. In the first I argue that Rawls' theory supports a *prima facie* liberty to copy. In fact, neither Rawls' writings, nor philosophers working within his theory, ever make reference to intellectual property.[2] But on the basis of Rawls' defence of the Aristotelian principle (Rawls, 1971, § 65), one can conjecture that people having a fundamental interest in exercising their talents in complex and new activities are generally averse to intellectual property rights. However, limited curtailments of the liberty to copy can be conceded in so far as they provide incentives for talented people to create new and original products. Then, the question of whether intellectual property rights are as *just* as other efficient incentives becomes relevant.

In the second section, I turn to two related features, which prevent Rawls' theory from assessing incentives based on unequal rights from the point of view of justice. One is the decision to define questions of justice as distributive issues arising in contexts of scarcity. The other is the second principle's focus on economic inequalities.

The Aristotelian principle

Intellectual property rights are exclusive rights. Their holders have the right to prevent others from using, fabricating or selling the patented invention. An invention is patentable if it is new (previously unavailable to the public), unobvious for persons skilled in the art and useful (or of industrial application). The correlative duty[3] of patent holder's claim rights is the third party's obligation to refrain from copying patented inventions. Should a just society recognise such an obligation?

Except for personal property, which is protected as a basic right, Rawls' theory neither defends nor rejects ownership rights.[4] Instead, it contains some elements conceding that a just society should protect the liberty to copy novel products. The foundation of such a liberty can be found in Rawls' thin theory of the good. In Rawls' theory of justice, a theory of the good is needed in order to specify the fundamental interests of the persons and the rules of rational choice, enabling parties to choose the principles governing a just society.[5] Rawls lists a couple of principles of rational choice, the Aristotelian principle being one of them.

The Aristotelian principle is stated as follows:

> other things being equal, human beings enjoy the exercise of their realized capacities (their innate and trained abilities), and this enjoyment increases the more the capacity is realized, or the greater its complexity.
>
> (1971, p. 426)

If this principle is a genuine rule of rational choice, and if the duty to refrain from copying could be shown to be contrary to the Aristotelian principle, then the preference for intellectual property rights will appear to be *prima facie* irrational. At first sight, the Aristotelian principle is a general principle of human motivation concerning the satisfaction derived from complex activities. What does it have to do with the liberty to copy novel products?

The preference for novelty

There is both an explanatory and conceptual link between the satisfaction obtained from complex activities and the preference for novelty. The Aristotelian principle states that the satisfaction obtained through the realisation of one's capacities increases with the complexity of the activities undertaken. This correlation can be explained, according to Rawls, by a more fundamental desire which complex activities satisfy: 'the desire for variety and novelty of experience... for feats of ingenuity and invention' (1971, p. 427). Such a desire is assumed to be universal: 'human beings', claims Rawls, 'take pleasure in the novelty and the occasions for ingenuity and invention that such activities provide' (1971, p. 431).

The conceptual link is as follows. If the satisfaction increases with the complexity of activities, activities can be ordered in a chain: the n + 1th activity includes the nth activity and one other in addition. Moreover, the Aristotelian principle is a version of a rational choice rule which Rawls calls the 'principle of inclusiveness' which states that, from two options, it is rational to prefer the one whose execution would achieve all the aims of the other option and one more (1971, p. 412). There are indefinitely many such chains, and the Aristotelian principle aims to remain neutral as to which is to be preferred. But as far as one chain is concerned, there is a general preference for ascending it, for innovating within the chain (Rawls, 1971, p. 430). Here, the sense of 'innovation' is certainly relative to one's chain of activities, and not every activity added to one's chain is objectively new. But once all known ways of acting and aims are exhausted, one's preference always to move up in a chain corresponds, at the limit, to a disposition to invent and to solve new problems.

Now, assuming that the pleasure of novelty is as widespread as the Aristotelian principle implies, one can still object that this simply means that people are inclined to invent themselves, not that they are disposed to deny exclusive rights to the more inventive. But why should one's preference for novelty lessen whenever novelty is someone else's invention? In fact, the sole limit Rawls envisages for the tendency to enjoy novelty is set by the balance between the amount of the final satisfaction of performing the n + 1th activity and the burdens of further practice and study needed to pass from the nth to the n + 1th activity (1971, p. 428). Now, this burden is clearly lower when the new activity is accomplished by copying someone else than by inventing oneself. Therefore, if the preference to innovate, to progress in a chain so long as the burdens are not unbearable, is universal, nobody will have an interest in establishing rights that prohibit further ingenuity.

How the Aristotelian principle protects imitators

One inevitable objection to this is that the rationale behind the intellectual property system is, on the contrary, to encourage ingenuity by publicly acknowledging it. What exclusive rights prohibit is only copying, not inventiveness. Indeed, once someone has invented a new device, how can others reasonably complain that being prevented from fabricating the same object obstructs *their* ingenuity? As Heraclites might have said, no object is new twice.

This objection relies on the distinction between the objective and subjective meaning of novelty and inventiveness. The meaning of novelty endorsed by the Aristotelian principle is subjective. This is not the case with the concept consecrated by the intellectual property system: novelty is equated with what was previously unavailable to the public, not to a particular individual. As a consequence, there is always a single inventor of a device, be it an individual or a group. Someone having 'independently invented' a device already available to the public is ineligible for monopoly rights and is liable for patent infringement if the device is patented. This narrow sense of novelty is tightened by the doctrine of equivalents. According to this, if one device performs the same function as another, in substantially the same way and with substantially the same result, it is the same as the second even though they differ in name, form or shape. Its 'inventor' is consequently liable for patent infringement.

Yet, the Aristotelian principle protects not only independent inventors but also imitators. This comes as no surprise to anyone aware that the principle is centred on individual activity. Invention is valued insofar as it is a new activity to an individual, not for the sake of society's general advancement. In other words, the Aristotelian principle is not intended to function as a perfectionist proviso and its role is not to support some constitutional clause for 'promoting progress and useful arts, by securing for limited times, to authors and inventors, the exclusive right to their respective writings and discoveries'.[6] Rather, from the Aristotelian principle perspective, creation and invention are valued as occasions, for an individual, to exercise her capacities and talents through new and more complex activities.

The Aristotelian principle, insofar as it is centred on activity and not on the production of novelty as such, supports a *prima facie* liberty to copy. It even encourages it by means of a corollary. 'A companion effect', Rawls maintains, of the Aristotelian principle is the general tendency to appreciate, learn and imitate products of human excellence: 'as we witness the exercise of well-trained abilities by others, these displays are enjoyed by us and arouse a desire to do the same things ourselves' (1971, p. 428). Therefore, a duty to refrain from copying, from 'doing the same things ourselves', seems to conflict with the Aristotelian principle. In addition, if the 'companion effect' is a genuine principle of rational choice and, as Rawls argues, an essential constituent of everyone's self-respect (1971, pp. 440–1), a preference for establishing intellectual property rights will appear as irrational.

The problem the intellectual property system poses, by forbidding duplication, is that it establishes monopoly rights on those activities which have permitted the realisation of the protected intellectual products. Without the consent of the exclusive rights holder, people are not allowed to exercise their skills by copying, even though these activities involve adding to novelty and complexity for the imitator herself.

Which institutions promote the Aristotelian principle's goals?

Should the liberty to copy be protected by the basic structure of a just society? Rawls explicitly acknowledges that 'granted that the [Aristotelian] principle characterizes human nature as we know it' the question is not so much how to justify it, but rather 'to what extent is it to be encouraged and supported'? (1971, p. 432). Since the tendency to invent and to perform increasingly complex activities 'is strong and not easily counterbalanced', Rawls believes 'that in the design of social institutions a large place should be made for it'. If not, 'human beings will find their culture and form of life dull and empty' (1971, p. 429).

At an institutional level, however, there are two strategies to prevent culture from becoming 'dull and empty'. The first is to trust the Aristotelian principle and its 'companion effect' and grant the liberty to copy. The second is to consider the interests expressed by the Aristotelian principle only as a starting point. Equally rational maximisers can choose to curtail the liberty to copy if the goals expressed by the

Aristotelian principle are promoted to everyone's advantage. In other words, it would be rational to concede limited curtailments on the liberty to copy if they constitute the only incentives for talented people to create original products.

The second strategy seems more promising. In a system protecting everyone's liberty to copy, the most talented people will be tempted to use their right to disclosure strategically. Even if they 'do [novel activities] without the incentive of evident reward', as the Aristotelian principle presupposes (Rawls, 1971, p. 432), talented people may want to recover their investment through sales. Some inventors will then choose not to disclose their products to the public, relying instead on trade secrets. But confidentiality is a strategy available only for inventions that are difficult to copy by reverse engineering. The rest are bound to be disclosed once they are sold. In order to minimise losses, inventors may try to charge the first buyer the full amount of their investment, or alternatively distribute it among more buyers, by imposing conditions on the sale of their products. They could, for instance, include in the transaction contract a clause prohibiting further disclosure, which will enable them to sue 'pirates' for breaching the contract.[7] Nevertheless, inventive people who know that secrecy is generally revealed or uncovered will have little incentive to divulge their work. As basic economic analysis teaches us, 'for a new work to be created, the expected return must exceed the expected cost of producing it' (Landes and Posner, 1989, p. 327).

Indeed, intellectual property rights are conceived of as a bargain for disclosure: society grants an inventor monopoly rights for a limited period in exchange for disclosure of their new product. However, there are various solutions available to this bargaining problem: reputation or financial rewards are alternative incentives for the most talented, and monopoly rights themselves could be arranged in different schemes. Among equally efficient incentives, which are the just ones?

Just incentives for the most talented

A theory of justice must be able to say what kind of incentives, for whom and on what products are just.[8] Are monopoly rights better incentives than direct financial reward? If monopoly rights are the just incentives, should their duration and scope be strengthened or weakened?

Unfortunately, a Rawlsian theory of justice is not able to compare monopoly rights to other forms of incentives or to various schemes of intellectual property rights. It lacks, as I shall argue, appropriate tools to take into account the nature of intellectual products, the type of inequality implied by monopoly rights and the kind of competition talented people are engaged in. First, in a theory of *distributive* justice restricted to conflicts of interests in conditions of scarcity, claims related to non-rival goods would not be regarded as claims for justice. Second, a theory centred on *economic* disparities will tend to assess all incentives in terms of these disparities, thus failing to address the question of whether inequality of (monopoly) rights is unjust, independently of economic contingencies. Third, a theory of equal opportunities centred on fair *initial conditions* disregards the question of why winner-takes-all competitions among talented people could be unjust.

Justice without rivalry

New devices have special properties. They share with other public goods two characteristics: non-rivalrous consumption and non-excludability. A good is *non-excludable* when it is difficult, if not impossible, to provide to one person without providing it to everyone. National defence and environmental conditions are examples of such goods. *Non-rivalry* means that each individual's consumption does not subtract the good from any other individual (Samuelson, 1954). Unlike machines, which are ordinary goods of private consumption, ideas embodied in new machines are of non-rivalrous consumption in the sense that 'no one possesses the less, because every other possesses the whole of it' (Jefferson, 1813). As Jefferson famously put it, 'he who receives an idea from me, receives instruction himself without lessening mine'.

Rawls' theory of justice seems to be tailored for goods of private, rival consumption. The theory is built on the fundamental assumption that scarcity of resources and competing interests are the two features explaining why questions of justice arise. They also explain why questions of justice are supposed to be mainly about the *distribution of benefits*. Following Hume, Rawls maintains that circumstances of justice 'obtain whenever mutually disinterested persons put forward conflicting claims to the division of social advantages under conditions of moderate scarcity' (1971, p. 128). Both features, scarcity and diverging interests, are assumed to be *necessary* conditions for justice: 'unless these circumstances existed, there would be *no occasion* for the virtue of justice' (ibid.; emphasis added). In other words, according to this account, if resources are abundant and benefits from cooperation do not fall short of the demands people make, questions of justice will not arise. Scarcity is the 'objective' side of the circumstances of justice.

It should be noted that conflicts of interest, the 'subjective' part of circumstances of justice, are wider in scope, and should not be confused with, the idea of 'rivalry'. Rivalry is an inherent property of some kind of goods, describing the impossibility of joint consumption.[9] Rivalry accounts for some, but not all, conflicts of interests. Some of them, perhaps the most significant, stem from the fact of value pluralism since, as Rawls put it, 'in an association of saints agreeing on a common ideal... disputes over justice would not occur' (1971, p. 129). However, rivalry does account for the way Rawls designed the theory of justice as one primarily concerned with *distributive* issues.

Now, intellectual goods raise no allocation problem: there is a zero marginal cost for an additional individual to enjoy benefits of a public good. They are not scarce in the sense that they need to be distributed. It is then surprising that some scholars have argued that under Rawlsian contractualism, *information* should be included in the list of primary goods to be equally distributed (Drahos, 1966, ch. 8). Yet, no institution is necessary to adjust the distribution of information: once produced and divulged, information is available to all. Distributive concerns become relevant only when intellectual property rights are established, since they artificially create excludability.

Rather than allocation problems, information and, more generally, intellectual goods, give rise to collective action problems (Olson, 1965). This kind of problem occurs whenever individuals have an incentive to 'free ride' or take advantage of the efforts of others. Pure public goods, by being non-excludable, give everyone a sure benefit of consumption, and as such an incentive not to contribute. It is rational for an individual to wait for an intellectual product be created, and then to copy and enjoy it without incurring any of its production costs. By artificially creating excludability, intellectual property rights provide an institutional tool to avoid free riding.

Does free riding raise questions of justice? If Rawlsians agree that it does, they should also agree that scarcity of resources is not a *necessary* condition for qualifying claims as being made in the name of justice. A non-excludable good (or one that is difficult to exclude) could not be deemed to be in short supply, yet this is not a sufficient reason to leave free riding out of debates over justice. The definition of 'circumstances of justice' should then be revised to include those conditions favouring free riding, such as the non-excludability of some goods. This means that not only scarcity, but also *equal availability to all* raises questions of justice, and this constitutes a problematic result for any theory taking the aim of equal distribution of benefits as an axiom.

It might be objected either that the dismissal of scarcity does not follow from its premises or that free riding does not pose questions of justice. Let us look at the first point. What makes free riding the subject of justice, one could argue, is not the availability of intellectual goods to everyone, without contribution, but the way they become available, i.e. their production. Indeed, intellectual goods are created through people's work, talents and material resources. Indeed, Rawls included 'intelligence and imagination' (but not the information they are likely to produce) in the list of natural primary goods, useful for any life plan, thus implying that talents are scarce and unequally distributed (1971, p. 62). There would then be no need, the objection runs, to modifying the definition of the circumstances of justice in order to accommodate free riding.

This objection is misleading. By pointing out the scarcity of talents, it rightly suggests that the distribution of benefits should be linked to the distribution of costs. However, this link explains why (and which) acts of free riding could be unjust, and not why free riding raises questions of justice. These issues are independent. Depending on the theory endorsed, free riding will be considered a disincentive to, or a failure to reward, already scarce talents. But reproducing free of charge the nth copy of a drug or taking the bus without paying could be defined as free riding before establishing that they are just, according to one or another theory. The question of whether a criterion is relevant for an evaluation is distinct from the question of the result this evaluation leads to. Accordingly, one can agree that free riding raises questions of justice without condemning it as unjust conduct. For some philosophers, justice itself is a matter of 'not [taking] advantage of one's fellows either as a free-rider or as a parasite' (Gauthier, 1987, p. 252), but others will deny that benefiting from others' efforts is (always) unjust.[10]

One may also deny that free riding raises any questions of justice. Not only does this option seem counterintuitive, but Rawls' explicit position was to regard free riding as a version of egoistic *conceptions of justice* and to reject it (1971, p. 124). When he discusses the production of public goods (mainly, domestic safety and national defence), he suggests that coercion is both rationally and morally justified to enforce financing (1971, pp. 97 and 267).

First, as far as rationality is concerned, he argues that since a collective end is to everyone's advantage, it will also be in the individual's interest to contribute to its production. This argument fails to grasp the nature of a collective action problem by committing the fallacy of composition, that is, to infer from a group's having an interest in contributing to the provision of a good, the individual's interest to bear its cost.

Second, the moral argument against free riding is founded on the principle of fairness, which states that 'we are not to gain from the cooperative labour of others without doing our fair share' (Rawls, 1971, p. 112). One may then conclude that benefiting from others' labour gratuitously is *prima facie* contrary to fairness, but what counts as free riding will depend on what 'labour' and 'fair share' mean.

Moral evaluation of free riding seems to force Rawlsians into an uncomfortable dilemma. If they judge it to be unjust, their theory of justice needs to establish a stronger connection between distribution of benefits and the costs incurred to produce them. If, on the contrary, free riding is not unjust, then the fairness principle should be weakened. None of the alternatives is really convenient for Rawlsians and the dilemma is not specific to the production of intellectual goods.

The problem the principle of fairness raises for Rawlsians is the moral connection it establishes between one's own labour and others' obligations arising from that labour. According to Rawls, one deserves neither one's abilities, nor the willingness to make an effort: they are owed to natural lottery and social circumstances. Since labour depends on morally arbitrary characteristics, no one can claim to deserve its fruits either. Would, then, 'labour' be more able to impose *obligations on others* than to *entitle one* to its benefits? In the economy of Rawls' theory of justice, the scope of the principle of fairness must be gained at the expense of the moral arbitrariness thesis. Accordingly, what counts as free riding will depend both on what counts as labour and on how much we owe to what counts as labour. In the extreme case, if others are entitled to few benefits from their labour, and if *doing* our fair share means only *being* a cooperative member of society, few acts would be qualified as free riding.

To sum up, if Rawlsians agree that new and original ideas are the kind of goods that create incentives to free ride, and that free riding raises questions of justice however they are assessed, they should also agree to modify the definition of 'circumstances of justice'. Not only scarcity of rival goods, but also equal availability to all of intangible goods raises debates over justice. However none of the arguments suffices to reject free riding on intellectual goods.

Is anything wrong with monopoly rights?

As noted, intellectual property rights are monopoly rights. They are often justified as incentives to create and divulgate new and original products, and that is the way a Rawlsian would justify them too. Certainly, there are various institutional tools to encourage ingenuity (Polanyi, 1944; Croskery, 1993) and even as far as monopoly rights are concerned, the efficiency of stronger or weaker protection is widely debated. Let us suppose that direct financial reward of talented people through taxation was shown to be as efficient as monopoly rights are: is there something wrong, *from the point of view of justice*, with monopoly rights, as compared to financial reward?

Rawls' theory would answer this question by comparing the two systems from the point of view of the second principle of justice. If, let us assume, each incentive system creates economic inequalities that satisfy *to the same extent* fair equality of opportunity and improvement of the condition of the least advantaged, no further discrimination between the two forms of reward could be made. Monopoly rights and financial reward are equally just. However, if it can be shown that monopoly rights are unjust for reasons other than those related to optimal incentives and economic inequalities, it follows that Rawls' framework for analysing justice of institutions is at least *incomplete*.

Intellectual property rights provide us with reasons to believe that it is *unsuitable* as well. Rawls' followers tend to analyse the justice of an institution by focusing on its effects on economic inequalities. But monopoly rights entail first and foremost an *inequality of rights*. The focus on economic benefits explains why most criticism of intellectual property rights, and in particular of the patent system, is misguided. Usually, this criticism takes health care and an already existing drug for an important disease, such as HIV/AIDS, as a counter-example to show that a pharmaceutical firms' interest to maximise profits limits poor people's access to medicines.[11] While this argument is correct (as prices are greater when established by monopoly than by competition), it is not an argument against patents as such, or against patents in health care in particular. At best, it is an argument for compulsory licensing of a particular drug or alternatively, for progressive taxes and redirection of collective efforts in favour of poor AIDS sufferers.

In reality, monopoly rights are granted for inventions independently of their market value. While inventions should have some 'utility' or 'industrial application' to be patentable, no threshold of how much utility they should have is specified. A corkscrew inventor is granted the same monopoly rights as a molecule inventor. If the pharmaceutical researcher is not allowed to sell her molecule as a drug, while the corkscrew inventor manages to earn important benefits from his monopoly, will we say that the first patent is less unjust than the second? Alternatively, if the first inventor sells her drug at a lower price and in a smaller quantity than the successful corkscrew inventor, is this a valid reason to criticise patents on corkscrews rather than those on drugs? Economic benefits and their effects on inequalities, while deriving from monopoly rights, are contingent, in the sense that they depend on market demand and patent owner management of an invention.

It might be objected that these are isolated cases which, as with HIV/AIDS drugs, prove little about the institution of patents in general. But if it could be argued that researcher's monopoly rights can *harm* more than the corkscrew's inventor patent, then the example illustrates the idea that monopoly rights raise problems of justice *independently* of their economic benefits, and this question is our concern here.

Monopoly rights allow their holders to prevent third parties from using their product. They allow the pharmaceutical researcher, whose molecule is patented but not marketable, to sue any other researcher for the use of her molecule. Assuming that less subsequent inventions could be developed from the new corkscrew, it follows that economic benefits derived from a patent are not relevant for evaluating the right holder's capacity to limit others' conduct. The logical independence of monopoly rights from the economic benefits parallels Rawls' distinction between liberty and the worth of liberty (1971, p. 204). In other words, the ability or inability to take advantage of patent rights is not a criterion for evaluating the inequality of rights the patent system imposes. If this argument is correct, Rawls' second principle of justice, which deals with economic inequalities and not with unequal rights, is not the most suitable criterion to assess the justice of intellectual property rights.

One may ask how anything can be wrong, from the point of view of justice, with monopoly rights, once they are deemed to be both the best incentives for the most talented and to the greater advantage of all, including the least advantaged. This question assumes both a *consequentialist* position about justice and a conception privileging *distributive* justice. Nevertheless, if monopoly rights appear to be unjust, the stronger reasons we can press are primarily deontological and only secondarily consequentialist and distributive in nature.

Even if monopoly rights over an invention are justified as the best incentives, other facts will continue to trouble us from the point of view of justice. One is the salient inequality they establish between the rights holder and third parties. As noted, this inequality is not only of economic advantages (due to monopoly prices), but of rights (the patent holder has the right to decide when and at what price the invention will be produced and to whom it will be licensed). The right to exclude third parties applies over an extended domain: all possible instances of the patented device, be it a process or a composition of matter. But beyond distributive concerns, there is a further reason why monopoly rights over all instances of a device seem unjust. From the point of view of the patent holder, an *independent inventor* is on a par with someone who copies the patented device. They could equally be sued and fined without discrimination. We all have a strong intuition that treating someone who produces a device by her own efforts as a thief or a free rider is profoundly unjust, independently of the conception of justice we happen to endorse. This failure to distinguish a free rider from an independent inventor is intrinsic to monopoly rights. Here is also the difference to be made from the point of view of justice between incentives by monopoly rights and incentives by financial reward, a difference that neither a consequentialist nor a distributive conception of justice can grasp.

It might be objected that a system distinguishing between free riders and independent inventors is too costly, if not impossible, to enforce and the benefits of the actual system exceed its unjust side-effects. This is a utilitarian objection. But even such a theoretical framework can try to accommodate these side-effects. A utilitarian aiming to diminish the injustice of treating independent inventors as free riders has two institutional mechanisms at her disposal. One is to modify the length of patent rights: to have both more efficient and less unjust monopoly rights a reasonable rule of thumb would be to approximate how long it would have taken, in the absence of patent system, for a second inventor to produce the device.[12] Beyond this, incentives to create seem suboptimal. Another mechanism is to modify the breadth of a patent: by narrowing its scope, it allows improvements and subsequent innovators to reach the market (Schotchmer, 1991). While the question of the optimal length and breadth of patents is under debate (Nordhaus, 1969; Gilbert and Shapiro, 1990), the question of (deontological) justice seems to plead in favour of lessening them.

If Rawls' second principle seems unable to address questions of justice specific to monopoly rights, it may derive an important improvement from them. Assessed through the equal opportunity principle, intellectual property appears as just if the competition between talented people is open to all, including the least advantaged. Rawls' conception of equality of opportunities is highly concerned by procedures and initial conditions, while neglecting completely 'stake fairness' (Jacobs, 2004). An egalitarian conception of justice cannot fail to ask for which positions people should have equal opportunities to compete. From this perspective, the difference between competitions for direct financial reward and winner-takes-all competitions for monopoly rights will appear once again as salient from the point of view of justice.

Conclusion

There are two elements explaining why Rawls' theory is unable to assess the justice of intellectual property rights. The first is the decision to confine questions of justice to scarcity contexts, thus neglecting problems of justice related to non-rival goods. As a consequence, the theory of justice overemphasises the importance of the distribution of benefits at the expense of the distribution of costs. The second element is the exclusive focus on economic and social inequalities. According to Rawls' second principle of justice, once social and economic inequalities respect fair equality of opportunity and improve the least advantaged condition, no further discrimination between winner-takes-all competitions for monopoly rights and competition for direct financial reward for the most talented could be made. As a consequence, a theory focused exclusively on economic inequalities is unable to distinguish between free riders and independent inventors.

Notes

1. Thanks to Marc Rüegger, Nicola Riva, Alain Marciano, Lubomira Radoilska, Vincent Aubert, Axel Gosseries and to participants of the Chaire Hoover (UCL Belgium) seminar for their helpful comments on earlier versions of this chapter.
2. With very few exceptions, e.g. Rakowski (1991, pp. 84–7), discussing the amount of luck implied by inventions and discoveries; Nozick (1974, p. 182), discussing the optimal length of patents; and Pogge (2005), criticising patents on essential drugs.
3. Or the 'jural opposite', cf. Hohfeld (1913).
4. Private property is not a basic right, *pace* Resnik (2003)
5. The fundamental interests of the persons are specified by preferences for primary goods. The theory of the good should remain thin: while defining what is necessary to any life plan, it aims to be neutral on the content of each life plan.

6. US Constitution, § 8
7. This solution is consistent with the libertarian, contractualist approach, see e.g. Nozick (1974, p. 141).
8. This question was not explicitly addressed in the literature and as Friedman (2000, p. 135) notes, 'What we want, however, is not merely incentive but the right incentive'.
9. Some scholars disagree that being public is a characteristic inherent to goods, taking it rather as an attribute of institutions. See Cowen (1985).
10. For quite opposite justifications of this same view, see Nozick (1974, pp. 93–5) and Lemly (2005).
11. For a Rawlsian scholar who defends this solution, see Pogge (2005).
12. The suggestion is Nozick's (1974, p. 182).

References

Cowen, T. (1985) Public Goods and their Institutional Context: A Critique of Public Goods Theory, *Review of Social Economy*, 43: 53–63.

Croskery, P. (1993) Institutional Utilitarianism and Intellectual Property, *Chicago-Kent Law Review*, 68: 631–57.

Drahos, P. (1996) *A Philosophy of Intellectual Property*. Sudbury, MA: Dartmouth.

Friedman, D. (2000) *Law's Order*. Princeton, NJ: Princeton University Press.

Gauthier, D. (1987) *Morals by Agreement*. New York: Oxford University Press.

Gilbert, R. and Shapiro, C. (1990) Optimal Patent Length and Breadth, *RAND Journal of Economics*, 21.

Hohfeld, W. N. (1913) Some Fundamental Legal Conceptions as Applied to Judicial Reasoning, *Yale Law Journal*, 23: 16–59.

Jacobs, L. A. (2004) *Pursuing Equal Opportunities. The Theory and Practice of Egalitarian Justice*. Cambridge: Cambridge University Press.

Jefferson, T. (1905) Letter to Isaac McPherson, 13 August 1813, in A. Lipscomb and A. E. Bergh (eds.) *The Writings of Thomas Jefferson*, vol. XIII. Washington, pp. 326–38.

Landes, W. M. and Posner, R. A. (1989) An Economic Analysis of Copyright Law, *The Journal of Legal Studies*, 18: 325–63.

Lemley, M. (2005) Property, Intellectual Property and Free Riding, *Texas Law Review*, 83: 1031–75.

Nordhaus, W. D. (1969) *Invention, Growth, and Welfare: A Theoretical Treatment of Technological Change*. Cambridge, MA: MIT Press.

Nozick, R. (1974) *Anarchy, State, and Utopia*. Oxford and Cambridge, MA: Blackwell.

Olson, M. (1965) *The Logic of Collective Action*, Cambridge, MA: Harvard University Press.

Pogge, T. (2005) Human Rights and Global Health: A Research Program, *Metaphilosophy*, 36: 182–209.

Polanyi, M. (1944) Patent Reform, *Review of Economic Studies*, 11: 61–77.

Rakowski, E. (1991) *Equal Justice*. Oxford: Clarendon Press.

Resnik, D. B. (2003) A Pluralistic Account to Intellectual Property, *Journal of Business Ethics*, 46: 319–35.

Rawls, J. (1971) *A Theory of Justice*. Oxford: Oxford University Press.
Samuelson, P. A. (1954) The Pure Theory of Public Expenditure, *The Review of Economics and Statistics*, 36: 387–9.
Scotchmer, S. (1991) Standing on the Shoulders of Giants: Cumlative Research and Patent Law, *Journal of Economic Perspectives,* 5: 29–41

3

Access to vs. Exclusion from Knowledge: Intellectual Property, Efficiency and Social Justice

*Giovanni Battista Ramello**

Introduction

Property rights have been a powerful device for promoting trade development, markets and efficiency throughout human history. What is not owned cannot be traded. Hence, a well-defined set of property rights is central to trade.

In addition, commonly held resources cannot be subdivided without a specific set of rules assigning the various portions to individuals. Thus, the market as we define it today cannot exist without property rights. On the other hand, a system of allocating goods that does not rely on market exchange, such as war, theft or gift, seems unable in most cases to warrant the attainment of maximum welfare through the allocation of a scarce resource to the one who most values it. Therefore, as confirmed by a long tradition of economic theory, a well-defined set of property rights can play a crucial role in promoting the efficient allocation of scarce resources and social welfare.[1]

Further, in Western culture private property has been the cornerstone of capitalist society, to the point of being considered to some extent the necessary condition for the freedom of its citizens and the existence of the market, and hence an irrefutable component of individual liberty. These premises are incontestable, and the beneficial role of property rights should be duly acknowledged.

However, the converse cannot be equally endorsed: recognising the virtues of property rights should not mechanically translate into a blank cheque giving them the status of a panacea for any issue.

From the perspective of demand, even when promoting productive efficiency, the market order may be (and very often is) unable to serve the criterion of social justice, and there is no denying that under many circumstances it leaves basic needs unsatisfied for a significant number of people. This in turn places serious limits on the exercise of individual liberty.

From the supply standpoint too property rights do not always translate into efficiency, mainly because productive milieus present idiosyncratic features requiring different regulatory frameworks. Property rights are 'genetically' conceived to manage economic resources for which excludability plays a significant role in regulating their use or avoiding their depletion, as in the case of private goods or commons (a fishery, a pasture, etc.). By contrast, they do not apply in the same way or produce a similar result in domains with distinct characters where excludability can directly influence productivity.

This chapter is an attempt to gain further insight into one of these cases, i.e. knowledge, a distinctive entity that profoundly characterises human relationships and the semantic sphere of human groups. Knowledge relies heavily on sharing, long governed by exchange mechanisms that are different from the market – mainly communication – and is now broadly 'colonised' by the market paradigm through intellectual property rights (IPRs).

The main rationale for justifying the change and the appropriation of this resource relies on the widely held belief that IPRs promote efficiency by providing the owner/creator with the proper economic incentive for producing the optimal level of new knowledge and knowledge-intensive products. Noticeably, along the lines described above, this neglects the specific feature of knowledge and the consequences of the newly enforced excludability on its production.

Although not contesting the incentive effect provided by IPRs, this chapter discusses the consequences of this oversimplified assumption about knowledge. Using literature focusing on knowledge, it attempts to expose some of the shortcomings of traditional economic theory as applied to intellectual property (IP) and to elaborate an alternative economic model from which policy implications can be drawn.

The main findings support the thesis that while limited appropriation can indeed provide some incentive for knowledge production, over-extensive appropriation will tend to produce an adverse outcome for the total amount of knowledge feasible and for overall efficiency. Thus, it is crucial to preserve wide accessibility to knowledge in order to promote efficiency in this domain. Interestingly, this prescription seems to serve social justice equally well, once again confirming the idiosyncratic nature of knowledge as an economic resource.

The chapter is organised as follows. The first section introduces the standard thesis justifying IP and the functional role of exclusion. In the next I discuss the idiosyncratic nature of knowledge, which is simultaneously output, input and productive technology. I then systematise this assertion by means of a simple descriptive model that illustrates the effect of varying the strength of IPRs on knowledge. Finally, I argue that the paradigm equally serves the goal of social justice.

Knowledge, intellectual property and markets: the role of exclusion

Generally speaking, the traditional thesis advocated by the scientific literature depicts IPRs as devices designed to encourage creative and inventive activity. From this perspective, patents and copyrights – but also trade secrets and trade marks, although with different flavours[2] – are essentially viewed as incentives to create, in accordance with the utilitarian tradition summed up in this well-known quote from Jeremy Bentham:

> which one man has invented, all the world can imitate. Without the assistance of the laws, the inventor would almost always be driven out of the market by his rival, who finding himself, without any expense, in possession of a discovery which has cost the inventor much time and expense, would be able to deprive him of all his deserved advantages, by selling at a lower price.
>
> (1839, p. 71)

Consistent with this argument, IPRs are held to address a specific market failure: the underproduction of knowledge because of the lack of profitability for inventors/authors. Variations on this theme abound (Ramello, 2005a).

The previous interpretation is highly convenient for economics theory, as it likens knowledge production to a standard manufacturing process. In this vein, the creator is represented as an economic agent aiming at maximising his utility under the assumption that 'he who has no hope that he shall reap, will not take trouble to sow' (Bentham, 1839, p. 31). Hence, the pecuniary incentive obtained thanks to IPRs is needed in order to pay the opportunity costs of inventive and creative activity. Finally, the production process is treated as a typical manufacturing function, with knowledge as the standard output.[3]

All in all, if this stylisation is valid, IPRs are a good thing and the main critical concern is the exclusion from consumption of a number of individuals because of market power and consequent above-cost pricing. The latter implies that the exclusion from knowledge enforced by IPRs is a necessary condition of the newly devised economic mechanism. This point requires further discussion. Ever since Arrow (1962), the economic nature of knowledge has been identified with that of a public good. Once an individual is part of a human group, she cannot be excluded from the collective sharing of knowledge and her access to it is non-rival. Accordingly, from the standpoint of allocative efficiency, no market is the optimal solution.

Therefore, the market can be introduced in order to promote the attainment of productive efficiency, since, to quote Bentham again, 'without proper assistance of the laws' a suboptimal quantity of knowledge would be produced. This, at least, is the thesis supported by the incentive-to-create argument. Nonetheless, once the market is shaped, a positive price translates into exclusion of those consumers unable to afford it.

However, since in the knowledge domain the marginal cost of reproduction is close to zero, in perfect competition this would essentially mean no or very little exclusion. Unfortunately, as discussed below, perfect competition is not the market structure likely to arise within the IP domain, because the proper working of the incentive mechanism requires market power, which in turn produces the exclusionary effect.

It is worth noting that although the mere existence of IPRs, as with ordinary property rights, does not necessarily confer significant market power to the right-holders *per se*,[4] as the success of a given item of knowledge on the market and its exploitation are likely to produce market power, hence exclusion. This is consistent with the reward mechanism set up by the IP rationale. In fact, most knowledge protected by IPRs must necessarily be difficult to replace, otherwise there would be no need to set up a complex system of incentives in the first place. If the protected fragments of new knowledge were near or perfect substitutes for one another – as would be necessary to cancel out market power – then the IP system would make no sense, because it would be easier and cheaper to provide direct incentives to only one (or a few) inventors and creators. This notion is thus consistent with the concept of the welfare-enhancing effects of variety in ideas, but implies imperfect substitutability and consequently market power.

Also, in order to be effective, the incentive to create demands a profit and therefore above-cost pricing. In general, this profit has been likened, since the earliest writings, with the concept of quasi-rent (Nordhaus, 1969). If this were not the case, the outcome would be exactly the same as that of a market without IPRs.[5]

Further, the possibility for above-cost pricing brought about by IPRs is easy to observe in the real world, where mark-ups on such property are significant. This is the case with trade marks and fashion, copyrights and music, patents and pharmaceuticals. Taking that last example, the exclusionary effects and tragic consequences of uniformly enforcing patent laws have been widely debated with reference to antiretroviral drugs and HIV/AIDS in sub-Saharan Africa, and clearly illustrates the extent of the problem (Attaran and Gillespie-White, 2001; Scherer, 2004).

On the whole, above-cost pricing and the consequent exclusionary effects are the outcome of the IPRs system, but are also a major policy concern when it comes to distributive and egalitarian principles. Nonetheless, if the this justification holds, IPRs are necessary and the exclusionary effects on knowledge can be to a great extent likened to those involving private property and restricted access to protected resources such as food, land and water.[6] Knowledge is a valuable scarce resource – although being a public good, it is scarce in production and not in consumption – and requires that enclosures be built to avoid free riding and thus promote productive efficiency. This brings up the usual trade-off between efficiency and social justice, but the topics up for discussion seem, at first glance, not to differ from those pertaining to private property in general.

As discussed in the following sections, however, this is not the case. IPRs concern an idiosyncratic domain where the typical exclusionary effects they create are amplified in a way that affects not only the static efficiency in the manner with which we are familiar (i.e. by excluding those who are not able to pay for a good), but also the productive process (by causing underproduction of a public good and the depletion of production technology). This, it will be argued, affects not only efficiency but also social justice.

The idiosyncratic nature of knowledge

The standard economic argument about IPRs works if we think of knowledge as a typical private good or a sum of private goods. However, this is not the case, and such a perspective is also misleading when it comes to setting policy. Rather, in the knowledge domain, it will be argued, criteria of both efficiency and social justice require substantial access to knowledge, which is only possible if IPRs are weak.

Knowledge as a social entity

While property exists in almost all human groups, IP is essentially a peculiar institutional outcome of Western culture, and the recent proliferation of the literature justifying IPRs demonstrates that even in this specific legal culture, the concept behind it is not as trivial as it may seem. Rather, the design of a particular legal category for appropriating knowledge suggests that we are dealing with an idiosyncratic milieu, and what is standard elsewhere is not automatically transferable here. If one looks at the variety of IPRs and the differences in design, one can infer that knowledge is so different from the typical property subject matter that it requires distinct paradigms for its appropriation, which must be fine-tuned in order to obtain the expected outcome. In particular, the nature of knowledge and the specificity of its productive process must be taken into account.

Nonetheless, a detailed description is not a trivial task. Knowledge is not just a good or resource, defined and delimited like standard goods produced and exchanged on the markets, but a dynamic entity and a cognitive tool pertaining to social groups that is crucial to both the individual and to social action. Knowledge essentially belongs to the collective context in which it is created. It is brought to fruition in the symbolic and semantic sphere defined by society, and renewed through sharing among individuals, which is thus an indispensable feature for creative activity.[7]

Knowledge is public because meaning is, and obviously there can be no knowledge without meaning. Accordingly, there can be no meaning without a human group to share it. Therefore, although knowledge fragments are often created by individuals, this can only happen when embedded within the broader context of the collective semantic space to which the knowledge fragments are inextricably tied (Geertz, 1973).

Romney provides insight into this idea:

> knowledge, found mostly in humans, arises from human inventions, is learned and handed down from one generation to the next, and usually varies from one society to another. . . . it is shared among relevant participants and . . . it is learned as part of our social heritage. . . . In short, careful reflection reveals that the very notion of [knowledge] involves sharing of ideas, concepts, behaviors, etc., by more than one person.
>
> (1999, p. 104)

On the whole, this demonstrates two important features of knowledge: knowledge is both input and output, as recognised though not fully developed by selected articles in economics;[8] and the sharing process is necessary in order to make any creative effort effective, constituting from this perspective a sort of production technology (Weitzman, 1998; Ramello, 2005b).

Consistent with its social and dynamic nature, knowledge presents another puzzling feature not possessed by ordinary commodities – its 'indivisibility' – which implies two orders of nuisances somehow connected to one another: first, the definition of what can be appropriated by an IPR is not trivial; and second, the appropriation of a part always entails the whole entity (Rooney et al., 2003).

The first such concept, according to the nineteenth-century English legal scholar Augustine Birrell, is easily explained: while it is simple to draw the boundaries of a physical asset – a leg of a mutton, in Birrell's example – it is altogether impossible to determine how much a book truly belongs to an author, because any creative endeavour contracts a significant and indissoluble debt with its precursors and with the context in which it is generated (Goldstein, 1994). This is consistent with the nature of knowledge as a public good.

Hence, the atomisation process enforced via copyright, and via IPRs in general, is just a rough approximation of the division of physical assets – land, cattle, etc. – while any appropriation in the knowledge sphere will be more extensive than in physical property domain, generally appropriating parts that are socially owned or that have been created by someone else.

The second implication, again linked to its nature as a public good, is that because knowledge is a collective and dynamic entity, appropriation cannot concern only a specific number of bits, but also the process itself.

Taken together, these two notions can easily lead the IPR system into a hyper-appropriation, where the typical exclusionary effects generated by property rights are amplified since they simultaneously affect 'the product and the process'.

The main reason for this outcome is the atomisation procedure enforced by economic analysis representing human activities, which cancels from view all that resides in social relationships and which cannot be directly attributed to single individuals but pertains to groups (Granovetter, 1985).[9] On the whole, this over-simplification leads to a misrepresentation of knowledge viewed as the sum of discrete bits of information, thus neglecting the social dimension and its role in the productive process.

Codified and tacit knowledge

We can elaborate on the above by adopting the analytical framework introduced by Polanyi (1966), which mainly addresses the role of knowledge in the scientific domain, but is widely referenced in the literature for its accurate description of the multifaceted nature of knowledge.

Polanyi represents knowledge essentially as a dyadic structure, made up of two distinct but complementary components: 'codified knowledge', which can be articulated and encoded; and an immanent form of knowledge, defined as 'tacit knowledge', which does not lend itself to articulation or codification but which is nevertheless communicated and exists in interpersonal relations.[10] The former is a fragment of knowledge encoded in any one of the various media made available by society, such as language, writing, reproduction technologies, and so forth. Because it can be encoded in discrete units (e.g. a book, a CD, etc.), it can also be commodified, appropriated by means of IPRs and exchanged, giving rise to knowledge markets. Note that through the encoding process, knowledge becomes a static entity and can be more or less likened to traditional private property such as a parcel of land or a can of beer.[11] Indeed, the very purpose of the label 'intellectual property' is to bring appropriated knowledge into the realm of property.

On the other hand, the tacit form of knowledge is by nature a dynamic entity, and as such can never be entirely encoded and commodified. Consequently, as we shall see, it cannot be produced and directly exchanged on the markets, thus giving rise to specific property rights on it, but depends on interpersonal relationships for its production and dissemination. This is supported by various studies on technology transfer, which have stressed the difficulty of transferring the tacit portion of knowledge as compared with its codified portion, due precisely to the necessity of moving individuals as well as physical goods (i.e. of establishing ad hoc social relations), while demonstrating the inevitable need to promote both types of transfers if the policy is to have a favourable outcome (William and Gibson, 1990; Takii, 2004).[12] In effect, tacit knowledge grows out of the dynamic sphere of the communication process, which is a prerequisite for the very existence of knowledge, as well as for the sustenance of human groupings.

It is worth noting that in view of the dyadic structure, the knowledge set encompasses the sum of codified knowledge fragments and their exchange does not *per se* imply the transmission of the tacit dimension. Given its nature, tacit knowledge can only be transmitted within a context of social interaction. This explains, for example, the rationale behind typical educational systems: books are generally used to provide information, but the presence of a teacher is necessary to impart learning and in general to communicate those aspects of knowledge that cannot be statically encoded. Accordingly, Nelson (2003, p. 917) asserts that any 'classroom equipment… [is a] complement not a substitute for an effective teacher working with students'. What is missing, in fact, is the imparting of that tacit knowledge which books alone are unable to convey.[13]

On the whole, this has serious implications for knowledge production: tacit knowledge and the related social relationships are not only important parts of knowledge, but also crucial determinants for the productivity of the creative process.[14] In other words, the existence, transmission and development of knowledge, all at once representing the productive technology, require as a necessary condition social interactions. This is tantamount to asserting that knowledge, when construed as technology, presents increasing returns in the access.

Several studies in fields as diverse as the medical sciences, organisational sciences and economic growth essentially confirm this assertion.[15]

Access to vs. exclusion from knowledge: a simple economic model

Furthermore, the effects of IPRs are various and all should be properly taken into account in order to evaluate the overall outcome. In particular, considering the joint nature of knowledge as an output, an input and a productive technology, the appropriation set up by IP produces three categories of consequences.

1 There is the pecuniary incentive that can play the useful role of attracting individuals to the inventive process; this is not challenged here *per se*. Of course, for anyone who has to earn a living, expecting economic benefits to exceed opportunity costs thanks to specific property rights can make knowledge production an attractive endeavour. This is not the only feasible incentive, but is certainly an important one.
2 As pointed out by Arrow (1962) and more weakly by Landes and Posner (1989), the incentive mechanism will tend to increase the cost

of knowledge as an input. Hence, the total incentive effects will be discounted by the increase in production costs.

3 The exclusion enforced by IPRs will impair the sharing process according to what is discussed, and thus the productivity of knowledge as a technology.

The net balance of the three effects is not obvious and must be properly considered when setting policies. In particular, the last feature is crucial for understanding the overall consequence of exclusion, and provides an important new argument for preserving extended access to knowledge in view of efficiency. This, in turn, suggests a convergence between the promotion of efficiency and the pursuit of social justice in the knowledge domain, as investigated in the next section.

The model shown below captures this view by proposing a bridge between standard economic reasoning and the hypothesis concerning the idiosyncratic nature of knowledge. Figure 1, helpful for positive purposes, highlights the consequence of neglecting the nature of knowledge as a productive technology. It starts from a standard representation of the 'incentive to create', then introduces the changes occurring once the effect on the production side are considered by

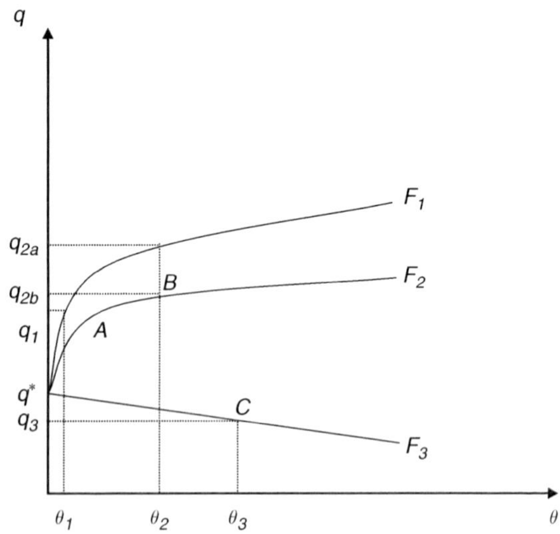

Figure 1 The puzzling issue of appropriation, incentives and productivity in knowledge domain

overlapping a number of different pictures corresponding to varying levels of appropriation via IP. Figure 2 presents the new setting once all the knowledge features are considered, and is useful for normative purposes.

Let us imagine, for the sake of simplicity, that the production of new knowledge depends only on a variable θ representing the strength of the IPR and thus negatively affecting access to knowledge.[16] In other words, θ measures the degree of appropriation permitted by an IPR. Let us assume $0 \leq \theta \leq 1$, though this assumption will be more practical in Figure 2. Thus, $\theta = 0$ means no appropriation; $\theta = 1$ implies the strongest level of appropriation and, in accordance with incentive theory, should stimulate greater revenue for the owners of the rights.

The value of θ depends on several variables, including the right duration (time span) and scope (breadth of appropriation), the strength of law enforcement (hence the infringer's likelihood of being caught), the extent of fines and criminal sanctions, the selectiveness of entitlement criteria, the extension of spill-over spaces intended as derogation of appropriation, and so forth.[17] Consequently, while the definition of θ is easy in the abstract, it is difficult as a matter of practice, meaning that it is simple to talk about weak or strong appropriation but hard or even

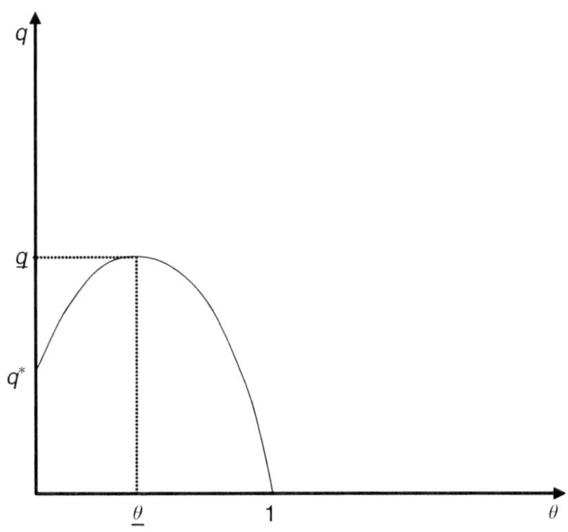

Figure 2 Appropriation and knowledge productivity.

impossible to define a precise level. This observation, discussed further below, is useful for policy prescriptions.

The F_i curves with $I = 1, 2, \ldots n$ in Figure 1 represent a set of knowledge production functions, i.e. technologies, such as $q = F_i(\theta)$ where q is the level of knowledge produced and $q^* = F_i(0)$, with $q^* > 0$, the level of knowledge freely produced in a given state of nature. The latter value is easily demonstrated by the observation that knowledge production exists throughout human history and societies, even in the absence of IPRs.

The slope of F_i production functions is determined by the ratio between the incentive effect and the increase in production costs determined by appropriation via IPRs: the stronger the appropriation, the higher the cost of knowledge as an input. Accordingly, the incentive effect along a given curve (e.g. F_1) diminishes with the increase in θ.

Nonetheless, it has been argued that appropriation will also affect the productivity of knowledge, decreasing in θ due to the negative effect on the sharing process. Hence, a significant increase in θ will negatively impact on creative technology; this can be taken into account by the shift from a given production function, say F_1, to another to the left, say F_2, where any given level of θ will generate a lower level of q.

This impairment process will continue as long as appropriation is strengthened, and for a certain level of θ, the effect will become totally negative and the production function will be downward sloping, as in the case of F_n thus always undermining q^*.

This contradicts the standard incentive theory, for which the production of knowledge is positively related to appropriation; hence the production function should not change. The idea behind the standard incentive rationale is therefore that if one raises the level of θ, q will also increase. For a low IPR strength, say θ_1, the production function in a given time will be described, for instance, as F_1 and the level of knowledge produced will be q_1 which is greater than q^*. Hence, IPRs have the desired incentive effect on the production of knowledge.

By this reasoning, a stronger appropriation regime θ_2 should thus produce a higher quantity of new knowledge, say q_{2a}, and accordingly exclusion will always enhance welfare.

As discussed above, however, this does not happen if we introduce the idiosyncratic nature of knowledge. Expectations will be only partially fulfilled because the stronger IP regime will negatively affect the sharing process, and hence productivity. In Figure 1 this effect causes the shift from F_1 to F_2, the new production function characterised by lower productivity. Consequently, there will be significantly less new knowledge, since $q_{2b} < q_{2a}$.

Nevertheless, in this case the incentive seems to work as the quantity of knowledge still increases in θ. Things change when θ grows even stronger, up to θ_n for example, for the production function will continuously shift to the left: let us assume this has become F_3. Clearly, in this case the knowledge produced will be less than in the absence of IPRs, because $q_3 < q^*$.

Taking this to an extreme, when IPR strength is high enough, the quantity of new knowledge produced will tend towards zero, meaning that the entire sharing process will be impaired, that is to say tacit knowledge will be erased and creative activities will come to a halt. This outcome is essentially the effect of an excessive appropriation of IP on knowledge as a technology and corresponds to an extreme situation ($\theta = 1$), which is difficult to verify since no law yet designed permits total appropriation.[18] In a sense it represents the upper boundary of appropriation.

The pattern for productivity described above can be further clarified by linking all the points corresponding to different pairs of (q, θ) – q^*,A, B, C, etc., as shown in Figure 1. The outcome is the curve presented in Figure 2.

It is straightforward to note that q increases with appropriation at lower levels and decreases when appropriation is greater. In particular, Figure 2 shows that below a certain level $\underline{\theta}$, corresponding to a weak appropriation level, IPRs do indeed produce a positive effect on knowledge production; though for higher levels the overall effect will be negative. In other words, appropriation by means of IP, similar to what happens with trade tariffs or taxes, acts like a tax on the production of knowledge: a certain level of appropriation has positive effects on productivity up to a given threshold, after which the effects become negative.

At this juncture, the next logical step for economists would be to find the optimal level of appropriation by means of the usual mathematical tools, which in Figure 2 happens to be $\underline{\theta}$. Unfortunately, this is easy in theory but almost impossible to do in practice, because the model indicates just the essence of what happens in the real world. Considering the high variability of creative and inventive environments, the differences in knowledge produced in distinct domains and the number of all variables defining θ, the search for this figure could be fruitless.

Nonetheless, from a qualitative perspective the previous result has an important consequence in terms of normative implications. Indeed, at least one important policy prescription can be inferred: the total appropriation of knowledge will never lead to an efficient outcome. Accordingly, the general rule that emerges is that weak IPRs will usually have a more efficient outcome than strong ones.

All in all, if IP can do some good, this will occur in a region of limited appropriation which implies lower productive costs for follow-on creators, wider access to knowledge and the possibility of free riding, understood as unpaid access to knowledge for a considerable number of individuals.[19] Stated differently, efficiency in the knowledge domain requires the preservation of broad access.

Social justice meets efficiency

The policy-setting concept described above has another interesting feature, as it also serves the aim of social justice with regard to the provision of a range of welfare rights outside the sphere of income and the satisfaction of basic needs, regardless of individual merit (Stapleton, 1998).[20]

As economic theory broadly attests, entitlement to property rights affects the distribution of resources and is essentially geared towards promoting efficiency. The idea is that property rights attempt to achieve the optimal allocation of scarce resources in order to enhance social welfare, roughly interpreted in the Pigouvian tradition as the maximum production of wealth. In other words, the only distributive principle in economics asserts that a given resource should be allocated by the most efficient user, regardless of other individuals or fairness.

From an egalitarian perspective, however, the concept of social justice demands that the distribution of scarce resources preserve the equal right of individuals to 'the most extensive total system of equal basic liberties compatible with a similar liberty for others' (Rawls, 1971).

Clearly, although both principles deal with the allocation of scarce resources, they are guided by distinct and somewhat divergent goals. While the former essentially aims to determine the optimal use of a given (scarce) resource in order to achieve a higher level of wealth no matter who benefits, the latter hinges on the principle of equality among individuals, and thus specifically takes into account the distribution of that resource and the provision to every individual of a range of welfare rights (Barry, 1989; Munzer, 1990).

In other words, while economic theory trusts in the assignment of rights and in the power of the market to produce efficient outcomes, completely disregarding the issue of distribution, the social justice rationale focuses on distribution and on the asymmetries created by economic mechanisms, possibly recognising the need for an authority to take action on distributive matters.

Generally speaking, the two principles produce a trade-off that can be solved only on the basis of political considerations. This is the typical dilemma raised, for instance, by the general equilibrium theory, where most efficient solutions (almost) never meet the criterion of social justice. What is more, economic theory is totally unequipped to deal with this.[21] Given the considerable number of efficient solutions lying on the contract curve, economics has no guiding principle for choosing a specific solution. Even a very asymmetrical distribution of resources – e.g. one party has all and the others nothing – is acceptable on the grounds of efficiency.

Social justice sets a different condition: the choice should be guided by the achievement of a common level of 'well-being,' i.e. the satisfaction of basic needs, regardless of personal merit, that are deserved simply because one is a human being living in a given society (Rawls, 1971; Miller, 1976). This principle relates neither to the claim of an identical level of material resources, nor to a minimal standard of living, nor to the goal of efficiency. Rather, it concerns 'the willingness to recognize the rights and liberties of others and to share fairly in the benefits and burdens of social co-operation' (Rawls, 1971, pp. 60–1).

Clearly, the creation of new property rights for a social entity such as knowledge addresses the concept of social justice, since it impacts not only on the distribution of knowledge and rights over knowledge, but also the social relationships, communication processes and self-expression that access implies. All in all, appropriation and the resulting exclusion conflict with social justice.

It is worth noting that the feasibility of a higher level of knowledge does not imply an increase in social justice *per se*. In Figure 1, for instance, the q_1 quantity of knowledge produced is, in economic terms, better than q^*. However, since it is achieved by increasing the property of a few individuals and consequently prejudicing access to knowledge by a large number of individuals, it can negatively affect distribution, increase exclusion and thus hinder social justice. This effect is more likely when the level of appropriation θ is higher. Nonetheless, since in terms of efficiency there is an upper boundary to appropriability, the previous equally preserves a significant degree of accessibility thus serving indirectly social justice.

When appropriation is excessive, the outcome is a reduction in the total amount of knowledge that is socially feasible ($q < q^*$ in Figure 2).

This renders the impairment of social justice more likely as it significantly reduces not only access to but also the total amount of resources. It also violates social justice from an inter-temporal perspective, because appropriation by a given generation depletes the resource for the next generation, again, now accessing a stock of knowledge $q < q^*$. It is intuitively clear that, from an economic viewpoint, the society in time t produces an externality over $t+1$ and subsequent generations. Accordingly, extended appropriation at time t not only impairs social justice for the current generation, but can prejudice the attainment of it for any future generation. Indeed, the egalitarian principle embedded in social justice dictates that no generation has a greater right to a given resource, so 'each generation accepts the dual role of beneficiary and trustee' (Frischmann, 2005, pp. 464–5). This means that individuals are prohibited from compromising the interests of future generations in a given resource, intended as their right to inherit the resource in at least the same conditions as previous generations have had.[22]

On the whole, the social justice rationale argues again (although on different grounds) for as little appropriation as possible. This is also valid from the perspective of efficiency: given the idiosyncratic nature of knowledge as a dynamic entity, its existence requires the preservation of sufficiently wide accessibility, while extensive appropriation impairs the resource and its productivity. When increasing returns in the number of users do matter, as in the case of knowledge, the scarcity concept is simply reversed (Ramello, 2005b). Then the exhaustion of knowledge is caused by under-exploitation, which calls for weak propertisation. Hence, in the knowledge domain, efficiency seems to shake hands with social justice.

The earliest structure of IPRs appeared to be consistent with the enounced rationale, as the rights were originally conceived to give individuals incentive and entailed marginal private appropriation. This feature kept the impact on the public dimension and the sharing process as low as possible. Copyright, for example, originally expired 14 years after the publication date. The fair use doctrine, again concerning copyright, permitted several exceptions to the exclusive right granted to the owner. In science, wide swathes of the public domain were recognised in order to preserve the basic tools of research.

The current extension of copyright to 70 years after the author's death, the progressive erosion of fair use space and the possibility to copyright and patent an increasing number of subject matters are now changing the entire framework, with apparent disregard for the original criteria. Analogous dynamics characterise other IPRs.[23]

Concluding remarks

The main rationale for justifying IP relies on the thesis of the incentive to create. Creators and inventors are economic agents attracted by the returns they expect from their effort. This depiction is practical and widely endorsed by law and economic theory, but does not give due weight to the complexity of knowledge production.

This work does not contest the potential benefit of the opportunity for creators and inventors to reap some profit from their work. Rather, it considers the idiosyncratic nature of knowledge, which is simultaneously input, output and productive technology, and is closely linked to the social dimension. This provides further insight into the production process and suggests a significantly different framework for policy.

More specifically, because of the increasing returns governing creative technology, the efficiency criterion used to guide economic choice calls for weak IPRs, thus preserving wide access to knowledge. A stronger appropriation regime would significantly impair the total outcome of the creative processes.

Interestingly, this appears to apply equally from a social justice perspective, perhaps in an effortless solution to the age-old trade-off between economic efficiency and social justice.

Acknowledgement

* I am greatly indebted to participants to the Workshop on IP and Justice and to an anonymous referee for thoughtful suggestions. This research was supported by PRIN. The usual disclaimer applies.

Notes

1. For references, see Ramello (2007) and the book in which that article is published.
2. In the case of trade secrets, appropriation is pursued by protecting the secrecy of the discovery, while in the case of trade marks the incentive is to produce information that does not represent the product *per se* – at least in the original rationale – but an ancillary device to the market and competitive process (see Ramello, 2005a).
3. The same criticism has been raised by others. Among them, Weitzman (1998, p. 332) asks whether 'production of knowledge [is] a process that can be

modeled by analogy with fishing new ponds or discovering new oil reserves.' and answers 'that something fundamentally different is involved here'.

4. A land owner has an exclusive right over his/her parcels, but this does not imply that he/she is a monopolist. Neighbouring parcels can be almost perfect substitutes.
5. In accordance with anti-trust literature and practice, IPRs *per se* do not confer any market power, as repeatedly affirmed by the European Union, European Court of Justice and by the US Federal Trade Commission and Department of Justice. IPR-protected information, if not successful, will not allow the legal monopoly granted by IPRs to translate into an economic monopoly. However, it is the prospect of securing supra-profits that constitutes the incentive to create, since a perfectly competitive market would deliver no extra profits and therefore zero incentive. The logic behind IPRs is thus to reward successful ideas with market power (Ramello, 2005a).
6. In the case of private property, prices are exclusionary in the competitive regime as well because they must cover significant costs. By contrast, in the knowledge domain competitive pricing would imply prices close to zero since marginal costs are very low. It is the incentive mechanism that requires pricing above marginal cost.
7. It is worth noting that I avoid using the term 'information' and the related 'information goods' in favour of 'knowledge', in accordance with extensive economics literature. Although the two terms are sometime used interchangeably, they refer to distinct concepts. An item of information is a message containing structured data, while knowledge addresses the cognitive context of economic agents. It bears the expanded meaning commonly associated with 'the state or fact of knowing', and corresponds to the more general definition of 'the sum or range of what has been perceived, discovered' (*American Heritage Dictionary of the English Language*, 4th edition, 2000). It is dynamic in nature, and can therefore never be entirely encoded or commodified as a whole. Although fragments can be encoded and somewhat appropriated, it is only an attribute of a collectivity of individuals (Cowan, David and Foray, 2000; Rooney, 2003). In effect, the dynamic character arising from the process of communication is necessary not only for the existence of knowledge, but also for the sustenance of human groupings (Polanyi, 1966).
8. Few economics papers take this feature into account. For a discussion, see Ramello (2005b).
9. This representation of human action 'disallows by hypothesis any impact of social structure and social relations on production, distribution, or consumption' and thus produces a poorly descriptive picture (Granovetter, 1985, p. 483).
10. For an overview, see Cowan et al. (2000). The fact that tacit knowledge is physically held by individuals does not negate its social nature, since, generally speaking, there is no such thing as a physical entity called 'social relationships'. In other words, individuals are the 'bearers' of this type of knowledge, but the expression and transmission of tacit knowledge nevertheless requires interaction between individuals to take place. Von Hayek (1945) equally distinguished the portion of scientific knowledge that can be encoded from the 'unorganised knowledge' which is essentially inalienable

and demands the participation of several individuals in order to be exploited

11. Interestingly, Edison used the term 'canned sound' to describe the possibility of recording sound in a wax cylinder thanks to his 1877 invention, the phonograph.
12. This assertion does not deny that in specific cases, IPRs can play some role in transferring both codified and the related tacit knowledge by facilitating contracting and interpersonal interaction. However, this can be seen as more an exception than a rule and strengthens the argument that in IP a more conscious balance should be considered between various effects (Ramello, 2005c).
13. Nelson and Winter (1982, p. 78) further argue that 'a trait that distinguishes a good instructor is the ability to discover introspectively, and then articulate for the student, much of the knowledge that ordinarily remains tacit'.
14. Nelson and Winter (1982) explicitly introduce the productive role of tacit knowledge.
15. Willison and MacLeod (2002), Liebeskind et al. (1996), Romer (1990), Weitzman (1998). Legal knowledge also, governed by an open access model, can be interpreted in the same vein (Harnay and Marciano, 2007).
16. The exercise of the exclusive right granted by IPRs, as discussed above, implies above-cost pricing and by consequence exclusion.
17. The strength of appropriability is linked to the design of the law and other law enforcement variables. For a discussion of distinct IPRs and references to further literature, see Ramello (2005).
18. The best example of the described outcome is brought by what happens when all the individuals belonging to a specific culture die. It is possible to preserve objects and relics, cultural products and literary texts, i.e. codified knowledge, but the elements pertaining to interactions among individuals are lost and no new knowledge is produced.
19. To put it differently: '[a] culture could not exist if all free riding were prohibited within it' (Gordon, 1992, p. 167). This is consistent with the literature claiming the central role of free riding and knowledge spill-over in its production.
20. The concept and the definition of social justice have been disputed and questioned ever since Plato's *Republic*. I am endorsing here the modern thesis that social justice 'has less to do with individual conduct than a "fair" distribution of material benefits and burdens in society and in this perspective it represents a major function played by states'(Stapleton, 1998, pp. 468–9).
21. Naturally, this assertion refers mainly to the mainstream neoclassical tradition and does not consider the heterodox perspectives. Thus far, however, there is a widespread idea that the needs of many, if not most, individuals are unmet in the market order and in the theoretical representation of it (Stapleton, 1998).
22. It goes without saying that this concept should be equally applied to other resources such as the environment. However there is a significant difference in the case of knowledge relying on the concept of scarcity, again highlighting its distinctive nature: while in the former, depletion of the resource stems from its over-utilization – this is the typical case of commons that exhibit

diminishing returns with a growing number of users – in the latter, depletion is caused by under-utilization since the creative commons present increasing returns with number of users (Ramello, 2005b).

23. Ramello (2005b).

References

Attaran, A. and Gillespie-White, L. (2001) Do Patents for Antiretroviral Drugs Constrain Access to AIDS Treatment in Africa? *Journal of the American Medical Association*, 286: 1886–92.

Barry, B. (1989) *A Treatise on Social Justice*. London: Harvester-Wheatsheaf.

Bentham, J. (1839/1962) A Manual of Political Economy', in John Bowring, *Works of Jeremy Bentham*. vol 3, New York: Russell & Russell (reprint).

Cowan, R., David P. A. and Foray, D. (2000) The Explicit Economics of Knowledge Codification and Tacitness, *Industrial and Corporate Change*, 9: 211–53.

Frischmann, B. (2005) Some Thoughts on Shortsightedness and Intergenerational Equity, *Loyola University Chicago Law Journal*, 36: 457–67.

Granovetter, M. (1985) Economic Action and Social Structure: The Problem of Embeddedness, *American Journal of Sociology*, 91: 481–510.

Geertz, C. (1973) *The Interpretation of Cultures*. New York: Basic Books.

Goldstein, P. (1994). *Copyright's Highway*. New York: Hill and Wang.

Gordon, W. (1992) On Owning Information: Intellectual Property and the Restitutionary Impulse, *Vanderbilt Law Review*, 78: 149, 167.

Harnay, S. and Marciano, M. (2007) Intellectual Property Rights and Judge-Made Law: An Economic Analysis of the Production and Diffusion of Precedent', in D. Porrini and G. B. Ramello (eds) *Property Rights Dynamics. A Law and Economics Perspective*. London and New York: Routledge.

Landes, W. M. and Posner, R. A. (1989) An Economic Analysis of Copyright Law, *Journal of Legal Studies*, 18: 325–63.

Liebeskind, J. P., Lumerman. O. A., Zucker, L. and Brewer, M. (1996) Social Networks, Learning, and Flexibility: Sourcing Scientific Knowledge in New Biotechnology Firms, *Organization Science*, 7: 428–43.

Miller, D. (1976) *Social Justice*. Oxford: Clarendon Press.

Munzer, S. R. (1990). *A Theory of Property*. Cambridge: Cambridge University Press.

Nelson, R. R. and Winter, S. G. (1982) *An Evolutionary Theory of the Economic Change*. Cambridge, MA: Belknap Press.

Nelson, R. R. (2003) On the Uneven Evolution of Human Know-how, *Research Policy*, 32: 909–22.

Nordhaus, W. D. (1969) *Invention, Growth and Welfare*. Cambridge MA: MIT Press.

Polanyi, M. (1966) *The Tacit Dimension*. New York: Doubleday.

Ramello, G. B. (2005a) Intellectual Property and the Markets of Ideas, *Review of Network Economics*, 4: 68–87.

Ramello, G. B. (2005b) Private Appropriability and Knowledge Sharing: Contradiction or Convergence? The Opposite Tragedy of Creative Commons, in L. Takeyama L., W. Gordon and R. Towse (eds) *Developments in the Economics of Copyright*. Cheltenham and Northampton, MA: Edward Elgar.

Ramello, G. B. (2005c) Property Rights, Firm Boundaries and the Republic of Science, *Industrial and Corporate Change*, 14: 1195–1204.

Ramello, G. B. (2007) Property Rights Dynamics: Current Issues in Law and Economics', in D. Porrini, and G. B. Ramello (eds) *Property Rights Dynamics. A Law and Economics Perspective*. London and New York: Routledge.
Romer, P. (1990) Endogenous Technological Change, *Journal of Political Economy*, 98: 71–102.
Romney, A. K. (1999) Culture Consensus as a Statistical Model, *Current Antrhopology*, 40: 103–15.
Rooney, D., Hearn, G., Mandeville, T. and Joseph, R (2003) *Public Policy in Knowledge-Based Economies*. Cheltenham and Northampton, MA: Edward Elgar.
Scherer, F. M. (2004) A Note on Global Welfare in Pharmaceutical Patenting, *World Economy* 27: 1127–42.
Stapleton, J. (1998) Social Justice, in P. Newman (ed.) *The New Palgrave Dictionary of Economics and the Law*. London: Macmillan/New York: Stockton, vol. 3, 468–76.
Takii, K. (2004) A Barrier to the Diffusion of Tacit Knowledge, *Review of Development Economics*, 8: 81–90.
von Hayek, F. (1945) The Use of Knowledge in Society, *American Economic Review*, 25: 519–30.
Weitzman, M. L. (1998) Recombinant Growth, *Quarterly Journal of Economics*, 113: 331–60.
Williams, F. and Gibson, D. V. (eds) (1990) *Technology Transfer: A Communication Perspective*. Newbury Park, CA: Sage.
Willison, D. J. and MacLeod, S. M. (2002) Patenting of Genetic Material: Are the Benefits to Society Being Realized? *Canadian Medical Association Journal*, 167: 259–62.

4
The Incentives Argument for Intellectual Property Protection[1]

Seana Valentine Shiffrin

The incentives argument for intellectual property contends that intellectual property protections must be given to creators in order to give them the incentive to create their works. The incentives argument for intellectual property differs from other incentives arguments because the intellectual property incentive works in a distinctive way, by offering a form of monopoly control as the incentive. In theory, that incentive operates to stimulate creation of some work by promising the power to prevent other, similar works from being produced or distributed. I will argue that by enabling creators to prevent the creation or dissemination of other, similar works, the incentives argument for intellectual property is prey to unique philosophical difficulties that do not arise for other incentive arguments, or at least not to the same degree.

To situate the issues I raise, I first comment on some arguments I wish to distinguish and set aside, namely Lockean natural rights arguments for intellectual property. In earlier work I have argued against interpreting the Lockean tradition to support strong individual natural rights to intellectual property, including rights to forbid others' use or consumption of materials, as well as the right to prohibit the production of derivative works (see Shiffrin, 2001; 2007, pp. 653–68). Despite its frequent invocation in support of strong intellectual property rights, the Lockean tradition, as I understand it, is suspicious of such rights. This tradition begins with the idea that we own the world in common, and then directs that property be allocated in such a way as to promote its full and effective use. It is only when exclusive use is necessary for full and effective use that a Lockean natural individual right to the exclusive use of property should be acknowledged.

Although Locke argues that the full and effective use of real property requires certain forms of exclusive control and direction, it is much harder to extend that claim to intellectual property. Generally, full and effective use of intellectual property does not depend on its exclusive use. On the contrary, typically, intellectual property can be used by many people simultaneously and to different ends without frustrating or impeding others' use.

From a number of philosophical perspectives, whether Lockean or not, this feature of intellectual property – its capacity to be used simultaneously by an indefinite number of people – makes arguments for its exclusive control by private agents suspect. With respect to copyright, this suspicion is justifiably heightened within legal and cultural contexts, such as the United States, that prize uninhibited freedom of expression.[2]

The problems with natural rights arguments, as well as our continued affirmation of the value of uninhibited expression, have focused recent legal and philosophical attention on a different kind of justification for our private intellectual property regime: namely, the claim that rights of exclusive use and control for a limited duration must be granted because they provide the necessary incentives for the creation of useful inventions and expressive works, works that contribute to a robust speech culture.[3] Despite the frequent invocation of the incentives argument, it is surprising how little attention and research has been devoted to assessing the claim that copyright and patent terms of the sort we have are in fact *necessary* to incent creative production.[4] Whether such terms do provide necessary incentives is a difficult and more complex question than is usually acknowledged. Here, I will set out a few philosophical problems associated with understanding and justifying the incentives argument and the uses to which it is put. I will focus on difficulties with the argument for strong forms of intellectual property protection. These include a fairly long-term ability to control who uses a product, how it is used and, most important, whether similar products may be generated and distributed.

The diverse array of persons who create, produce and distribute intellectual products poses difficulties for making the general incentives claims about them all. Take the claim that strong copyright terms are necessary to provide creators (as distinguished from publishers or distributors) with an incentive to create because such terms offer the greatest leverage for obtaining pecuniary rewards in exchange for production. For many artists, although there is a need to recoup labour and production costs, their primary motivation to create does not hinge on whether substantial pecuniary rewards are offered and does not increase when higher rewards are offered. Their primary interest is often just in their art and in the process of creation, and for many in its wide dissemination to others. There is some experimental evidence that high levels of reward may deter some creative artists rather than act as an incentive.[5] Notwithstanding the cynical speculations of a culture permeated by simplistic models of greed and self-interest, many medical researchers' primary motivation is to create products that will cure diseases and promote health. Most academics, as we know, work from these sorts of motives as well as from interests in gaining status and earning a reputation.

To justify anything like our current intellectual property regime, the incentives argument must advance beyond the modest claim that creators need funding to recoup creation and labour costs; and that given the ability of competitors to make cheap copies, the funds creators need may exceed what would be available through the unprotected release of their products and creations on the market. Those considerations do not justify strong schemes of copyright, including the wide sweep of derivative work protection as well as injunctions and criminal penalties. Creators' expenses could be adequately covered through salaries, stipends, compulsory licensing schemes, simple restrictions on direct copying or other schemes, without ceding the full panoply of rights of exclusive use and control over the work and its derivatives. We must distinguish between those situations in which the prospect of control over a work directly or indirectly (as leverage for indefinite amounts of financial gain) operates as a motivation for creation and those situations in which some funding and control over the work during creation may be necessary to make creation feasible. In the latter case, control and funding only facilitate the creation, but their prospect is not the aim of creation. I do not know of any evidence that strong copyright or strong patent protection is the *only* way to facilitate creation in situations of the latter kind. Thus, to justify strong intellectual property protection with an incentives argument, the argument must begin with the strong claim the prospect of strong copyright protection over works (and their derivatives) is itself a necessary motivation for creation, or offers the prospect of significant financial leverage in future bargaining, which is a necessary motivation for creation. It is this argument I address here.

There are difficulties I will set aside about how we could ascertain the optimal incentive level, the least we need to offer in order to motivate creators to produce.[6] Assuming that we know that strong intellectual property protection is necessary to motivate some creators, there are two other, more philosophical problems about incentives that run deep. One concerns the evaluation conditions of the claim that strong intellectual property protection is a necessary incentive for creation; the other concerns the justification conditions for the claim that we should provide such protection if necessary.

I will focus on the argument that a derivative works protection of the sort the US copyright regime provides is a necessary incentive for production and creation and is justified where necessary.[7] (Although my focus is on copyright, many of these arguments apply also to a patent scheme that offers long terms of exclusive use and control over an invention, even to preclude the release of independently invented infringing works.) If these incentives work, they do so by providing a monopoly for a producer of a given work of a particular sort. The producer's work will not have to compete with related versions or derivatives that might otherwise be created. As Rebecca Tushnet put it, copyright law suppresses some speech in order to make other speech more likely (2000, p. 3). Suppose it is true that the derivative works protection provides some incentives for creators to make derivative works of their own, or even to make primary works that they would not otherwise create. Even if this is true to a significant degree, it should not be assumed that for the production of *all* original creative works it is absolutely necessary that there be protection for derivative works.

There is some historical evidence for my scepticism. Wide control over derivative works is a relatively recent component of copyright protection (Goldstein, 1983, p. 209). Books, artworks and other creative works were certainly produced before the introduction of derivative works protection. Nonetheless, even creators who would create without derivative works protection may nonetheless wield that protection to penalise infringers. Legally, they are permitted to do so; they may elect to do so for financial gain even if they did not need this power as a prerequisite for production. Those who want to create derivative works will be deterred by the prospect of liability and criminal prosecution. So, what will be deterred by strong copyright protection includes both derivative works of original works that themselves would not have been created but for the monopoly right as well as derivative works of original works that *would* have been created absent the granting of the monopoly right.

The uncertain net effect of derivative works protection

The justificatory problem is as follows: how can we know and assert with confidence that the works incented through the derivative works protection are superior in some relevant respect (quality? quantity?) to the works whose production is deterred by this form of copyright protection? How *could* we know this? We are comparing works that now exist with works that have been legally precluded from being created or disseminated. Even if we had examples, how could we generalise from them?

If no creative original work at all were produced absent the derivative works protection, then this justificatory problem would dissolve. If that were the case, all precluded derivative works would depend on the existence of primary works that would not be created without the derivative works protection. If creation entirely ceased without derivative works protection, there would be nothing to compare. But the historical evidence, as well as our knowledge of the motivations of at least some creators, strongly suggests that this is not the case. Some primary works will be created regardless of derivative works protection. An artist may be motivated to produce for other reasons – for instance, a sufficiently powerful interest in writing, painting or sculpting, possibly coupled with a satisfaction with whatever compensation is available for producing the primary work. If some primary works will be created without a derivative works protection, then the question that we face with regard to the incentive provided by derivative works protection becomes far more complicated. The question then becomes whether the quantity or quality of work that we believe derivative works protection incents is superior in either quantity or quality to the precluded work that infringing creators would produce absent such protection.

Suppose that we could run cross-cultural experiments to show that societies offering derivative works protection have one type of culture and societies lacking derivative works protection have another. Even if these cultures were otherwise comparable, and even if we could identify the effects of the derivative works protection (or any other form of copyright incentive), to make sense of the derivative works argument, it would still be necessary to evaluate these cultures and assess which culture is superior. This might prove rather difficult, We would confront hard questions, including how to assess the qualitative merits of the different cultural outputs; how qualitative considerations should weigh against considerations of quantity; how these factors relate to the value of easy, inexpensive public access to creative works; whether it is better for a wide or narrow range of the population to participate in creative activity; how simple and inexpensive consumer access to interesting forms of expression should be; and how these factors interrelate.

We cannot say with any confidence that we have even begun to think about how difficult these questions are, much less approximate an answer to them. Rather, we have ducked them. I do not know whether this is deliberate or whether, implicitly, we are appealing to the kinds of natural rights considerations that favour the first creator but that, properly understood, do not have a firm foothold in the area of intellectual property.

There is an argument for moving in the opposite direction from what appears to be the default presumption of many that accords strong intellectual property protections to the first creator. Our free speech commitments are to robust, open and widespread public production and consumption of intellectual materials. When we find ourselves in the condition of profound uncertainty I have just articulated (uncertainty about whether copyright protections are in fact necessary incentives for the kind of culture we aim to nurture and uncertainty about whether the work incented by prohibiting the creation of other work is superior to that which we suppress), our free speech commitments should incline us against the deliberate suppression of speech. This is a minimal principle: we should not actively suppress speech on the grounds that suppression will incent better or more speech than is suppressed unless, at the least, we have strong grounds for believing that the speech that is suppressed is on some significant dimension worse.

The problem that I have articulated concerns the evaluation and assessment of the claim that copyright protections provide necessary incentives for optimal cultural production. To rely on this claim, we must be able to articulate criteria for assessing the success of such incentives, but we lack the knowledge of what those criteria are and we lack the information necessary to apply them.

Fair and unfair demands for incentives

Even if the incentives claim could be evaluated, there is another problem with the incentives argument, namely whether it is justified to act on the idea that such incentives are necessary to promote optimal cultural production. Over the last decade, there has been much work done in political philosophy about incentives in a different context.[8] Although this work has not been applied to intellectual property, it is worth considering what light it casts on the role of and need for incentives in copyright law.

The incentives argument for strong copyright protections bears similarity to a familiar incentives argument in contemporary political philosophy. John Rawls famously argued that in a just society the basic structure would aim to distribute social primary goods equally unless an unequal distribution would be to the maximal advantage of the least well-off. If those enjoying the smallest allotment of social primary goods under an unequal distribution would be better off than they would be under an equal distribution, Rawls argued that it may be justified, even required, to distribute resources unequally.

When would these conditions hold? Rawls hypothesised that there may be conditions under which the promise of higher salaries or rewards would operate as an incentive to those positioned by talent or social position to be extraordinarily productive (Rawls, 1971,p. 151). So long as a distributive scheme were structured so as to share as much surplus production as possible so that everyone in society would benefit from it – in particular those who end up at the bottom of an unequal distribution – then such incentives, as well as the inequalities they engender, would be justified.

The incentives argument for copyright could be viewed as having an analogous structure. Our society's commitment to freedom of speech creates a presumption of free and equal access to, and use of, expressive materials. The incentives argument suggests the following. If unequal access to cultural materials produces a richer array of such materials that benefit everyone, particularly those whose use is more restricted, then restrictions on speech necessary for such incentives may be justified.

G. A. Cohen's work, in what I think of as the virtue theory of political philosophy, has suggested that the justification for the incentives arguments in Rawls' work has to be made more complex than its standard presentations. As Cohen argues, the mere fact that an incentive is required for production does not necessarily mean that its provision is justified or that the conditions that make it requisite are justified. We should ask why the incentive is required instead of taking it as a given. If the incentive is required because the extra production is especially taxing or time-consuming, that would be one thing. It would be quite another if the incentive is required because talented people ransom their talents, withholding their creative products in order to demand greater compensation. In the latter case, the talented person's motives are inconsistent with the motives of a just person. Cohen argues that such motives are inconsistent with the idea that inequalities are justified only if they are to benefit the worst off, because such a person would be creating an inequality for her own gain. She could be just as productive and accept an equal share of the surplus.

I might put the argument differently, though to the same end. In a Rawlsian just society, a just citizen accepts both the theory of justice and its justification. So a just citizen accepts that social and natural talents as well as one's market position are arbitrary from a moral point of view. One could not accept these tenets and also use one's happenstance command over socially useful talents for private advantage by demanding premiums for an especially productive work. This would be to treat one's talents and market position as morally relevant, which is inconsistent with believing they are morally arbitrary.[9] When people demand incentives, one might think that they are acting in an unjustified way; so one might also think that responding to these incentives raises new questions of justice, namely whether one is acquiescing in, endorsing or encouraging injustice. The lesson of this argument is that it is not sufficient to assert that an incentive is required for production; rather, one might want to inquire as to the reason the incentive is required and as to the motives of those who demand the incentive.

I outline this argument not to endorse Rawls' theory in general, or to endorse Cohen's position. Instead, I raise it because there is a parallel to copyright that has not yet been articulated.

The parallel argument about copyright goes something like this. One may ask whether creators who demand incentives are operating from motives that are consistent with their accepting free speech protections and their underlying justifications. We might imagine a range of motives underlying why creators need exceptional incentives for production. If a limited monopoly were necessary to recoup the costs of production, as well as to allow for sufficient resources to ensure producers an adequate livelihood, that would provide strong justification for limited terms of copyright over direct copies of primary works. But, as I suggested earlier, it is hard to believe (and there is no strong empirical support) that the stronger rights of our copyright regime are the minimum necessary to recoup labour and material costs.

There are other reasons for demanding incentives that would be more suspect. For instance, some might be motivated by the idea that copyright protection focuses cultural attention on the creator, by deterring competing or similar types of work. Others may be motivated by the power that strong copyright protection affords the creator to police the quality of derivative works. Some may regard copyright protection as desirable because it gives creators the tools to fend off certain forms of criticism or what they may regard as inferior forms of parroting and endorsement or affiliation. Some seek copyright protection because the limited monopoly allows for more profit than is necessary for an adequate livelihood. Although the first motive, simply aiming to recoup one's costs of production and have an adequate livelihood, is perfectly consistent with free speech values, the consistency of these other four with such values is doubtful. A person who claims to be in favour of free, robust and open discussion, uninhibited self-expression and a sincere exchange and evaluation of ideas, but who seeks copyright protection in order to try to limit criticism, to suppress disagreement or to stifle creative reaction and mimicry, would seem to be acting from inconsistent motives.

In the United States, private citizens are not constrained directly by the First Amendment which codifies the US constitutional commitment to freedom of speech. Their motives need not comport with its values. But, morally, private citizens are constrained as virtuous democratic citizens. The First Amendment is not merely a constraint on government activity; it represents a public commitment to a free speech culture. Our community must decide how it wants to respond to those who act from motives that are inconsistent with endorsement of the First Amendment. Whether or not it is justified to suppress speech in order to incent more or better speech is already a vexed question. Whether we should do so to indulge motives that are fundamentally at odds with the motives necessary for a well-operating free speech culture poses an even greater challenge.

These difficulties suggest that we should question the structure and empirical basis of the incentives argument in greater depth. Further, we should inquire what motives make it necessary (if this is true) to provide monopoly incentives for creative production, and then ask whether, given our free speech commitments, we should acquiesce in such motivations.

Notes

1. This is an edited and footnoted transcript of remarks made on the 'Philosophical Perspectives' Panel of the Symposium on the Rule of Law in the Information Age at The Catholic University of America, 10 October 2002. A shorter version of some of the points appears in Shiffrin (2007, pp. 653–68). I am grateful to William Wagner, Susanna Fischer, C. Ed Baker, David Goldman, Lisa Lucas and Collin O'Neil for helpful comments.
2. Others have explored the First Amendment/copyright tension in depth. See, Baker (2002, p. 891); Benkler (1999, p. 354); Gordon (1989, pp. 1435–65; 1992, p. 149; 1993, pp. 1533–40); Lemley and Volokh (1998, p. 147); Lessig (2001, p. 1057); Nimmer (1970, p. 1180); Litman (1990, pp. 965–1063); Netanel (1996, p. 283; 2001, p. 1).
3. This is the justification articulated in the US Constitution (Article 1, §8, clause 8).

4. For a broader examination of incentives (and where we lack information about them) in the creation and exploitation of intellectual property, see Landes and Posner (2003, pp. 9–10): '[T]he economic arguments we make for intellectual property protection are not based primarily on a belief that without legal protection the incentives to create such property would be inadequate. That belief cannot be defended confidently on the basis of current knowledge.'
5. See Amabile (1996); Hennessey and Amabile (1998, pp. 674–5). Of course, artists are not the only players in this field. Many of the actors are not creative people, but rather distributors or publishers whose motives may differ substantially from those of creators.
6. For those artists who do meet the motivation profile presupposed by the argument, those who require significant financial incentives to produce, the problem is to understand and develop an independent criterion for what the least necessary incentive would be, as opposed to the price the creator would most prefer. In some cases there may be close rivals or substitutes, but in other cases, there may not be: the works may be unique and this may form some of the motivation for wishing in particular to incent them. For some sorts of work, creators often have, or, depending on your point of view, necessarily have, an exclusive relation to the material that they produce. Hence, it is difficult to develop arguments about the ceiling for an incentive that would have a source independent of the testimony of the person who demands it. Unlike other kinds of markets, there are no other possible providers. One cannot claim that one could obtain the same material more cheaply and thus have an independent criterion for the ceiling for these incentives. Where there are no close substitutes or rivals, there may be situations in which the creator is willing to call our bluff merely for the sake of establishing a strong bargaining position now or for the future. She may hold out for what she asks because the possibility is open that holding out will get her what she wants. Were there no such potential, she would create for a lower reward and would prefer those terms to not creating at all. In such cases, what appears to be a 'necessary' incentive could represent a higher level than is in fact necessary. See also Shavell and Ypersele (2001, p. 525), who argue that even where maximal reward is the incentive of the creator, reward systems may be comparable to or better than intellectual property systems and may avoid the social costs associated with monopoly pricing.
7. The Copyright Act defines a 'derivative work' as 'a work based upon one or more preexisting works, such as a translation, musical arrangement, dramatization, fictionalization, motion picture version, sound recording, art reproduction, abridgment, condensation, or any other form in which a work may be recast, transformed, or adapted. A work consisting of editorial revisions, annotations, elaborations, or other modifications which, as a whole, represent an original work of authorship, is a "derivative work"' (17 USC §101). The right to prepare derivative works is reserved to the owner of a copyright (17 USC §106(2)). For an attempt to determine the optimal scope of copyright with a focus on derivative works protection as an incentive, see Lunney (1996, p. 483).
8. G. Cohen (1995a, pp. 160–85; 1995b; 1997, pp. 3–30; 2000); J. Cohen (2001, p. 363); Estlund (1998, p. 99); Williams (1998, p. 225).

9. This form of the argument requires citizens to know and accept the justificatory basis behind the principles of justice. In that sense, it rests on a stronger premise than Cohen's. But this formulation avoids the controversial claim that the principles of justice that regulate the social structure should also serve directly to regulate individuals within the structure.

References

Amabile, T. M. (1996) *Creativity in Context* Boulder, CO: Westview Press.

Amabile, T. and Hennessey, B. A. (1998) Reward, Intrinsic Motivation, and Creativity, *American Psychologist*, 53: 674–5.

Baker, C. E. (2002) First Amendment Limits on Copyright, *Vanderbilt Law Review*, 55: 891–952.

Benkler, Y. (1999) Free as the Air to Common Use: First Amendment Constraints on Enclosure of the Public Domain, *New York University Law Review*, 74: 354–446.

Cohen, G. A. (1995a) The Pareto Argument for Inequality, *Social Philosophy & Policy*, 12: 160–85.

Cohen, G. A. (1995b) Incentives, Inequality and Community, in S. Darwall (ed.) *Equal Freedom*. Ann Arbor.MI: University of Michigan Press, pp. 261–329.

Cohen, G. A. (1997) Where the Action is: On the Site of Distributive Justice, *Philosophy & Public Affairs*, 26: 3–30.

Cohen, G. A. (2000) *If You're An Egalitarian, How Come You're So Rich?* Cambridge, MA: Harvard University Press.

Cohen, J. (2001) Taking People as They Are? *Philosophy & Public Affairs*, 30: 363–86.

Estlund, D. (1998) Liberalism, Equality, And Fraternity in Cohen's Critique of Rawls, *Journal of Political Philosophy*, 6: 99–112.

Goldstein, P. (1983) Derivative Rights and Derivative Works In Copyright, *Journal of the Copyright Society of USA*, 30: 209–52.

Cohen, G. A. (1993) A Property Right in Self-expression: Equality and Individualism in the Natural Law of Intellectual Property, *Yale Law Journal*, 102: 1533–40.

Cohen, G. A. (1989) An Inquiry into the Merits of Copyright: the Challenges of Consistency, Consent, and Encouragement Theory, *Stanford Law Review*, 41: 1435–65.

Cohen, G. A. (1992) On Owning Information: Intellectual Property and the Restitutionary Impulse, *Virginia Law Review*, 78: 149–281.

Landes, W. M. and Posner, R. A. (2003) *The Economic Structure of Intellectual Property Law*. Cambridge, MA: Harvard University Press.

Lemley, M. A. and Volokh, E. (1998) Freedom of Speech and Injunctions in Intellectual Property Cases, *Duke Law Review*, 48: 147–217.

Lessig, L. (2001) Copyright's First Amendment, *UCLA Law Review*, 48: 1057–73.

Litman, J. (1990) The Public Domain, *Emory Law Journal*, 39: 965–1023.

Lloyd, S. A. (n.d.) Self-interest, Citizen Virtue, and Justice in a Liberal Democracy: A Rawlsian Reply to G. A. Cohen (unpublished; on file with author).

Lunney, Jr., G. S. (1996) Reexamining Copyright's Incentives-Access Paradigm, *Vanderbilt Law Review*, 49: 483–571.

Nimmer, M. B. (1970) Does Copyright Abridge the First Amendment Guarantees of Free Speech and Press? *UCLA Law Review*, 17: 1180–1204.

Netanel, N. W. (1996) Copyright and a Democratic Civil Society, *Yale Law Journal*, 106, 283–387.

Netanel, N. W. (2001) Locating Copyright within the First Amendment Skein, *Stanford Law Review*, 54: 1–86.

Rawls, J. (1971) *A Theory of Justice*. Cambridge, MA: Harvard University Press.

Shavell, S. and Ypersele, T. V. (2001) Rewards versus Intellectual Property Rights, *Journal of Law and Economics*, 44: 525–47.

Shiffrin, S. V. (2001) Lockean Arguments for Private Intellectual Property', in S. Munzer (ed.) *New Essays in the Legal and Political Theory of Property*. Cambridge: Cambridge University Press.

Shiffrin, S. V. (2007) Intellectual Property Theory, in R. Goodin and P. Pettit (eds.) *Blackwell's Companion to Contemporary Political Philosophy*. Oxford: Blackwell, 2, pp. 653–68.

Tushnet, R. (2000) Copyright as a Model for Free Speech Law, *Boston College Law Review*, 42: 1–79.

Williams, A. (1998) Incentives, Inequality, and Publicity, *Philosophy & Public Affairs*, 27: 225–47.

5
When Property is Something Else: Understanding Intellectual Property through the Lens of Regulatory Justice

Shubha Ghosh

Introduction

While everyone agrees that the subject of intellectual property is copyrights, patents, trade marks and related legal concepts, such as trade secrets, there is increasing doubt that this subject can or should be described as property (Carrier, 2004; Lemley, 2005). *Blackstone's Commentaries* discusses patents and copyright as a species of monopoly (1979b, pp. 407, 159). Contemporary economic theorists, uninfluenced by the legal theorist William Blackstone, analyse intellectual property as a species of the monopoly problem (Levine and Boldrin, 2002). Even the concession that intellectual property is a set of property rights does not resolve the issue, for the rights created by copyright, patents, trade marks and related concepts are decidedly different from the rights granted to land or other tangible assets (Heald, 2005). Even intangibility cannot serve as a marker for differentiation since what is labelled intellectual property is different from intangible assets such as securities and other financial instruments. Scholarly pages are expended debating what intellectual property is not. In this chapter, I explore what intellectual property is. My concern is less with the name, and even though the term 'intellectual property' is unfortunate, it is acceptable if properly understood for the concept being referenced.

My claim is that intellectual property can best be understood as a system of laws meant to define and regulate creative activity. This chapter explains what I mean by 'regulate' and 'creative activity'. Put succinctly, intellectual property establishes a system of rights and obligations that order the processes of creating novel products and services that are valuable to society. Novelty does not imply that the products and services are created *ex nihilo*. Instead, the creative processes can be broad, ranging from the activities of a lone, individual creator living in isolation from society, to the activities of groups of individuals acting in concert according to norms and customs.

Two implications follow from my claim. First, intellectual property is not about things (or *res* to use the legal jargon), but about activities. A focus on activities allows us to examine intellectual property in descriptive terms. Second, intellectual property as regulation of activities allows deeper consideration of the normative goals driving the structure of intellectual property law. These normative goals are what I refer to in the title as 'regulatory justice'. This chapter, therefore, has both positive and normative dimensions. I am claiming not only that intellectual property can be understood as regulation of creative activities, but also that this description is desirable for certain normative reasons that follow.

The claim is developed in three sections. I first show what it means to describe intellectual property as a system of regulation through examples from patent and copyright law. I conclude this section by examining the arguments for and against conceptualising intellectual property as regulatory. In the next section I develop the normative implications by identifying four notions of regulatory justice that can be gleaned from the scholarly literature on regulation: expertise, civic participation, market failure and management. I argue that each has an application to understanding intellectual property with civic participation and market failure having the greatest relevance. Finally, I demonstrate how understanding intellectual property as regulation helps us to understand two important areas of intellectual property law: pharmaceutical patents and fair use in copyright.

Intellectual property as regulation

Patents and copyrights, when understood as property, are reduced to things that can be alienated in the marketplace. As property, they can allow the owner to enforce rights of exclusivity in order to manage the thing in which ownership vests more effectively. The spectre of John Locke informs patents and copyrights as property, with all the attendant controversy (Gordon, 1993). What is strange is that the reduction of patents and copyrights to things ignores several aspects of patent and copyright law as they exist in the United States and elsewhere. The aspects I discuss below are the subject of frequent debate in international circles, particularly in the context of the implementation of the

Trade Related Intellectual Property Systems (TRIPS) Agreement, which is central to the World Trade Organisation (Ryan, 1998). While it is an empirical fact that patents and copyrights are treated like property, it would be wrong to reduce patent and copyright law to a species of property law. Instead, patent law and copyright law regulate primary activity, as I shall demonstrate.

Consider first patent law as it exists in the United States, the model through which the law is to be exported to the rest of the world. A patent is a grant from a state authority that allows the owner of the patent to exclude others from using, making, selling or importing the invention described within the patent instrument. The state authority granting the patent is called the Patent Office, the responsibility of which includes reviewing a patent application and publishing the patent instrument when the application is granted and the patent issued. The application process, often referred to as prosecution, requires a disclosure by the applicant of the claimed invention and a review by the Patent Office to ensure that the claimed invention is novel and non-obvious. The determination of novelty and non-obviousness entails a review of prior art, or the legally recognised prior knowledge and usage in a given field. If the claimed invention is strictly identical to or a trivial variation of inventions in the prior art, the application will be not granted.

Once the application is approved and a patent is issued, the owner of the patent has the right for a given period of time (usually 20 years from the date of issue), to exclude others from using, making, selling or importing the claimed invention. This right is exercised through a lawsuit, called an infringement action, brought against a party that has made an unauthorised use, manufacture, sale or import of the claimed invention. In addition, the patent owner will typically license the claimed invention to parties who want to make some use of the work. Since a patent is a valuable asset, it can also be used in commercial transactions, particularly as collateral for a debt obligation or as an asset that can be bought and sold like any other.

Superficially, patents resemble property. But it would be wrong to assume from that family resemblance that patent law is simply a branch of property law. There are several important aspects of patent law that cannot be understood solely by an appeal to the category of property and its attendant principles. For example, the concept of prior art is not as expansive as one may initially think. Under US law, prior art includes what was known or used in the US and what was patented or published anywhere in the world before the date of invention. The fact that what was known or used outside the US is excluded from prior art is revealing. If patent law was about establishing boundaries like those that exist in real property, then it does not make sense to exclude foreign knowledge and usage from the scope of prior art. The exclusion is sometimes justified in terms of administrative convenience, sometimes by the need for incentives to borrow knowledge and usage from foreign countries to use within the US. This fairly common instance of patent law suggests that there is more happening with patent law than the creation and protection of property.

Equally telling is the on sale bar which disallows the grant of a patent if the applicant has sold the invention for a statutory period before filing the application. The disposition of the invention by the future patent owner seems antithetical to the treatment of patents as property. One of the hallmarks of property ownerships is the ability to alienate and dispose of one's property as one sees fit, absent harm to others. The on sale bar seems to eliminate a key right of the property owner. The bar, however, is understood as providing incentives for the inventor to expeditiously file for a patent application rather than exploit his invention outside the scope of the patent system. The incentive for expeditious filing is justified by the benefits of public disclosure of the invention and the protection of reliance interests vested in members of the public who have bought and used the invention and face the risk of forfeiting that right if a patent is subsequently granted on the invention. The bar on sale effectively regulates how an inventor can commercially exploit his invention in the shadow of the patent application process.

Patent infringement also demonstrates the incongruity between patent law and property. To prevail in a patent infringement suit, the patent owner must prove that the infringing invention falls within the claimed description in the patent instrument. This requirement is superficially similar to the legal action of trespass to land. Often, in a trespass cause of action, the court will refer to the legal description of a parcel of law to determine the metes and bounds of the property and to see if they have been invaded. Even though judges in patent infringement cases refer to the claims in a patent instrument as setting forth the metes and bounds of the patent owner's legal interest, this usage is metaphorical and obscures differences between patent infringement and trespass. A legal description of land refers to natural boundaries and indicators that help to demarcate the parcels. Patent claims, however, are verbal descriptions of the underlying conception that the patent owner has invented. Legal descriptions of an invention are wholly linguistic, as evidenced by the heated scholarly and judicial debates over the proper interpretation of claims. Furthermore, patent infringement allows for legal actions against equivalent inventions, meaning inventions that can be equivalently described by the language of the patent claims. By contrast, there is no such thing as a trespass action brought against an equivalent parcel.

Copyright law consists of analogous incongruities with property. Unlike patents, copyrights are established as soon as an author fixes an original work of authorship in a tangible medium of expression. In other words, as soon as the writer places pen to paper and writes the words or a musician records his song or a film maker tapes his video, copyright is created. There is no need for review by the Copyright Office, whose job is largely to record registrations of copyrighted works. This automatic creation of rights may make copyright seem more property-like than patent, but many copyright doctrines belie equating copyright with property. First of all, copyright infringement does not require consideration of any legal description of the written expression. There is no analogy to the patent claims or to the legal description of land in copyright. Instead, copyright infringement mandates a visual or aural comparison of the copyrighted work with the infringing work to determine substantial similarity. If the works are substantially similar, then there is infringement. If they are not similar, then there is no infringement. The fuzzy determination of rights in copyright contrasts with the usage of metes and bounds of trespass causes of action. As with patent infringement, copyright infringement is wholly a matter of linguistic interpretation.

Fair use and protected uses also distinguish copyright from property. Under the broad doctrine of fair use, an infringer can defend against the claim of infringement by showing that the use was justified. Although the defence of justification is recognised in property law, fair use has contours that allow the use of copyrighted materials in situations where such use is necessary for the creation of critical commentaries and expressive works that build on copyrighted works. The use is fair if it does not unduly interfere with the rights of the copyright holder, particularly the right to market the work. The doctrine of fair use requires analysis of the use to which the copyrighted work is put. In addition, uses of copyrighted works are protected through statutory safe harbours that exempt certain performances of copyrighted works in school, religious and commercial settings that are deemed necessary for instructional, religious or promotional reasons. Furthermore, copyright law makes generous use of compulsory licensing, requiring the copyright owner to license works in such situations as the creation of a cover recording, cable and satellite transmittal of broadcast content and digital audio transmission of certain radio broadcasts. Compulsory licensing, like fair use and protected uses, creates a class of uses that are exempt from claims for copyright infringement.

The category of property, while capturing some dimensions of patents and copyrights, does not adequately describe or explain the full reach and dimensions of the two sets of statutory law. One striking aspect of the details of patent and copyright laws that I have presented is the emphasis on usage. Many patent rules affect the use of the invention by the inventor and applicant. Copyright rules, analogously, focus on the use and activity by non-owners of the copyrighted expression. For these reasons, copyright and patent (and, by extension, other intellectual property) can best be understood as a system of rules that regulate creative activities. While my description does not deny that in many ways intellectual property is like property (i.e. an asset that can be alienated), treating intellectual property as property focuses solely on the thingness of intellectual property, as *res* , rather the activity of creating. At the minimum, the examples I provide support the claim that intellectual property can be described as regulating creative activity, rather than a thing that can be acquired and managed.

Before I proceed to the normative implications of characterising intellectual property as regulation, I will respond to several potentially salient criticisms of treating intellectual property as regulation of creative activity.

First, there is the vagueness of the term 'creative activity'. It may seem both under- and over-inclusive, and ultimately an unhelpful category for the application of law. It is under-inclusive since much of what patent and copyright deal with, such as the buying and selling of inventions and expressive works, is not particularly creative. For example, the on sale bar deals solely with the sale of an invention, which perhaps is better described as a business activity rather than an act of creation. However, this objection ignores the fact that commercial transactions, while subsidiary to creation, are an important part of the creative process. Many artists create in order to survive; therefore, regulation of creative activity may bring in non-creative activity that is necessary to make the pursuit of creation meaningful. While the problem of under-inclusiveness can be dealt with by more carefully situating creative activities in broader social and market exchanges, the criticism of over-inclusiveness would point to the well-known observation that much creative activity is not addressed by intellectual property. Therefore, to say that intellectual property encompasses the regulation of creative activity would ignore the fact that copyright does not apply to live performances or that patent law does not apply to discoveries of mathematical propositions or scientific principles. But to say that X regulates Y does not imply that X regulates every instance of Y. For my characterisation to hold, I need to show that intellectual property regulates some creative activities. As for those activities that are seemingly unregulated, my characterisation forces us to ask why these activities are excluded from intellectual property. Property characterisation, on the other hand, would support broad protection for all creations very well. Treating intellectual property as regulation requires us to ask whether all creations should be treated similarly, including whether all creations should be covered by intellectual property law.

The second objection to characterising intellectual property as regulation stems from the law's use of private enforcement mechanisms and private incentives to police intellectual property infringement. Although the Patent Office and Copyright Office are important state agencies, they do not enforce intellectual property rights. The Patent Office grants the rights based on certain statutory requirements, and the Copyright Office maintains a registration of copyrights submitted by the owners. As for violation of rights, it is up to the patent and copyright owners to bring private lawsuits against alleged infringers. In this way, intellectual property seems closer in spirit to real property or personal property law rather than regulatory law, which principally relies on litigation brought by governmental agencies to protect individual rights. The salient examples in the US are the Environmental Protection Agency, the Federal Trade Commission and the Securities and Exchange Commission. Admittedly, private rights of actions exist for the enforcement of environmental law, unfair competition law and securities law. By contrast, intellectual property law relies solely on private enforcement. This objection, however, is not fatal to my characterisation of intellectual property as regulation. If regulation of certain activities (such as the buying and selling of securities or polluting the environment) can occur through a mix of private and public enforcement, there is no reason to think that such enforcement could not occur solely through private enforcement.

Finally, conceiving of intellectual property as regulation seems inconsistent with the generally accepted notion of regulation as centralised designed to control activities. Intellectual property does not command anything. Instead, it defines a set of rights that are enforced through private causes of action. This objection differs from the second by evoking a conception of regulation as command. The salience of the objection rests on acceptance of a fairly strained notion of regulation. The deregulation movement, particularly in the US, has taken the form in part of privatising previous government decisions and opening the use of markets. But it would be erroneous to think that deregulation has meant the absence of regulation and the expansion of *laissez-faire*. Most deregulated environments still operate under rules and these rules are designed to regulate private activity. The third objection rests on a false dichotomy between free markets and regulation. Since intellectual property is about the market for inventions and creative works, it is argued that intellectual property cannot be about regulation. But all markets are subject to rules and regulations, whether formal statutory law or the laws of property, contract and tort. Furthermore, the market itself is a regulatory mechanism, sometimes established privately, sometimes, as in the case of tradable emissions or securities, established by the government. A totally free market without any rules would be anarchic. Intellectual property recognises the regulated nature of any market by establishing rule for creative activity that permit the creation of markets and other institutions for the creation and dissemination of inventions and expressive works.

In addition to rejecting the criticisms of my description, there are several affirmative reasons to adopt the description of intellectual property as a system of regulation. Understanding intellectual property as regulation is consistent with the institutions, such as the Patent Office and Copyright Office, that are instrumental to the implementation of intellectual property law. The existence of these governmental agencies can be explained only by examining the regulatory and administrative dimensions of intellectual property. Furthermore, the regulatory approach offers a unifying explanation that addresses the various aspects of intellectual property, which has elements of property, tort, contract, competition law and health law and policy. Finally, for the many who are sceptical of intellectual property's status as property, the regulatory approach offers an alternative that allows us to understand and criticise the elements of intellectual property law and its application.

In this section, I have made the case for describing intellectual property as regulation of creative activity. In the next section, I elaborate on the normative implications of this description.

The normative shift

To argue that intellectual property is regulation is to espouse a normative position about intellectual property law that is in opposition to the normative implications of conceiving of intellectual property as property. Intellectual property as property suggests that intellectual property law should protect the autonomous decisions of the intellectual property owner in managing, alienating and devising the subject matter of intellectual property (Landes and Posner, 2003). Intellectual property as regulation situates intellectual property law beyond the domain of individual decision-making and control. Patents, copyrights, trade marks and the other species of intellectual property are understood to have a social dimension. They are the means to a social end beyond the protection of individual self-interest.

There are several possible normative implications for what I have called regulatory justice. The four I will analyse here are referred to as 1) the model of expertise (Breyer, 2004); 2) the model of civic participation (Mashaw, 1997; Cuellar, 2005); 3) the model of market failure (Strauss, 1989; Ayres and Braithwaite, 1992); and 4) the model of management (Wilson, 1989). These four models are not mutually exclusive, but they are distinct. A specific intellectual property system may have elements of each or may be informed by only one. I emphasise here that the system of intellectual property laws that we design will reflect one or more of these four models. Alternatively, society through democratic institutions could pick one or more of these models and design an intellectual property system that reflects the normative choices. What I shall do in this section is explain each of these four normative models, highlighting the implications for the design of intellectual property law. My conclusion is that the second and third models offer the best normative rationales for the current state of intellectual property law in the US and the European Union and are the normative framework that informs international intellectual property law as promulgated through the TRIPS Agreement. After elucidating the normative implications of conceiving of intellectual property as regulation, I turn in the next section to two applications.

The model of expertise rests on the assumption that knowledge is distributed unequally among individuals in society. Some individuals are either better informed about events in the world or are better trained or more adept at using information. Individuals with more knowledge can use their superior position for private gain and most likely will do so. The model of expertise does not necessarily place limits on the use of superior knowledge for private gain. The key insight, however, is that those with superior knowledge should use their position to the benefit of society as a whole. Societal interests trump private gain. An example of this model is the learned professions. Physicians can use their expertise to heal themselves and to better themselves. But the model of expertise implies that physicians should have an obligation to help others and in some instances this obligation trumps the pursuit of profit. A similar argument can be made for other learned professions, such as law or accounting.

As illustrated with the example of the learned professions, the model of expertise has clear implications for the shape of regulation. While knowledge, as I have described it, can never be fully equal among all individuals in society, rules and institutions are structured in a way that imposes obligations on the better informed and sophisticated. The rules and institutions serve to redistribute the fruits of knowledge so that the more sophisticated do not harm the less. Furthermore, rules and institutions have to be structured in such a way as not to create a permanent underclass of the uninformed. The model of expertise does not justify or support ignorance. It simply recognises that the possession of and ability to process information is unequally distributed for various reasons. The model of expertise implies that regulation should be structured to prevent exploitation of the unsophisticated and to impose obligations on the sophisticated.

Health and safety regulations as well as environmental regulations can be understood through the model of regulation. So can intellectual property law. For regulations pertaining to health, safety and the environment, in many instances some parties will be better informed or in a better position to be informed about the harmful effects of a product or service. Under the model of expertise, those who are in a position to prevent or mitigate the harmful consequences of a product or service must be accountable for their superior position. More importantly, when society is uncertain about the harmful consequences of certain activities, it should spend resources to uncover the harmful consequences and inform individuals to be aware of them. Intellectual property plays an important role in this. To the extent that intellectual property law protects the generation and creation of information, intellectual property provides a mechanism for knowledge creation. The problem is that if intellectual property law is too proprietary, the benefits of knowledge-sharing are lost. Therefore, the model of expertise can help us understand intellectual property in terms of the limits that must be placed on exclusion for knowledge creation to be effective.

The model of civic participation recognises that legislative processes can be closed off and subject to capture by special interests if the processes are not made open to participants. Regulation therefore is needed to ensure that legislative processes are subject to public scrutiny and review. Much of administrative law and constitutional law in the US can be understood through the model of civic participation. The model's applicability to intellectual property may be less apparent. At one level, the model can explain such phenomena as copyright protection for legal materials, an issue that is handled in the US by offering little or no copyright protection to statutes, judicial opinions and other materials that constitute public law. At a deeper level, many of the rules of intellectual property demonstrate a concern with public access to the fruits of the arts and the sciences. The requirement, for example, that the duration of intellectual property protection be time-limited represents a commitment to the public domain and public access to works of art and scientific inventions. Furthermore, the existence of administrative institutions like the Patent Office, and to a more limited extent the Copyright Office, show a commitment to governmental review and criticism of what types of products count as innovative for the purposes of intellectual property law. Through the agencies, individuals can virtually participate in the process of innovation and invention by helping to set standards for the creative and inventive processes.

The model of market failure is a well-understood rationale for regulation and a particularly well-acknowledged justification for intellectual property. The term market failure covers a variety of phenomena that lead to the inability to establish mechanisms that generate price information which can measure the social desirability of projects. For example, the existence of polluting activities that are not fully reflected in the price of a final product because someone outside the market is forced to bear the costs of pollution is an example of market failure. In the realm of intellectual property, the inability to gauge the innovativeness or originality of a new product or service without in some way observing the new product or service creates a market failure. The famous Arrow paradox implies that it will be difficult to market new knowledge because no one will buy the knowledge until they are given a sense of what the knowledge is (Arrow, 1962). But once the knowledge is disclosed, the incentive to buy vanishes because one need not purchase what has already been revealed. The range of intellectual property law, from trade secret law and common law misappropriation to the more sophisticated statutory schemes of patent, copyright and trade mark, are designed to resolve the Arrow paradox and help to create markets for information and new knowledge that is embodied in products and services.

Finally, the model of management follows from the existence of resources that need to be collectively managed in order to maximise social value from the resources. Natural habitats, parklands and coastal properties are typical examples of such resources that require collective management. The domain of intellectual property may also include such resources. Artwork, antiquities and scientific breakthroughs are perhaps examples of resources whose management we do not want to delegate to an individual, but are better managed through collective entities, whether these are the state, museums, universities, libraries or other institutions. The model of management can help to explain the existence of institutions like museums and libraries and help in recognising the obligations of intellectual property owners to manage their creations for the general public. The problem is that the model of management, as applied to creative works, speaks more to preservation than to the process of innovation and creation. Because of the emphasis on preservation, the model of management provides a more conservative, backward-looking normative criterion than the forward-looking criteria of innovation and progress which are associated with intellectual property. I mention the model only because there is a sizeable literature that focuses on the use of intellectual property as a tool for collective management of cultural resources.

I have presented the four principal normative models that are implied by a regulatory theory of intellectual property. I turn now to the implications of the regulatory theory for specific problems within intellectual property.

Implications

In this section, I focus on a contemporary problem found in intellectual property: pharmaceutical patents. I use this example to make two points. The first is to illustrate the weaknesses of conceiving of intellectual property as property and to show the regulatory theory aids in addressing the weaknesses. The second is to apply the four normative models described above as tools to address the problems.

Patents protect useful, novel and non-obvious pharmaceutical products and the useful, novel and non-obvious processes that produce them. Pharmaceuticals are also subject to health and safety regulation and, in many instances, must be approved by a government agency before they are allowed to be sold in the marketplace. The difficulty is the conflict that can arise between patent protection and health and safety regulation at the end of the life of the patent. When a patent expires, competing manufacturers (often referred to as generics) can produce and sell the pharmaceutical product and use the process to make the drug without seeking approval from the patent owner. However, the generic manufacturers must obtain approval from the government agency to review the safety and efficacy of the product before entering the market. Because of this review process, there is a delay in competition to the previously patented pharmaceutical. In effect, the delay from the review process effectively extends the life of the patent beyond its expiration date. One way to resolve this problem is to obtain review of the generic product before patent expiration so that the generic products can enter the marketplace upon expiration. The problem is that reviewing the generic product will entail using or experimenting on the patented product. This use or experiment during the patent term would constitute patent infringement. Many countries have resolved this conundrum by permitting the use of patented pharmaceuticals during the life of the patent as long as the use is to seek governmental review of the safety and efficacy of the product. This exception from patent law is referred to as a type of experimental use. I shall call it the statutory experimental use exception.

This discussion highlights the intensely regulatory nature of patent law, particularly in the pharmaceutical field. Patent law interacts with and often needs to be harmonised with other regulatory systems. Furthermore, conceiving of patents as property does not help in addressing the role of patents within the regulatory system. Patents share a superficial similarity to property by creating a right to exclude, and the statutory experimental use exception imposes some limits on this right to exclude. But the family resemblance to property does not help in understanding how the right to exclude is shaped to regulate market entry in the pharmaceutical industry in particular, and in other industries more generally. More importantly, the conception of patents as property may be harmful to the implementation of patent law, as illustrated by another dimension of the issue of generic pharmaceuticals.

The statutory experimental use exception in the US requires the potential generic drug manufacturer to warrant that it is not infringing the patented pharmaceutical when preparing studies of the safety and efficacy of the generic product. This warrant usually requires a statement about both the generic drug manufacturer's activities and its position regarding the validity of the patent. Since the safety and efficacy review is an open process, the patent owner is aware of the potential generic drug manufacturer. It is, in fact, quite common for the patent owner to bring a legal action against the potential generic drug manufacturer upon the initiation of the review. The law suit alleges that the potential generic drug manufacturer may be making infringing uses of the patent outside the scope of the statutory experimental use exception. Furthermore, if the potential generic drug manufacturer attests that the patent is invalid, the patent owner raises the claim of validity in defence of his patent rights. These law suits have been controversial because often they settle with the generic drug manufacturer agreeing not to enter the market for a specific period of time. The legality of these settlements have been the subject of legal controversy in the US, with one court ruling that these settlement agreements are a violation of the competition laws.[1] Other courts, however, have ruled differently, with one court finding no violation[2] and another stating that a more careful factual analysis of the anti-competitive effects needed to be considered in order to determine the legality of the agreements.[3] Given this controversy, it is very likely that the Supreme Court will consider the issue in the next few years.

The controversy over these settlements exemplifies both the weakness and the real hazard of conceiving of patents solely in terms of property. The weakness is demonstrated by the inability of the language of property to resolve the controversy, except in terms of protecting the patent owner's right to exclude. The hazard stems from concluding that the patent owner's right to exclude trumps other values, such as competition or access to pharmaceuticals. The regulatory perspective provides a richer way to address the problem posed by these settlements and the broader problem of pharmaceutical patents.

The four normative models aid in expanding our perspective beyond the narrow paradigm of property. The model of expertise emphasises that the grant of a patent reflects the judgement of the Patent Office on the novelty, usefulness and non-obviousness of the invention. There is no administrative judgement on the effects of the patent on market competition. Therefore, it is within the jurisdiction and obligation of agencies whose expertise is in competition policy to police the anti-competitive uses of patents. The rights granted by patent law are subject to these limitations from competition law. Furthermore, the model of civic participation would recognise the grant of a patent as requiring public scrutiny both of the innovativeness of the invention and of potential misuses of the patent. The model of market failure squarely recognises the use of patents to create markets and the need to limit the patent right if the market is being harmed or compromised. Finally, the model of management suggests that inventions are public resources that should be managed in a way that benefits the public. Therefore, the model of management would call for limitations on the private right to exclude granted by the patent.

The case of pharmaceutical patents demonstrates the limitations and dangers of conceiving of patents as a species of property. The regulatory model that I have presented provides an alternative which helps us to identify the problem and construct solutions.

Conclusion

The status of intellectual property as property is the subject of lively debate. However, less attention has been paid to what conception should replace the property paradigm. In this chapter, I have made the argument that intellectual property should be understood as a system of regulation. This shift has both descriptive and normative implications and offers a basis for addressing pressing legal and policy issues within intellectual property, such as the problem of pharmaceutical patents.

Notes

1. *In re Cardizem CD Antitrust Litigation*, 332 F.3d 896 (6th Cir. 2003).
2. *In re Tamoxifen Citrate Litigation*, 2005 WL 2864654 (2nd Cir. 2005).
3. *Schering-Plough v. F.T.C.*, 402 F.3d 1056 (11th Cir. 2005).

References

Arrow K. J. (1962) Economic Welfare and the Allocation of Resources for Invention, in NBER, *The Rate and Direction of Inventive Activity: Economic and Social Factors*. Princeton, NJ: Princeton University Press.

Ayres, I. and Braithwaite, J. (1992) *Responsive Regulation: Transcending the Deregulation Debate*. Oxford: Oxford University Press.

Blackstone, W. (1979a) *Commentaries on the Laws of England: Of the Rights of Things*. Chicago: University of Chicago Press.

Blackstone, W. (1979b) *Commentaries on the Laws of England: Of Public Wrongs*. Chicago: University of Chicago Press.

Breyer, S. (2004) *Breaking the Vicious Circle: Toward Effective Risk Regulation*. Cambridge, MA: Harvard University Press.

Carrier, M. A. (2004) Cabining Intellectual Property through a Property Paradigm', *Duke Law Journal*, 54: 1–135.

Cuellar, M-F. (2005) Rethinking Regulatory Democracy', *Administrative Law Review*, 57: 411–91.

Gordon, W. J. (1993) A Property Right in Self-expression: Equality and Individualism in the Natural Law of Intellectual Property', *Yale Law Journal*, 102: 1533–1610.

Heald, P. J. (2005) A Transaction Costs Theory of Patent Law, *Ohio State Law Journal*, 66: 473–507.

In re Cardizem CD Antitrust Litigation, 332 F.3d 896 (6th Cir. 2003).

In re Tamoxifen Citrate Litigation, 2005 WL 2864654 (2nd Cir. 2005).

Landes, W. M. and Posner, R. A. (2003) *The Economic Structure of Intellectual Property Law*. New York: Belknap Press.
Lemley, M. A. (2005) Property, Intellectual Property, and Free Riding, *Texas Law Review*, 83: 1031–75.
Levine, D. and Boldrin, M. (2002) The Case against Intellectual Property, *American Economic Review Papers and Proceedings*, 92: 209–12.
Mashaw, J. L. (1997) *Greed, Chaos, & Governance: Using Public Choice to Improve Public Law*. New Haven, CT: Yale University Press.
Ryan, M. P. (1998) *Knowledge Diplomacy: Global Competition and the Politics of Intellectual Property*. Washington, DC: Brookings Institution.
Schering-Plough v. F.T.C., 402 F.3d 1056 (11th Cir. 2005).
Strauss, P. L. (1989) *An Introduction to Administrative Justice in the United States*. Durham, NC: Carolina Academic Press.
Wilson, J. Q. (1989) *Bureaucracy: What Government Agencies Do and Why They Do it*. New York: Basic Books.

6
Liberty and the Rejection of Strong Intellectual Property Rights

Jonathan Trerise

In this chapter I argue that a particular form of intellectual property protection is unjustified; this is the *strong type* of intellectual property right. What is meant by this I shall illuminate shortly; here, note that this is the form of the Anglo-American patent system and its crucial objectionable feature is that it makes no room for independent discoverers or inventors to own and/or use the ideas they discover during the period of protection; thus my objection to this form of property right is from a concern for liberty. I favour a weakening of intellectual property protection; and the view I support can be called Weak-Type Protection.[1]

I will be criticising strong-type protection from both consequentialist and deontological concerns for liberty (I define 'liberty' soon). Due to space considerations, it is necessary that I simplify the liberty-respecting consequentialist view to a *pure* liberty consequentialist one, disregarding other consequentialist values. Now, it may be that few people would actually embrace this pure position. However, one does not have to hold the view explicitly to be moved by my concerns, which are to show that there is reason to reject strong intellectual property rights and embrace a weaker form, according to a liberty consequentialist perspective.[2]

The type/token distinction

I have noted that IP regimes are often *type*-protecting. This is in contrast to *token*-protecting systems (our concrete property rights – like those over land or cars – are token-protecting). A token is a specific object located in a particular spatio-temporal location; types are abstract categories and tokens members of those categories.[3] I shall consider the distinction roughly to be this: tokens are members of categories, which are types, and exemplify or instantiate types. The particular computer that I am typing on is a *token* of a *type* – specifically, the computer I am using is a token of the type *computer*, or perhaps *PC computer*.[4]

The type/token distinction is not simply that between the general and the specific, although there are similarities. Types might actually be fairly specific yet still admit of *multiple realisability* – the ability to be instantiated in more than one place at a time. For example, 'blue table having 16 legs' is a fairly specific type; it is specific in being described more carefully, yet it is still a type in being a category that can be instantiated in multiple places.[5]

I do not pretend that this distinction is unproblematic, nor do I wish here to further any philosophical discussion regarding it. Instead, I propose an application of this distinction to the question of intellectual property rights. It is my contention that IP rights are not like paradigmatic property rights (over concrete things) in a particularly striking way: intellectual property rights are often conceived of as rights over *all the potential tokens of a type*, whereas paradigmatic property rights over physical items are rights over *single tokens*. For example, when one owns a patent over a drug type, one has the right to control other drugs like it wherever they occur within the jurisdiction of the legal system, and however they occur. This is not the case, for instance, with car ownership; when one owns a car, one owns only that particular car, not others like it. Thus, IP rights often give rights over all tokens of a type, rather than over individual tokens.

Strong type-protection and weak type-protection

Strong type-protection

I said above that the Anglo-American patent system is a *strong type-protecting* (STP) system of IP rights. It gives rights over *types*, rather than over *tokens*, and, as an STP system, it gives rights over all the concrete instantiations of ideas wherever and however they occur (within the jurisdiction of the legal system).[6] This means it gives strong protection, since there is no regard for *causal history*.

The strong type-protection that the patent system affords works this way: ownership of a patent over X gives one rights over the making, using and selling of X, *wherever and however* X occurs; that is, patent ownership of X gives ownership of $X_1, X_2, \ldots X_n$, regardless of the history of $X_1, X_2, \ldots X_n$. So, if agent S has a patent over X, and some other agent T develops her own X_2 *independently* of S's initial token X, S has a claim on X_2.[7] That is, regardless of how T came up with X_2, T has infringed upon

S; S has type-protection in that all tokens of that type are protected, regardless of how they came about. This is, of course, in contrast to material property rights – that is, token rights – in which each person's rights do not have any bearing on another person's rights over a similar object; my rights over my car say nothing about your owning your car. I shall argue against this position that it restricts the liberties of others.

Weak type-protection

An intellectual property regime weaker than STP can be named, aptly, weak type-protection (WTP). WTP is the view that one has ownership over one's original token(s),[8] as well as a claim right on the *rivalrous uses of copies* of one's original token(s). A use of X is rivalrous if and only if use of X by one person reduces the availability or value of use of X by another person. For example, my use of the sun to grow plants is non-rivalrous use of the sun; it does not impact on your ability to use the sun to grow plants (or do anything else).[9] My use of a pencil, however, is rivalrous – it impacts on your ability to use that pencil. Now, this means that when people copy your token(s), you have a claim on some *uses* of those copies.[10]

I will provide more detail about this view at the end of the chapter. I simply note here that WTP allows one to own ideas in that others are not free to copy and profit from those copies, thereby impacting your ability to make a profit. WTP also does not, in contrast to STP, restrict one's ability to make independent and yet qualitatively identical items; that is, WTP regards the *causal history* of putative copies as relevant to determining their status as ownables. However, others are free to copy ideas and make personal use from those copies.

Liberty and the rejection of strong type-protection

My claim is that theorists concerned with liberty should be against STP, since that form of IP protection involves significant infractions against liberty. I will explain what these infractions are; following that, I will explain that this argument applies for all those theorists concerned with liberty – from the deontological to the consequentialist.[11]

What exactly is the liberty violation involved with STP? Put succinctly, it is that STP limits the liberty of others to too great a degree. It does this by limiting what independent agents can do with their time, labour and resources. If one owns a patent over X, subsequent agents cannot develop or use X on their own. In contrast, one's claim over one's car involves only *that* car. This is *token*-ownership – one owns one particular tokened object – paradigmatic property rights, rights over things like cars and land, are token ownership and give a claim on only one particular object in time and space.[12]

Type-protection, however, by definition, increases the amount of possible protection. It gives a claim over a class of objects based on function and/or composition; further, however, *strong* type-protection gives this kind of protection regardless of the causal history of any member of that class of objects. Strong type-ownership, then, involves owning much more than the particular object one has created (or the instantiated idea one has discovered and developed); it gives a right over what other people do, as I have noted, with their own labour, in their own time and with their own resources; even independent inventors, with labour and material they own, are barred from making and using what is owned (when, suppose, there has been no contractual agreement to hand over what is laboured upon). This is far too powerful a right for people to have, since others are not free to do what they want with their own labour, time and resources. But this is precisely the right people who own a patent have.[13] Far too much restriction of the liberties of others occurs when one owns a type in a strong manner.

Deontological and consequentialist concerns for liberty: against STP

I must clarify that I will be speaking of specifically non-moral (or empirical) liberty; that is, when I say that those concerned with liberty should reject STP, I am speaking about empirical liberties. This stands in contrast to specifically moral liberties, where one might have the moral permission to do X, even if X is illegal or physically impossible for one to do. Thus one might have the moral liberty to fly, even if flying is illegal where one lives (and is clearly impossible). One does not, however, have the empirical liberty to fly – it is simply something one is not able to do. So, one has empirical liberty to X if and only if one is physically able to X, *and* one lacks empirical liberty when one cannot X because of the action(s) (or disposition(s) to perform some action) of some other person(s); that is, an agent is empirically unfree (not at liberty) when, were it not for this other person's action or disposition, the agent could X.[14] It is this notion of liberty that I will use.

Consequentialist concerns for liberty

I will first try to explain more precisely the consequentialist side of the problem of liberty for STP. The liberty consequentialist claims that we should maximise individual liberty in the world.[15] Consider the following argument. It is sound, according to Liberty Consequentialism:

The Total Liberty Consequentialist Argument against strong type-protection:

P1: If X promotes the overall morally relevant liberty of persons less than an available alternative, X is unjustified
P2: Strong-type protection promotes the overall morally relevant liberty of persons less than an available alternative (WTP)
C: Therefore, strong type-protection is unjustified

P1 is simply a statement of the political theory of the Total Liberty Consequentialist.[16] P2 is the important premise.[17] Now, the *counting* of liberties is notoriously difficult. It is difficult to determine how one system is more liberty-promoting than another, in that a precise answer not only involves listing the potential liberty violations involved under each system, but also requires a comparison of the different severities of each liberty violation. Such a task would be difficult, to say the least. Still, however, we can conclude that the premise is true.

To see this, we need to know what liberty violations are involved with the alternative(s) to STP. If we can identify a system which does not have some of the liberty violations that STP has and adds no liberty violations, then P2 is true, and consequentialists concerned with liberty should reject strong type-ownership. Specifically, then, consider weak type-protection (again, WTP). Under this system, subsequent and independent inventors are not considered in breach of an ownership of a particular type. This system of type-protection gives ownership over a type to an agent, but allows others the creation, use and even ownership of independently arrived at tokens of the same type. Thus, under this system, if agent S has ownership over a type of drug X, then S has a claim on all tokens X, unless some other agent T develops some X independently.[18] In this case, S has no claim against T.

Let us observe whether more or less liberty is violated under WTP than under STP. What is clear is that WTP does not violate the liberty of others to do what they will with their own time, labour and resources as STP does. That is, there is at least this one liberty violation more under STP than under WTP.

However, under WTP there is one liberty violation added. Under WTP, agents cannot exclusively market and/or use whatever it is they own, whereas they can do so under strong type-ownership. For example, under STP, agent S can exclusively market and/or use their cure for cancer; under WTP, this is no longer the case. Thus, the liberty of agents to exclusively market and/or use items is not present under WTP; this system contains a liberty violation that STP does not.

P2 (which states that STP promotes the overall liberty of persons less than an available alternative) may still be true, however. Let us be clear about the trade we have made with regard to the liberty violations of each system. In abandoning STP in favour of WTP, we have eliminated the liberty violation of limiting what other people can do with their time, labour and resources, and added the liberty violation of disallowing people to exclusively market and/or use items. While I noted above that counting liberties is difficult, I claim that there simply is no way to count liberties such that the Liberty Consequentialist should still favour STP. This is because of 1) the raw number of *people* whose liberties are violated under STP as compared to WTP; and 2) the sheer number of *activities* that are prevented in these cases.

Under STP, more people's liberties are violated than under WTP since (1) under the latter only one agent's liberty can be violated (namely, the agent who would exclusively use/market). It may be true that everyone in the world's liberty is violated in not being able to exclusively use/market, but only one person actually could exclusively use/market the item. Hence, really only one person's liberty to exclusively use/market is lost. Compare this to when STP is the case; here, the liberty of everyone who could have used (in any way) what is protected is infringed in that none of them is at liberty to use an owned item (except for the owner).[19] Consider an example. Suppose again agent S invents a cure for cancer. Under STP, all agents who are not S who could make use of the cure for cancer (by, for example, at least making their own) lose liberty in that they cannot use the cure for cancer freely. Under WTP, though everyone loses the liberty to exclusively market, effectively only agent S actually loses the liberty to exclusively use/market the cure for cancer. There is less liberty lost in terms of the number of people who lose liberty in the case of WTP.

Also, (2) the sheer number of activities that are prevented shows that more liberty is lost under STP 2. Under this type of system, one cannot use what is owned by another *in any way*. This stands in contrast to WTP, which adds only one kind of restriction that was not present in the case of strong type-ownership: WTP only denies people exclusive use and exclusive access to the market. Thus, since WTP removes more restrictions of liberty than it adds (for example, it allows others to use items independently *in any way* they please), it clearly has fewer liberty violations. Exclusive use is a subset of use in general and there are clearly examples of non-exclusive use. It is thus clear that the liberty violations involved in denying exclusive use are fewer in number than the liberty violations involved in denying anyone the ability to use any token of a type in any way.

WTP, then, has fewer liberty violations in terms of the number of people whose liberty is lost, as well as in terms of how many actions they are not at liberty to pursue. The Liberty Consequentialist, then, should reject STP in favour of WTP, *unless* it can be shown that the lost liberties under WTP have a greater weight than the lost liberties I argued are present under STP. That is, it would have to be the case that the lost liberty to exclusively market and/or use an item is more important in terms of liberty than the lost liberty that everyone else (but the putative owner) experiences in all of their lost liberties to use. It is difficult to see, however, how the weight of the lost liberty to exclusively market and use could be so great as to outweigh all of the lost liberties of all of the non-owners. It is unclear how we could construe *one person's* lost liberty to exclusively market and use an item as having greater significance than another *one* person's liberty to do what they will with their own resources, let alone *everyone* who could use the item. I conclude, then, that the Liberty Consequentialist must reject STP, since less liberty is lost under WTP.

The deontological concern for liberty

The deontological concern for liberty does not require that we maximise liberty. This position simply says that, all things being equal, those actions are right that respect liberty, and those actions are wrong that restrict liberty. According to this position, a system is wrong if it restricts the liberties of individuals more than is necessary to be consistent with the respect for the liberty of others.[20] Let us, for ease of argument, call this the Libertarian position.[21] Our question, then, is this: what would the Libertarian say about STP?

The Libertarian would reject it. Such a system involves extensive restrictions of liberty. But, the reader may note, there is a concomitant restriction of liberty involved in the rejection of a strong type-ownership system. This restriction is the same as the one noted above: one no longer has the liberty to exclusively market and/or exclusively use an item. What, then, should the Libertarian conclude? Is the Libertarian forced into a contradiction, saying that we should both reject strong type-ownership and reject its rejection?

No, for we can try to determine which of the restrictions of liberty the Libertarian finds more disrespectful. It is clear that Libertarians would privilege some liberties over others; for example, one's liberty to make one's own choices in life (so long as one respects the choices of others) is clearly more important to Libertarians than, say, one's liberty to move a particular pebble from one location to another. Thus, we can recognise that Libertarians will regard some liberties as privileged. So, which of these would the Libertarian think violates a privileged liberty, if any: 1) the restriction that non-owners cannot do what they will with their own time, labour and resources? Or 2) the restriction that no one can exclusively market and/or use items?

It would, of course, be difficult to enumerate all the privileged liberties; it would also at some point become a matter of debate. However, I think we can quite easily see that WTP violates no privileged liberties, while STP does. In order to explain why I think the Libertarian will regard the lost liberty to do what one will with one's time, labour and resources as the violation of a privileged liberty, consider the following example, with different cases. In both cases, I have manicured my garden in a particularly efficient and artistic way, and you have done the same thing with your garden (in the same way). However, in case A, this is purely accidental – your garden is completely independent of mine; you've never seen or heard of mine. In case B, however, you have observed my garden, taken some photographs and applied what you have learned in your own. Also, in case A, all the use you make of it is personal use. In case B, you write a book about garden manicuring and make a decent profit.

The possible liberty restrictions are these: if you were to be prevented from doing what you have done, you would lose the liberty to do what you will with your time, labour and resources (that is, build your own garden, and so on). If I was prevented from stopping you from doing what you have done, I would lose the liberty to *exclusively* market and/or use the garden (or books about the garden).[22] Now, it is easy to see that my loss of the liberty to exclusively use and/or market my garden is not the loss of a privileged liberty. For, at least in this case, not only can I still use my garden, but I can also still market my garden (though for admittedly less than under STP). Whereas if you lose the ability to do what you will in your own time with your own materials, this is a significant disrespecting of liberty, since you are completely bereft of options *vis-à-vis* the owned garden (under STP). Under STP, agents are not at liberty with regard to their own inventions, simply because someone else beat them to it chronologically. Being free to do what one will – as long as one does not disrespect others – seems clearly to be a part of the privileged set, encompassing as much as it does.

This stands in contrast to WTP, under which I can still use and market my garden, and you can have your copy of the garden for personal use. The only thing I cannot do is use/market the garden exclusively. That is, the only liberty I have lost is the ability to restrict others' liberties in a particular kind of way. It is implausible to consider as a privileged liberty the ability to exclusively market items, since marketing them non-exclusively remains an option (and since exclusive marketing means the limitation of others' liberties).

So, while both systems restrict liberty, and while it may be difficult to spell out exactly what constitutes the privileged set of liberties, the ability to do what one will in one's own time with one's own materials and labour seems crucial and wide-ranging. STP, then, in denying this denies a privileged empirical liberty. Also, the liberty restricted under WTP is simply not part of the privileged set. The deontologist concerned with liberty should thus reject STP.

Details about weak type-protection

STP is rejected by both deontological and consequentialist views concerned with liberty. WTP is to be preferred. WTP, then, is in desperate need of further explication. I do so in this section; however, my treatment here will still be incomplete.[23]

I propose calling WTP weak since, though it is a type-protecting system,[24] it does not give as broad or as strong protection as the standard STP system does. Let us return to the garden example. I claim that WTP more closely fits our intuitions than STP does. What WTP will claim is this: if you happen to design the same garden totally independently (as in case A), then I have no claim against you at all. In case B you copy me, perhaps even *exactly* copy me, and profit from your copy. WTP calls this a violation.

Suppose now there are cases C and D. In case C, you do copy me (and, as in case B, perhaps even exactly copy me), but you make no rivalrous use of the resource. That is, you use the copy solely for personal enjoyment. WTP says this is no violation as it does not rival the investment return that I, as the original owner, could make.[25]

In case D, you make a profit from the garden that is now in your possession, but it is not entirely clear that you have 'copied' me; say, for instance, you have merely driven past my house and got a glimpse of my garden. You certainly *got the idea* from me in this case, but this does not necessarily constitute a copy. So, there will certainly be some difficult cases for WTP.[26] The important point, however, is that there are clear cases as well. In cases A and C, WTP sees no problem with what you have done; in case B, you have violated me and owe me some sort of compensation.[27] This is intuitive. In cases A and C, where you have no impact on me, WTP correctly claims you owe me nothing. On the other hand, in case B, where you do impact on me, WTP claims you owe me. Let us try to be more precise about this.

As noted above, WTP is the view that one has ownership over one's original token(s), as well as a claim right on the *rivalrous uses of copies* of one's original token(s). And this means that when people copy your token(s), you have a claim on some uses of those copies. So, I do not have a claim on all uses; as explained, in the garden case, if you use the garden you have created in a non-rivalrous manner (for example, for enjoyment), I have no claim against you. I do have a claim against you, however, in case B, as you impede my ability to make a profit from my token.

Remember that my complaint earlier against STP is that it does not allow for independent invention. Now, we need to be able to distinguish between a copy and an independent invention, so that WTP can be distinguishable from STP. What does it take for something to be a copy of something else (and not simply independent)? Two factors are important. First, note the most important difference between WTP and STP: WTP regards the *causal history* of ideas as relevant for their ownership. So, for X to count as a copy of Y, X must in some way be dependent for its existence on Y. Also, however, some functional and/or compositional similarity between X and Y is necessary, since we would not say that something which simply depends on some earlier thing therefore counts as a copy (for example, the car is not a copy of the internal combustion engine). These are, then, the necessary conditions for X to be considered a copy of Y: X must be derivative of Y and be functionally and/or compositionally similar.[28]

Let me conclude this section with applications for real life.[29] One cannot simply take ideas from others and profit from them. However, one can copy ideas that others have not protected by other means (by fencing in those ideas, for instance) and use those ideas. This means, for instance, that while one cannot download music from illegal internet websites (which have their music via the violation of a contract which says explicitly that one cannot redistribute the music, and one knows this), one is free to make as many copies for oneself as one desires of something one has bought. One cannot, however, distribute those copies and rival the investment return of the original owner.

Or, if a cure for cancer is owned by someone, whether or not others can distribute that idea depends on the details about how those others came to know about the drug. If the drug *was not* protected by the original owner, copies may be distributed but not profited from; however, this does not preclude the drug's owner from taking other measures to secure the drug, including securing contracts restricting the ways in which others (who obtain the drug) spread the information. And, if the drug was protected, we must ask in what way an agent came to know the details of the drug. If simple awareness of its existence and effects stimulated the agent to make their own drug, there is no violation as no copy has been made. If the agent reverse-engineered a copy of the drug they had purchased, the same rules apply as in the downloaded music case: they cannot distribute that information and rival the investment return of the original owner.

Conclusion

Less liberty is lost under WTP than under STP. We can also see that WTP accords well with our intuitions. WTP allows for independent invention and ownership, as well as free copying in cases where no damage has been done to the original owner's ability to use or derive economic value from their original token (that is, where the use made of the copy is not rivalrous). The liberty restrictions under WTP are not members of the most important set of liberties, while those under STP are. My description of WTP has been admittedly cursory and is in need of more definite delineation, but those concerned with liberty[30] should favour it over STP in shaping our IP rights.

Acknowledgement

I thank Axel Gosseries and another editor, as well as Peter Vallentyne and Brian Kierland, for extremely helpful comments. Any remaining errors are, of course, my own.

Notes

1. Full defence of this view would require a comparison of Weak-Type Protection to no intellectual property protection whatsoever. I do not have the space for this defence here.

2. In my dissertation, I also argue against having no intellectual property rights. Further, I argue that other consequentialist concerns do not swing the balance back in favour of either no intellectual property rights or the strong type protecting system (with a possible exception for the pharmaceutical industry). This is the case even with utilitarian concerns, which constitute the most popular defence of strong intellectual property rights since it is thought that, to have incentives to keep on producing ideas – which is good for everybody – agents need the promise of strong property rights. For reasons to doubt the effectiveness of strong intellectual property protection, see Edwin Mansfield (1990) 'Intellectual Property, Technology and Economic Growth', in Francis W. Rushing and Carole Ganz Brown (eds.) *Intellectual Property Rights in Science, Technology, and Economic Performance: International Comparisons*. London: Westview Press, pp. 17–30. I should note that Mansfield is specific that he is not against IP rights. Also see David K. Levine and Michele Boldrin (2005), 'Intellectual Property and the Efficient Allocation of Social Surplus from Creation', *Review of Economic Research on Copyright Issues*, 2(1): 45-66. Cf. note 30 for more on this. My dissertation is available at the University of Missouri archives: http://edt.missouri.edu/Summer2007/Dissertation/TreriseJ-073007-D8217/research.pdf.
3. The distinction between types and tokens (in these words) comes first from Peirce. See Charles S. Peirce (1931–58) *Collected Papers of Charles Sanders Peirce*, vols. 1–6, ed. Hartshorne and Weiss. Cambridge, MA: Harvard University Press).
4. There are complications to the distinction mostly irrelevant for our purposes here. One issue which I will note is that types come in varying levels of generality. There can be many or few tokens of a type depending on how *finely* or *coarsely* individuated a type is. 'Male student' is a coarsely individuated type, while 'Male college student in Midwestern America' is a more finely individuated type than the first. Still finer is 'Male college student at the University of Missouri-Columbia on 30 January, 1982'.
5. Cf. note 4 and the issue of varying levels of generality. In addition, the type/token distinction is not equivalent to the idea/expression dichotomy, as particular ideas can be tokens as well as types (my particular idea of desegregation is a token of the type of the same name).
6. This is the last time I will explicitly make this qualification, but it continues to apply below.
7. There is an important side-issue here. In the above example, X_2 is putatively *the same as* S's original token X. But this may not always exactly be the case in the real world. So, consider that X is a drug; say, a cure for cancer. Agent S comes up with (X); at a later time, agent T comes up with her cure for cancer (X_2). Again, in the above example, if X_2 is qualitatively identical to X, then S has a claim on T's X_2. But what if, as is often the case, there are functional or compositional differences between X and X_2, but both of them still act as cures for cancer? In these cases, does S still have a claim on T's X_2? This is a complication that I cannot fully address, as there is no clear and complete answer. When one owns a patent over X, one does not simply have ownership over *only* qualitatively identical separate Xs. One also owns, at least in Anglo-American patent law,

items which, while not qualitatively identical, are 'similar enough' to warrant protection (according to the law). This is known as the 'doctrine of equivalents'. This doctrine, which gives protection over objects which lie outside the explicit bounds of the patent, is necessary for patent protection, since otherwise would-be infringers could simply add something trivial to a patented item to avoid infringement. See Steven C. Carlson (1999) 'Patent Pools and the Antitrust Dilemma', *Yale Journal on Regulation*, 16(2): 359–400. Also see www.ladas.com/BULLETINS/2002/0802Bulletin/US_Doctrine Equivalents.html.

8. How exactly one obtains ownership on one's original token is a question I leave open; I intend for WTP to be neutral on this matter. Hence, whatever view one ascribes to for property rights in general, apply this view to ownership of one's original token. That is, there need be nothing specifically *intellectual* about one's original token ownership. Even if the original token is an idea, it will be instantiated in a concrete physical object, and that object can come to be owned according to typical property ownership justifications. I assume that some justifications of private property work.
9. Except, perhaps, to use the sun *exclusively* to do something else. That is, any use of a resource is rivalrous in the sense that others can no longer exclusively use that resource. So this description technically is not logically precise; I am simply using the term, however, as economists generally use it. This means that, while the definition of rivalry as presented will allow for some examples that show all resources to be rivalrous (in at least one sense), for our purposes, the definition will do. It is trivial that my use of a resource clearly impacts on your ability to keep me from using the resource; hence, we are justified in ignoring this possibility. What matters is when my use of a resource has a more significant impact on your use. This significant impact can be measured economically, if need be.
10. I define what it takes for something to be a copy below.
11. Those concerned with values other than liberty, I argue in my dissertation (see reference in n. 2 above), should still reject STP. I cannot flesh out this position here, but my larger project is to argue for my view (Weak Type-Protection) from many plausible theoretical perspectives, and therefore establish a strong presumption for it.
12. It might also be objectionable, from a liberty perspective, to come to own all tokens of a type; and this would be without the ownership of a type *per se*. I do not preclude this possibility; indeed I find it likely that in many cases a concern for liberty will find such token ownership unjust. However, my concern here is to distinguish just from unjust type-protecting systems, as well as the just IP system; I thus set this issue aside.
13. It is probably the case that other IP rights do not give this sort of power.
14. This is a simplification of Matthew Kramer's notion of non-moral freedom. See Kramer (2003) *The Quality of Freedom*. Oxford: Oxford University Press, p. 3.
15. I here assume a maximising or aggregative strategy in my discussion of consequentialism and liberty. But, one might think that the distribution of liberty (from a consequentialist perspective) is the relevant strategy, not the aggregation. While I am indeed moved by this and find distributive concerns very important, I believe I can set aside this concern. This is because

distributive concerns will not change what I argue for because the only kinds of distributive concern that might change the position I argue for here are those that are aimed at helping the least well-off. It may be that, on some views like an *equality of opportunity for liberty* consequentialist view, the least well-off (in terms of liberty) needs to be favoured in order to equalise opportunities. While this is plausible it (perhaps surprisingly) does not change what will be our conclusion looking at the aggregative position. It does not, that is, force us to embrace STP (or even the no-IP position) in order to equalise opportunities. This is because IP protection is simply one legal institution within a larger institution of laws and distributions of goods. To say that STP (or no-IP) is necessary to favour the least well-off, under this theory (or one like it), means that there is no other way (or no other better way) to equalise opportunities. This would be surprising. Again, an IP regime is simply one legal institution among others; others which would probably be better suited to equalise opportunities (by, for instance, directly funding or educating the least well-off). So, the distributive consequentialist concerns that might actually affect my position will be better addressed via other means, and we can thus focus on which IP regime best aggregates liberty.

16. The qualification that we should promote morally relevant liberties is necessary, as there may be numerous, irrelevant liberties that any system can justifiably ignore, restrict or do whatever with; for example, we might think stacking grains of salt is a morally irrelevant liberty and need not be promoted. However, if it could be (and was) argued that this was a morally relevant liberty, the argument would then pay attention to it.
17. I would also claim, but will not defend here, that strong type-ownership promotes the overall liberty of persons less than a position of no IP protection. I claim this while still rejecting, all things considered, no IP protection (though I do not have space to defend this latter claim, either); I say more about this in the final note.
18. What it takes for an innovation to be independent is complicated. I will say more about this below; however, please note that, in practice, the identification of independent innovation will no doubt in some cases be complicated. This is a practical issue with details that need to be worked out. There are, however, some clear cases of independent innovation.
19. The number of people who could use an item is potentially huge. It might also be small in some cases, but there is no reason to suppose it will be small on average.
20. I here simplify a truly complex issue. An entire treatise could be (and has been) written spelling out exactly what this means. I put the position as broadly as possible to encompass different possible deontological views concerned with liberty. It is necessary, incidentally, to put the clause about remaining consistent with the respect for the liberty of all, since Libertarians will allow limitations of the liberty of those who violate others' liberties.
21. Though I do believe various deontological views that are concerned with liberty all bear strong relations with the ethical and political theory of Libertarianism, I do not mean here to identify all these views

with that theory (however it is construed). I only use this term for convenience.

22. The reader may think that the garden is not an 'idea'. I would point out that what has been copied is the garden's manicure. There is actually a complicated issue in the vicinity here; specifically, we may wonder whether IP rights (both in theory and in practice) protect material or ideational resources. It is clear, though perhaps surprising, that the Anglo-American patent system covers *material resources*. This is because if one has a patent over X, one has rights not over the idea of X, but over physical instantiations of X. Patent rights, then, are *material-type* rights. *Ideational*-type rights would be absurd; it would mean one would own the *idea* of X, wherever X occurred (even in other people's heads).
23. As noted before, I attempt to give a more complete treatment of this system in my dissertation (see n. 2 for reference), as well as show that many plausible theories would select my system as the form for IP rights.
24. Since it covers a class of objects, namely, original tokens and some copies thereof.
25. The only damage done to the original owner here is that the original owner can no longer profit from the copier's copy. This refers to the issue raised in note 9 above; there is some, trivial, impact in any case of copying – the owner of the original can no longer exclusively contain the item copied by another. In this case, if the owner did not want others to make copies for personal use, he should protect that item from being copied via privacy and secrecy. To require an owner to keep ideas from being copied and *profited from* via privacy and secrecy – which is, incidentally, to embrace the no IP position – is to put more significant restrictions on owners than the minimal restriction placed on them to conceal whatever they do not want others to copy and *use*.
26. I believe we should expect there to be difficult cases; this fits our intuitions. It is often very difficult to tell in the real world to what extent a subsequent innovation is in/dependent of an earlier one. Hence, if we are to construct a system that would distribute rights in a way which we find intuitive, it is obvious that there will be some difficult cases.
27. Whether compensation is sufficient or whether you must cease profiting from the copy you possess is an issue I leave for another time.
28. I will not attempt to answer whether complete functional similarity but compositional difference still counts as a copy (or whether functional difference but compositional similarity also counts). I suspect that, in each case, they do, though not as significant a copy as a functionally and compositionally similar pair. Nor will I be able to spell out more carefully to what extent X must be functionally and/or compositionally similar to count as a copy. It seems clear that there are controversial and uncontroversial cases on both sides.

    a) Recall garden case D, above, where you got your idea of the garden from mine, but make no precise measurements. Certainly, your idea is dependent on mine; also, it might be somewhat functionally and/or compositionally similar. But we may want to resist calling it a copy if you have put much of your own time and ingenuity into the creation of your own garden. In this case, incidentally, I believe WTP would proclaim that, if the copy (on which you make rivalrous use) is violative at all, it may only be so to a small degree and thus require only a small amount of compensation. (The details here can, of course, be elaborated; how exactly to compensate is complicated, but we can set up different scales of compensation for different levels of violation.) That is, we can construct WTP to reflect how significant the copying is in the cases where rivalrous use is made of copies.

b) However, case B is much more clearly a copy; its functional and/or compositional similarity is obvious (it is presupposed in the case) and it is clearly dependent on the original token. Thus, WTP says – and this accords with our intuitions – that you owe me compensation in this case.

29. Some readers may note the similarity between my system and the Anglo-American copyright system. This is unintentional, but I do recognise it. The copyright system does not have that most objectionable feature of the patent system – that independent innovators are denied the liberty to use their innovations. I do not, however, wish to explore the similarities and differences here. There are no doubt many similarities, and probably at least some differences (for example, the copyright system as it exists today in the US has some issues regarding vague contracts that are problematic). It is clear, then, that my position has the patent system looking more like the copyright system.
30. Again, I have simplified matters in setting aside other consequentialist values and simplifying distributive concerns. With regard to the former I would again like to note that I would claim these other consequentialist values (such as a utilitarian concern for overall well-being, or a concern for desert) will not change our conclusions (with an important exception in the case of pharmaceuticals). It is simply not the case that STP gives agents what they deserve (since it denies other, independent inventors what they deserve), nor is it the case that such protection promotes overall well-being the most (since strong protection actually can cause a disincentive to innovate). The no IP position does not fare much better, since it clearly does not give inventing agents what they deserve, nor does it provide any incentive for people to create to promote overall well-being. I argue this more completely in my dissertation; WTP fares better than STP and the no IP position on all counts (with an important exception for pharmaceuticals, where strong type protection may be necessary for adequate incentive). Cf. note 2 above.

Part II

Specific Issues

7

Is P2P Sharing of MP3 Files an Objectionable Form of Free Riding?

Geert Demuijnck

Introduction

As soon as my 15-year-old daughter hears a song she likes, she tries to find out the name of the band or the singer, then goes online and downloads the song to her MP3 player, either from *eMule* or from *Limewire*. When I tell her that this is illegal, she laughs and says that everyone in her class downloads music.[1] She is absolutely not disturbed by any sense of injustice or unfairness, nor are her friends.[2] In this chapter, I want to argue that, despite the illegal character of these practices, the moral intuitions of these young people are, on a fundamental normative level, not so obviously wrong. More precisely, I want to argue that the kind of peer-to-peer (P2P) downloading of music files they are practising is only exceptionally an objectionable kind of free riding.

Copyright protection of digital artistic production is a quickly evolving area, not only in its legal aspects, but also concerning the technical possibilities of copying and protecting. Moreover, it is surprisingly unclear what the economic effects of the growing possibilities of piracy as well as of commercialisation based on downloading or 'streaming' (interactively choosing music tracks without storage on the computer of the consumer) will be in the long run.[3] This chapter neither aims to explore these possibilities nor to predict what will happen. It merely focuses on the moral legitimacy of the current copyright rules. More particularly, it examines whether or not people who share music files on the internet are acting like *unfair free riders*.

Two main arguments in favour of P2P sharing – that is arguments that show that P2P sharing is not always an unfair form of free riding – are advanced, both, perhaps surprisingly, starting from, but not fully endorsing, the ideas defended by David Gauthier, one of the main contemporary defenders of Lockean property rights. The first defends the idea that, although copyright is an institutional scheme which aims to cope with the 'public good' aspect of information goods like shared files, free riding may not nevertheless be morally condemnable insofar as the scheme as such is unfair. The second argument starts from Gauthier's version of the Lockean proviso: negative externalities imposed on others with whom there is no market interaction at all does not deteriorate the terms of trade and should therefore not be compensated. Some piracy does not replace any market interaction and falls, therefore, under this scheme. This point will be related to some aspects of the 'fair use' exception.

None of the arguments is conclusive, but they all show nevertheless that piracy is not morally condemnable, in many cases, on the basis of the free riding argument. The arguments point out that in general the current copyright protection system, even if one fully accepts the objective of stimulating creativity, is ill adapted, at least in some respects. The quick development of digitalisation and sharing techniques simply makes this more obvious.

Is free riding immoral?

One moral objection to P2P downloading is that downloaders are *free riders* and, therefore, behave unfairly. The validity of this objection depends crucially on how we defend free riding and whether or not all cases of free riding, according to the definition we adopt, are unfair.

A good starting point for a discussion of the possible unfairness of free riding is Gauthier's contractarian theory of economic justice. According to Gauthier (1986), perfect market interaction is the paradigm of rational and moral interaction. If I sell goods that I have produced, I am the legitimate owner of what the transaction yields. Market exchanges, like selling my products, are both rational and impartial, and beyond the debate about distributive justice. Two important conditions have to be respected though. First, production should be based on my labour and on resources that are also available to others at the current market price. In other words, exchanges would become morally questionable if I were to take advantage of a monopolistic possession of a production factor, i.e. if I benefited from what Gauthier calls a 'factor rent'. Second, exchanges would also become morally questionable if I were to impose part of the production cost on others, i.e. if production created negative externalities, or, at least according to Gauthier, if production took advantage of positive externalities created by others' activities without paying for them.

The topic of free riding comes into focus when the second condition is not satisfied, that is in situations in which there are *externalities* at play, situations in which consumption or production decisions of some agents affect other agents' utility. These external effects, whether they are positive or negative, give rise, according to Gauthier, to two types of immoral behaviour: either being a free rider or being a parasite. 'A free rider obtains a benefit without paying all or part of its cost. A parasite in obtaining a benefit displaces all or part of the cost' (Gauthier, 1986, p. 96).

The aim of any set of moral rules and regulations is to eliminate free riders and parasites (ibid., p. 113). The whole purpose of moral rules in the economy can therefore be related to the failures of the market. Faced with these failures, rational people try to find solutions that are both impartial and rational. The discussion of Gauthier's particular solution is beyond the scope of this chapter. What matters here is the moral rejection of free riders and parasites. In general, Gauthier's moral objection is against what he calls 'taking advantage of' someone else. He defines justice as 'the disposition not to take advantage of one's fellows, not to seek free goods or to impose uncompensated costs, provided that one supposes others similarly disposed' (ibid., p. 113).

The concept of a parasite is quite clear: in more common language, it comes down to imposing negative externalities on others, in other words, harming other people. Gauthier gives an example: 'The factory owner who disposes of her gaseous wastes by polluting the atmosphere without compensating those who suffer the pollution she causes is a parasite, displacing part of the costs of her activities on to others' (ibid., p. 96). Parasitism is obviously unfair.

Gauthier also gives an example of free riding: 'The shipowners whose vessels take navigational advantage of a lighthouse although they have contributed neither to its erection nor to its maintenance are free riders' (ibid., p. 96). The shipowners 'obtain a benefit' from a positive externality. However, it is unclear whether 'obtaining a benefit' from a positive externality without paying *necessarily* means *unfairly* 'taking advantage of', as Gauthier's definition suggests. Consider the example of someone who has nice flowers in front of his house. Of course, the owner of the flowers is probably the person who sees them most often, but passers-by also enjoy the sight. And yet it seems completely absurd to claim that the owner of the flowers should be allowed to constrain the passers-by to pay for the view of the flowers they did not ask for.

Similarly, and more closely related to the issue at stake, my neighbour is a professional musician, and sometimes, when I am sitting in the garden, I enjoy listening to him playing the violin. Still, that is clearly not a sufficient reason for him to charge me. And yet, I benefit from an action which I did not pay for.[4]

Therefore, free riding as taking advantage of positive externalities seems *prima facie* morally acceptable.[5] The flipside of this point is that there is no reason to allow the producer of positive externalities to appropriate them.

Free riding and public goods

However, this is too quick. As Gauthier's lighthouse example suggests, free riding on externalities cannot always be condoned from a moral point of view. At first sight, the distinction between morally acceptable forms of free riding and unfair forms of free riding seems related to whether or not one is free riding on a good which is in some sense *public*. Technically, public goods are characterised by *non-excludability*: once they exist, no one can be excluded from benefiting from them. A further characteristic is *non-rivalry*: the fact that I enjoy the good does not impinge on other people enjoying the same good at the same time.[6]

If a good is a public good in this technical sense, free riding may lead to its non-production (Parsons, 2005, p. 643). Public goods are characterised by positive externalities to the extent that they cannot be produced by the standard market economy because their positive externalities prevent their production: the return on investment is less than the investment needed to produce them. For instance, it would never be worthwhile for an individual ship owner to bear the cost of the construction of a lighthouse.[7] To the extent that non-rivalry and non-excludability may be a matter of degree, goods may to some extent be 'public' and, as a consequence, under-produced.[8]

If goods are 'public' in this sense, citizens will not gain potential benefits unless they find an alternative to the ordinary combination of private entrepreneurship and a competitive market. Typically, many common collective goods (e.g. streetlighting, lighthouses and security) are technically public goods. If everyone were to free ride on them, they would not be provided. But in such cases, and only to the extent that we collectively judge that these goods are *socially desirable* and therefore *should* be produced, we can indeed opt for alternatives to the standard case, i.e. market production in which the appropriation of positive externalities is allowed.

A first possibility is that the government may provide the good. In this case taxpayers contribute, independently of whether or not they benefit from the good produced. If the decision to produce the good is taken democratically, we may assume that its total value exceeds the total cost. Moreover, the government, unlike a monopolist, does not capture this surplus.

A second solution is, in the case of tangible goods, to set up an institution such that the good is no longer a public good in the technical sense. One may, for example, grant a right to an investor to exploit privately the 'public' good. Concrete examples are private toll roads, but recently this strategy has also been used for the construction of tunnels and airports. This presupposes that excludability is to some extent realisable (Lemley, 2005, p. 1050). Unlike an ordinary street which may be used by anybody, private toll roads have access control. In this case it is important to stress that private investors need not capture *completely* the positive externalities created by their investment, but just *enough* for their investment to be profitable. This explains why governments grant temporary exploitation licences for which different companies compete. The latter strategy comes down to grant the right to internalise (part of) the positive externalities.

Whatever the specific exceptional institutional arrangement which copes with the public good characteristic is, it comes down to an institutional 'scheme' that 'confers benefits by making requirements of beneficiaries' (Cullity, 1995, p. 14), either tax revenue or specific fares, for the benefits. Free riding on such a scheme, which is only viable when most other people satisfy the requirements, seems *prima facie* unfair, as several authors have argued.[9] Not only would widespread free riding undermine the very institutional scheme, it is moreover unfair to accept the benefit from such an institutional arrangement by taking advantage of others' benefit-producing compliance.

However, this delineation between fair and unfair free riding (i.e. taking a free ride is acceptable unless it is on an institutional scheme which copes with a public good problem) is again too hasty. Garrett Cullity has convincingly argued that free riding on cooperative schemes which are set up to resolve 'public good' problems is only unfair when three conditions are satisfied. If they are not, free riding may, arguably, be fair. The conditions that allow us to say that taking a free ride on an institutional scheme is unfair are the following.

First, the practice of participation in the institutional schema represents a net benefit for the potential free rider. No free rider can be blamed if his regular participation in the scheme would have made him worse off than he would have been without the existence of the scheme. For example, suppose that I am poor and that there is a collectively organised cleaning system which sweeps the streets twice a day, bringing them to an exceptional standard of cleanness.[10] Even if the cost is fairly distributed among the citizens and street cleaning is a non-rival and non-excludable public good, my participation in the scheme (since I am poor and I am not really concerned with exceptionally clean streets) makes me worse off than I would be in the absence of the scheme. In this case, it seems questionable to condemn free riding as unfair. However, if I have a net benefit from the scheme, free riding is unfair, that is if the two other conditions are satisfied as well.

The second condition is that the scheme as a whole makes practically everyone better off when *fairly generalised*. Imagine a scheme that is organised in a fair way, that is the requirements it imposes on everyone are fairly distributed, but the scheme is inefficient overall: in this case it is not obvious to call free riding unfair. Cullity gives the example of a system in which everyone would be liable to pay all unsolicited benefits that are worth their cost (1995, p. 14). This system would be fair in the sense of the first condition, but so inefficient that it would impoverish most people.[11]

The third condition concerns the absence of general moral objection to the scheme. One could think of a scheme which is itself unfair or of a fairly distributed scheme among gangsters which exploits others. When these three conditions are met, taking a free ride on an institutional scheme which copes with a public good problem is unfair.[12]

Reframing these conditions to fit in better with the question at stake comes down to this. Insofar as copyright is an institutional device to cope with a public good problem, P2P sharing of music files would be unfair if 1) the potential downloader, if he did *not* download, still benefited from the current copyright protection, i.e. his utility would decrease if the system did not exist at all; 2) almost everyone concerned benefits from the current copyright protection; and 3) the copyright protection cannot be morally blamed in any aspect.

Intellectual goods as public goods

The 'public good' aspect of intellectual property is related to a particular technical characteristic of intellectual goods. The cost of creating goods such as films, songs and books is often high, but the cost of reproducing them is typically very low (Landes and Posner, 1989, p. 326). Strictly speaking, goods such as films, songs and books are excludable, and to some extent rival, goods. However, the marginal cost to produce a supplementary copy is extremely low, and since the introduction of digitalisation it is close to zero. Especially, the ratio of fixed to marginal costs is incomparably higher than that for material goods. Furthermore, as in all competitive markets, the price would be close to the marginal cost in the absence of an exclusive right to copy. Together, these elements imply that, given this particularly high fixed costs/marginal cost ratio, producers cannot cover their fixed cost investment. As a consequence, the good cannot be produced by the private market since no one will invest when there is a negative expected return. For example, if the price of a CD falls to the marginal cost of the production of the disk itself, the producers will not be able to capture the cost of making the recording.

Copyright, and intellectual property rights in general, are precisely a solution for this 'public good' problem. By limiting the right to copy, or the right to take advantage of a new idea, they create scarcity in order to boost returns on creative investments (Lemley, 2005, p. 31). To be clear, the expected return should cover not only the production costs, but also the risks, which are understandably high in creation (Landes and Posner, 1989, p. 327)

On the other hand, this exception to the general rule of the market mechanism – in which charging people for positive externalities is disallowed – does not imply that the creators of intellectual goods should have full control over these goods. On the contrary, a major goal of intellectual property rights is to prevent people keeping their ideas and inventions secret by guaranteeing a sufficiently long-term monopolistic exploitation. After this monopolistic term, the intellectual goods are 'free' and people are permitted to take advantage of uncompensated positive externalities (Lemley, 2005, p. 1052). This system has a lot of similarity with the system of private toll roads: it grants the right to internalise positive externalities. As a consequence; copyright necessarily produces deadweight loss (Gordon and Watt, 2003, p. xvii).

However, the point of copyright protection is also *to promote* uncompensated positive externalities:

> Copyright protection...trades off the costs of limiting access to a work against the benefits of providing incentives to create the work in the first place. Stringing the correct balance between access and incentives is the central problem in copyright law.
>
> (Landes and Posner, 1989, p. 326)

The exception to the general rule of free competition seems necessary in order to stimulate creativity, but it also seems important to minimise any market distortion and not to overprotect intellectual goods. From this perspective, it is important, as Lemley stresses, to take into consideration that intellectual property rights are 'a form of legal protection to deal with public goods problems' (Lemley, 2005, pp. 1030–1). Therefore, they should be compared with other forms of government intervention in the economy (e.g. subsidies, taxes, etc.) rather than with 'real' property. Whether or not free riding on this institutional scheme of legal protection is unfair depends on whether the three conditions outlined in the preceding section are satisfied.

Is P2P sharing of MP3 files unfairly free riding on 'public goods'?

Since the copyright system can be considered as an institutional scheme to overcome a public good problem, in order to qualify illegal downloading as unfair we have to ask whether Cullity's conditions are met. In this section we focus on the second and third condition, leaving the first to the next section.

Cullity's second condition states that the system should make (almost) everybody better off than either an alternative system or no system at all. The current system of copyright protection is highly questionable in this respect. For creativity seems to be overcompensated, and not unrelated to this phenomenon of overcompensation – insofar as the popular music market is a winner-takes-all market – creators are compensated very unequally.

One can quite confidently argue that famous rock stars are in factor rent situations (i.e. rent related to the monopolistic possession of a rare production factor, such as a special talent). Admittedly, precisely defining rent is a tricky matter. Gauthier defines factor rent as 'a premium certain factors services command, over and above the full cost of supply, because there is no alternative to meet the demand' (1986, p. 272). He specifies that this means, for the owner of a rare talent, 'to extract payment for his services over and above the cost to him, including the opportunity cost, of supplying those services' (ibid.). Although this definition may be to some extent imprecise, it is not difficult to suppose that, say, David Bowie would have composed his songs for less then he currently earns on the basis of copyright. The standard of living of famous rock stars is widely described and photographed in popular magazines. Insofar as children are illegally downloading music of this kind of contemporary nobility, they may justify it with a Robin Hood argument: these people are so rich that a small decrease in their copyright revenue is commendable.

The excessive incomes of famous rock stars are explained by the particular structure of the music business. The market of creation is of the 'winner-takes-all' type. In such a market, reward depends heavily on relative and not absolute performance. When a farmer is slightly less productive than his neighbour, he will have a slightly smaller income. In the world of music there is no such proportionality. The system of excessive reward creates 'a few big winners and lots of losers who have wasted their time'. As Lemley and others[13] point out: 'Virtually no musicians actually make money. Potential creators are drawn by the lure of the big score like moths to a flame, and most of the effort turns out to be wasted' (Lemley, 2005, p. 1103). Robert Frank and Philip Cook (1995) give the following example:

> At the turn of the century, Iowa alone had more than 1,500 of them [opera houses]. Thousands of sopranos earned adequate, if modest, livings from their live performances. But now, thanks to modern recordings, the world's best soprano can be literally everywhere at once.

The system of copyright protection combined with the typical winner-takes-all market structure explains why the great majority of the musicians earn relatively little from copyrights. Most of the income generated by copyright work goes to the publishers and to a small minority of high-earning performers (Regner, 2003, p. 109).[14] The second condition is clearly not met.

Nor is the third condition (i.e. the overall fairness of the system) satisfied because winner-takes-all markets are essentially unfair. Anyone who spends time where live music is performed knows that there are many excellent musicians around. Even during 'open mike' sessions, one often wonders why these people are not famous whereas others, barely better or sometimes worse performers, live like royalty. Of course, sometimes the 'system' picks up a street musician (Damien Rice is an example), but the artistic labour market is deeply divided between a few stars on the one hand and an army of losers on the other. Moreover, the high incentives for winners attract too many people to the market of creation, and all the more so the stronger the copyright protection is.[15]

On top of the unfairness of this system, it has some other troubling features which are worth spelling out. First, the winner-takes-all phenomenon is partly reinforced and explained by the rent-seeking behaviour of the publishers, who are the actual owners of the copyright.[16] The music industry is highly concentrated and the 'majors', which also own the channels through which the 'content' is distributed, want their artistic material (of which they own the copyright) distributed and bought. Marketing is aggressive, as Joost Smiers puts it, 'to the degree that alternate cultural options will be pushed away from many people's mental map' (2002, p. 121). Following the commercial logic, money for marketing and promotion creates 'stars'.

One obvious effect of this marketing system that aims at exploiting copyright property is the star system. The mechanism and its catastrophic artistic consequences were analysed in the 1940s by Max Horkheimer and Theodor Adorno, who showed how the mutual influence of the mass media, together with the development of a mass culture, would narrow artistic creation to standardised, fully interchangeable consumption products: i.e. songs of 3 minutes, TV soaps of 26 minutes, etc., based on stardom.[17] Their prediction turned out to be basically correct. The overall effect of this commercial culture industry is levelling down the intrinsic quality of cultural productions. Much of the music pupils are downloading is artistically more or less worthless. It is highly probable that a significant minority or even a majority of the population judges the music my daughter likes to be an ugly noise. The point is that the current copyright protection rules make investment in this kind of aggressively promoted records profitable, and pupils are the most obvious consumers. Therefore, it cannot be argued that the production of these goods demands an institutional device to overcome the 'public good' problem because they are rather the unlucky side-effect of the current overprotection of copyright.

Second, the flipside of this mass culture marketing system is that, paradoxically, current copyright protection may be insufficient as an incentive for artistic production. For example, copyright protection alone would never make it possible to record the wonderful traditional Baka music. I suppose that many people would be willing to pay a trivial sum to contribute to the recording of world heritage music such as the Baka's, but unwilling to pay the equivalent of the price of a CD. In this case, the typical 'public good' problem cannot be resolved by the current copyright protection. Although it overcompensates creators, it is, at least in some cases, insufficient. Luckily, public institutions like Unesco fill this gap.[18]

To conclude, it is obvious that, with respect to the musicians in general, the current system is not really an example of distributive justice.

Therefore, and *only* insofar as people mostly download winners' music, P2P sharing cannot be considered unfair, at least not unfair to these musicians. Some have even argued that one of the positive side-effects of the current crisis in the commercial music sector, arising from digitalisation and illegal downloading, might be that it leads to a less concentrated music offering and to a situation in which more people are able to make a living, albeit a less lavish one than famous rock stars enjoy.[19] In this sense, illegal downloading will contribute to more fairness.

Cullity's second and third conditions are clearly not met: the current system does not make (almost) everyone better off and the distribution of its advantages is, at least among creators, quite unfair, from which it follows, according to Cullity, that free riding on this system is not morally condemnable. There is though one sense in which P2P sharing may nevertheless be judged as unfair. This unfairness is about the radical market segmentation between payers and free riders. Film and music files that are downloaded with P2P sharing systems are made on the basis of real existing CDs and DVDs. The fact that the CDs are still produced and sold, albeit to a lesser extent, proves that they still can be produced by the market. The fact that profits diminish and that, therefore, the 'consumer surplus' increases is a normal phenomenon of the market economy. The question of whether P2P downloading makes their production impossible is pointless with respect to these files.

Piracy is only conceivable on the basis of produced work, and it therefore presupposes that the investment is valuable. Still, P2P sharing can only exist to the extent that some clients pay for their CDs. It presupposes, therefore, that in the market segment of CDs, copyright is not infringed. The only morally problematic point here concerns the division of the consumer surplus, i.e. the decrease of the deadweight loss due to P2P sharing: some consumers pay the former price (full deadweight included) and some pay nothing. This radical form of market segmentation is clearly unfair. However, it is unfair with respect to the paying consumers who finance the production, but not necessarily unfair to the creators.

Harmless copying in the absence of market interaction

Let me turn now to a second line of argument which shows that illegal downloading or copying is not necessarily a form of morally reprehensible free riding, even if the music market were not of the winner-takes-all type, and if copyright were pitched at an adequate level. It may be argued that some groups of downloaders do not have the means to buy some of the music they download – students, and also people living in poor regions. The point we defend here is, basically, that since these very poor free riders would never be able to buy CDs, they cannot be considered as unfair free riders. Four arguments may be deployed to support this view.

The first argument starts from Gauthier's theory of justice. Besides the basic conditions we mentioned above, Gauthier advances a further background condition to guarantee the impartiality of market exchanges – namely, that interacting parties should not worsen each other's initial position before they start their market relations. It is his very much weakened version of the well-known Lockean proviso, which says that one may convert natural resources into private property as long as one leaves sufficient of these to others. Gauthier gives the following example:

> Suppose that we live as fisherfolk along the banks of a river. . . . But if you, living upstream from me, merely use the river for the disposal of your wastes, then even though you thereby kill many of the fish in my part of the stream, you do not violate the proviso. For although you worsen my situation in relation to what I should expect in your absence, you do not better your own situation through interaction with me.
>
> (1986, pp. 211–12)

However, things change as soon as we start trading. The terms of trade are influenced by the supply of fish, which in turn is influenced by your polluting: 'You benefit from polluting my water; you better your situation through interaction that worsens mine' (ibid.). Gauthier argues that this harm should be compensated for in order to create fair market conditions.

The situation that interests us here is the first one, in which there is no commercial interaction. In that case, externalities, whether positive or negative, do not influence the terms of trade because there is no trade.[20] Imagine the not so implausible case that dumping your waste in the stream gives more food to the fish so that I benefit from positive externalities. In this case, the question of compensation in the absence of market interaction would be totally pointless. Moreover, it is not at all obvious that these positive externalities should be compensated for: insofar as the people downstream did not ask for them, claiming compensation would be illegitimate.

The relevance of this proviso for our topic is that, in the absence of regular market interaction, benefiting from externalities cannot make interactions unfair and is therefore not morally condemnable. This point becomes interesting if one takes into consideration that the reason why it may be impossible to establish a market interaction is not necessary, as in Gauthier's hypothetical example, ignorance of each other's existence, but, more commonly, poverty. Since poor 'pirates' could never have bought the CD, they do not worsen the market exchanges of the musicians (Gordon and Watt, 2003, p. 11).

A second argument relies on Cullity's first condition to qualify free riding as unfair. Free riding cannot be qualified as unfair if normal participation in the institutional scheme that is set up to overcome a 'public good' problem (here the non-rivalry of music files) does not bring about a net benefit to the participant compared to the absence of the scheme. The current copyright system does not improve the situation of very poor people, insofar as they lack the purchasing power to buy CDs. Therefore, their free riding cannot be qualified as unfair.

Our third argument is a variant of the second one. Its background is the 'fair use' jurisprudence which echoes to some extent the preceding point. 'Fair use' identifies some exceptional situations in which copying does not in any respect harm the copyright owner and can therefore not be considered as legally condemnable. (Note: we stressed earlier that free riding never causes harm directly, but causes harm to the extent that it undermines the institutional scheme that was set up to resolve a 'public good' problem. The basic argument here is the no harm principle.)

Fair use is a vague term used to refer to a set of exceptions that allows different kinds of exceptions to the copyright law. Some copying of a copyrighted work does not make the copier an infringer. Section 107 of the US Copyright Act 2000 mentions four major factors, drawn from prior judicial decisions, to be considered in judgments under the fair use doctrine.[21] The first factor is the purpose and character of the use. It indeed makes a difference, e.g. if the copier is a firm selling copies or not (Landes and Posner, 1989, p. 357).[22] Similarly, it seems obvious that we should be allowed to make a copy for personal use or share copies with our families. I come back to this point below. A second factor which justifies the fair use exception is the nature of the copyrighted work: it is considered less harmful to copy factual information than creative information, and already published material rather than unpublished. Third, the amount that is copied also matters. For example, less than a chapter of a book is acceptable. The last factor is the one which interests us here: the degree to which the effect of copying on the potential market for the copyrighted work is negligible. If the copier is not a potential purchaser of copies, his use does not affect the demand for them, nor the supply (ibid.). This is the factor most often invoked to justify the fair use exception (Beebe, 2007). One reason why the copier will not have an effect on the market may be poverty, which may explain why the copier would never buy copies. And, indeed, some of the explicitly mentioned exceptions in the jurisprudence of copyright concern the category of poor consumers.[23] Moreover, there are exceptions to the application of copyright related to the poverty of creators. For example, the US Copyright Act 'includes a provision that permits live performance of musical works and nondramatic literary works so long as the performance does not have a commercial purpose, the performers are not paid, and no admission fee is charged' (Shaffer Van Houweling, 2005, p. 1535).

A final, more fundamental reason why a comparison between copying without paying copyright and stealing tangible goods does not hold, and therefore why free riding may sometimes not be unfair, is that cultural goods have an intrinsic value, which has to be clearly distinguished from their market value. Creators want to make a living from their work, but they also want their work to be read, listened to or performed. Following this logic, creative artists want to be recognised in the first place. If a literary critic discusses a novel, the author will not bother to know whether the critic bought the book or borrowed it from a public library. Especially with respect to bona fide fans who do not have the means to buy an expensive copy, artistic creators somehow lose their artistic soul when they denounce illegal downloading.

This last argument needs some further comment related to the fair use exception. The ambition to be recognised and famous has implications for the use of copies. If you want renown you have to accept that people will talk about your work, share their opinions and occasionally borrow things from each other. This kind of sharing does not require any copying, but may nevertheless affect the market. Take the following example. A friend of mine is a member of a reading group of 12 who meet every year to discuss new novels that seem worth reading. They agree on a list, each buys one of the books, reads it and passes it on to another member the following month. At the end of the year, they have all read 12 books but have bought only one. Although their main motivation is not to save money, it is a quite strange device to be mutually stimulated to read because they think that reading novels is important, but constraining as well, since their sharing the books makes them avoid copyright payment. One could say that in this case there is no infringement of copyright since no copies are made. But the books are shared.[24]

The sharing or copyrighted material in small circles is explicitly accepted in the legislation. The French legislation on fair use, which is referred to as the 'private copy' exception, mentions the right to give free representation within 'the family circle'. [25]

However, although this justification of free riding is relevant, its scope is limited and does not apply to all P2P sharing. At first sight, one could argue that P2P sharing is just an extended version of sharing in a family environment, especially when it does not require any copying. However, this way of considering P2P sharing clearly contradicts the fourth justificatory ground of the fair use exception, i.e. the effect on the market. Unlike small-scale sharing, P2P sharing among people who do not know each other is likely to have a considerable impact on the demand side of the market. It would therefore probably imply much unfair behaviour.

Conclusion

This chapter is not an argument in favour of the abolition of copyright. We need to be aware of the reasons why copyright was invented in the first place: without copyright as a device to cope with the 'public good' character of art creations many authors and musicians would have been unable to create their work, to their detriment and to the detriment of consumers. However, faced with the new technological developments which tend to facilitate downloading, some are asking whether copyright is becoming obsolete. Technological as well as philosophical arguments to reconsider the legal framework of artistic creation and the market of cultural goods have been advanced. In this chapter, we have qualified an often heard argument, advanced by those who defend the prevailing copyright system, i.e. that illegal downloaders are morally objectionable 'free riders'. They may be, but certainly not all the time. We have indicated two configurations in which this qualification of unfair behaviour does not hold: insofar as they download 'winners', they take a free ride on an unfair system, and insofar as they lack purchasing power they are excluded from the regular market, which makes it questionable to call their free riding unfair. However, I am aware that in both cases it may be very difficult to draw a line between fair and unfair downloaders. The threshold which defines a musician as a 'winner' as well as the threshold of purchasing power which qualifies someone as poor enough to be excluded from the market are difficult to fix, and applying these thresholds would presuppose much empirical data we do not have.

Publishers may adopt a defensive strategy against free riding and try to develop 'self-help' systems, that is systems which make copying, including copying on your own computer, impossible. However, the development of such systems will be an infinite and costly race against people who break these systems. It might therefore be more fruitful to think of alternative ways of coping with the public good aspect of creative material, like a package deal in which people pay a copyright tax together with their internet bill. One positive side-effect of such an alternative might be a more equitable allocation among artists which, consequently, if my preceding arguments are correct, would make the scope of possibly 'unfair' free riding much smaller.

Acknowledgement

I am grateful to Axel Gosseries, Alain Marciano and Alain Strowel for their helpful comments.

Notes

1. Illegal downloading seems to be particularly widespread in France. Piracy is estimated to be twice as common there as in other OECD countries. See the estimations discussed in *Les Echos* (6 September 2007, p. 23) and *Le Monde* (24 November 2007, p. 24).
2. And neither are the teachers. Curtis Cook mentions a survey of teachers conducted in Illinois which shows that this group feels quite justified in infringing copyright law. See Cook (2002, pp. 124–5).
3. Einhorn (2004, p. 106) mentions the possibilities of streaming as substituted for actual downloading. Liebowitz (2003, p. 20) makes some predictions about the future of copyright infringement.
4. A similar example is given by Nozick: 'You may not decide to give me something, for example a book, and then grab money from me to pay for it, even if I have nothing better to spend the money on' (1974, p. 95). He argues especially against being coerced to participate involuntarily in a cooperative scheme. We will leave aside the whole issue of whether or not fair payments have to be voluntary: since we are talking of voluntary downloading, unsolicited benefits fall outside the scope of this chapter.
5. One could argue that diminishing prices caused by more aggressive competition similarly decrease profits and increase the consumer surplus. One could even argue that increasing the consumer surplus comes down to increasing the positive externalities (Lemley 2005, pp. 1046–7): The fact that I am willing to pay a particular amount for a book and that it is available for less thanks to market competition means that I do not have to pay what I consider to be the full price. See also Gordon and Watt (2003).

6. These are often cited as characteristics of public goods. However, the literature on public goods sometimes mentions other, mostly related characteristics, such as 'jointness in supply', i.e. once a good is available to one consumer, it is available to others at no extra cost, 'indivisiblity', etc. Cf. Cullity (1995, pp. 3–4).
7. Note that, as in the previous examples, free riding does not harm anyone.
8. Non-rivalry may be matter of degree: if I go to see 'Old Faithful', the geyser in Yellowstone Park, I am not bothered by the fact that someone else is there too. However, if there are several thousands of tourists present, that may diminish the pleasure I derive from the amazing phenomenon. Excludability may be a matter of degree when preventing someone from enjoying a good by making it excessively costly.
9. See e.g. Arneson (1982).
10. This example is taken from Cullity (1995, p. 17).
11. Most and not all because, as Cullity points out, it is possible to conceive overall inefficient systems of which some individuals would benefit.
12. We leave aside here the issue of whether or not the unfairness of free riding behaviour is a sufficient reason to coerce free riders to comply with the requirements of the scheme.
13. For example, Regner (2003) and Smiers (2002).
14. For a theoretical discussion of the particular winner-takes-all market of popular entertainment, see Rosen (1981). For the economics of superstars, see Adler (1985). A more intuitive approach is to be found in Robert Frank and Philip J. Cook. 'It's a Winner-Takes-All Market – Top Money Goes to Top Performing People or Products', *Washington Monthly*, December 1995.
15. Frank and Cook explain this by the fact that many people overestimate their chances of 'winning'. First, people see the winners much more often than the losers, and second, people are notoriously poor at estimating their own talents vis-á-vis those of others.
16. They pay so-called 'royalties' to the real creators. Artists receive a certain percentage of the revenue their songs generate. The initial rate is mostly between 7 and 15 per cent, but various deductions lead to a final royalty percentage of about 3 per cent. See Regner (2003, p.109).
17. Horkheimer and Adorno (1944, p. 109): 'In der Tat ist es der Zirkel von Manipulation und rückwirkenden Bedürfnis, indem die Einheit des Systems immer dichter zusammenschießt.' See also their analysis of the star system (ibid., pp. 120ff).
18. Cameroon Baka music. Unesco collection Auvidis. Musics & Musicians of the World. D8029.. © Auvidis/IICMSD/Unesco 1990.
19. See Smiers (2002, p. 133).
20. Gauthier's example only mentions negative externalities. This is not clear from the quote, but obvious in the passage from which it is taken. Gauthier says that my desire to buy your fish is increased by your pollution.
21. Similar laws apply in other legislations. For exemple, the French Code de la propriété intellectuelle, Art L122-5 mentions similar exceptions.
22. Recall the example of my listening to my neighbour playing the violin. I do not make recordings of his playing in order to sell them without paying him. If I did, I would make a profit by making him unknowingly part of the production cost. Therefore, there is an important difference between simply

enjoying a positive externality on the one hand, and using this externality to make a profit.

23. See Shaffer Van Houveling (2005, p. 1545) for examples.
24. This was explicitly defended by Proudhon: 'Défendrez-vous á l'amateur, qui vient de payer un livre, de réunir chez lui une douzaine d'amis, de faire des lectures, de prêter et faire circuler son volume?' (1862, p. 39).
25. Code de la propriété intellectuelle, Art. L122-5 : 'Lorsque l'œuvre a été divulguée, l'auteur ne peut interdire: 1° Les représentations privées et gratuites effectuées exclusivement dans un cercle de famille.'

References

Adler, M. (1985) Stardom and Talent, *American Economic Review*, 75: 208–12.

Arneson, R. (1982) The Principle of Fairness and Free-rider Problems, *Ethics*, 92: 616–33.

Beebe, B. (2007) An Empirical Study of U.S. Copyright Fair Use Opinions, 1978–2005. Unpublished working paper.

Blair, R. and Cotter, T. (2005) *Intellectual Property. Economic and Legal Dimensions of Rights and Remedies*. Cambridge: Cambridge University Press.

Cook, C. (2002) *Patents, Profits & Power. How Intellectual Property Rules the Global Economy*. London: Kogan Page.

Cullity, G. (1995) Moral Free Riding, *Philosophy and Public Affairs*, 24: 3–34.

Einhorn, M. (2004) *Media, Technology and Copyright. Integrating Law and Economics*. Cheltenham: Edward Elgar.

Frank, R. and Cook, P. J. (1995) It's a Winner-Takes-All Market – Top Money Goes to Top Performing People or Products, *Washington Monthly*, December.

Gauthier, D. (1986) *Morals by Agreement*. Oxford: Clarendon Press.

Gordon, W. and Watt, R. (eds.) (2003) *The Economics of Copyright. Developments in Research and Analysis*. Cheltenham: Edward Elgar.

Hettinger, E. (1989) Justifying Intellectual Property, *Philosophy and Public Affairs*, 18: 31–52.

Horkheimer, M. and Adorno, T. W. (1944/1971) Kulturindustrie, in *Dialektik der Aufklärung. Philosophische Fragmente*, Frankfurt: Frankfurt Fischer Verlag, pp. 108–50.

Kay, J. (1993) The Economics of Intellectual Property Rights, *International Review of Law and Economics*, 13: 337–48.

Landes, W. and Posner, R. (1989) An Economic Analysis of Copyright Law, *The Journal of Legal Studies*, 18: 325–6.

Lemley, M. (2005a) Property, Intellectual Property, and Free Riding, *Texas Law Review*, 83: 1031–75.

Lemley, M. (2005b) What's Different about Intellectual Property? *Texas Law Review*, 83: 1097–1104.

Liebowitz, S. (2003) Back to the Future: Can Copyright Owners Appropriate Revenue in the Face of New Copying Technologies? in Gordon, W. and Watt, R. (eds.) *The Economics of Copyright. Developments in Research and Analysis*. Cheltenham: Edward Elgar, pp. 1–25.

Nozick, R. (1974) *Anarchy, State, and Utopia*. New York: Basic Books.

Parsons, S. (2005) Fair-Play Obligations: A Critical Note on Free Riding, *Political Studies*, 53: 641–9.
Proudhon, P.-J. (1862) *Les Majorats littéraires. Examen d'un projet de loi ayant pour but de créer au profit des auteurs, inventeurs et artistes, un monopole perpétuel*. Brussels: Office de la publicité.
Regner, T. (2003) Innovation of Music, in Gordon, W. and Watt, R. (eds.) *The Economics of Copyright. Developments in Research and Analysis*. Cheltenham: Edward Elgar, pp. 104–17.
Shaffer Van Houweling, M. (2005) Distributive Values in Copyright, *Texas Law Review*, 83: 1535–79.
Rosen, S. (1981) The Economics of Superstars, *American Economic Review*, 71: 845–58.
Smiers, J. (2002) The Abolition of Copyrights: Better for Artists, Third World Countries and the Public Domain', in R. Towse (ed.) *Copyright in the Cultural Industries*. Cheltenham: Edward Elgar, pp. 119–39.

8
Copyright and Freedom of Expression: A Philosophical Map

Alexandra Couto

Introduction

Copyright law has an ambiguous relation with freedom of expression. On the one hand, copyright law protects the free expression of creators by ensuring that they reap the benefits of their own work. Without the existence of copyright law, any creator would fear the appropriation of her work by others. Copyright allows artists to express themselves without worrying about the potential reproduction of their words, art or music.[1] On the other hand, as is often noted, copyright law restricts the form that expression might take by forbidding the free use of copyrighted materials. In a rapidly changing environment with new technologies, it is not only the enforcement of copyright that has been put into question but also its moral legitimacy (Davies, 2002, p. 32). The conflict between freedom of expression and copyright raises a number of important normative issues. Not all of them can be addressed in this chapter. In particular, I will not address here the important normative issues raised by the direct copyright control that some corporations assert over the use of cultural and intellectual works.[2]

I start by outlining the argument of my chapter (appendix 1 provides further guidance in examining the possible interactions between freedom of expression and copyright). To begin with, the possibility of a conflict between copyright and freedom of expression requires the prior theoretical recognition of the general possibility of a conflict of rights. Some authors (e.g. Steiner, 1994) do not even recognise the possibility of conflict between rights. Assuming that one accepts the general possibility of conflict of rights, one might still hold that the *specific* rights of freedom of expression and copyright do not (or cannot) conflict with each other (1). Such a claim could be supported if any of the following claims were true. First, the enjoyment of freedom of expression does not require the reproduction of art works (1.1). Second, freedom of expression requires some access to copyrighted materials, but the allowances made in copyright law are sufficient for the protection of free speech (1.2). Third, the reproduction of copyrighted work does not constitute a violation of copyright because copyright is defined in a way that pre-empts conflict. For instance, copyright include either moral rights only or moral rights and a redefined set of economic rights (1.3).

The *specific* rights of freedom of expression and copyright *do not* conflict with each other if any of these claims is true. Moreover, they *cannot* conflict with each other if any of these claims is *always* true.

I will then turn to examine the possibility that the specific rights of freedom of expression and copyright *do* conflict (2). Given that neither freedom of expression nor copyright can be plausibly argued to be absolute rights – an absolute right is a right that cannot be overridden (Gewirth, 1981) – I will need to chart a step-by-step procedure to determine which right needs to yield when there is conflict. Assuming that the two rights conflict, I will examine two possible stands on their respective strengths: either both rights have the same status or they do not.[3] This will depend on the theory of justice adopted. On a Rawlsian theory of justice, both rights have the same status.

First, copyright and freedom of expression do not have the same status (Appendix 1.2.1 – henceforth numbers in parenthesis refer to the appendix):

- More likely, the solution is principled, as the stronger right trumps the other.
- One of the rights is clearly stronger, but there is an *overwhelming* balance of harm and benefit in favour of the weaker right such that the weaker right is favoured. This should be an exception, as rights are designed to pre-empt the consideration of interests, but I do not want to exclude this possibility. (2.1.2)

Second, copyright and freedom of expression might have the same status (2.2). I will claim that this is what would be the case in a Rawlsian theory of justice. In such a case, three alternative decision-making procedures can be employed to resolve the conflict:

1 Arbitrarily (2.2.1). I will not discuss this option.
2 By a non-consequentialist appeal to the values connected to the rights (2.2.2). I will provide a template for such a qualitative analysis and describe two similar qualitative methods used by Waldron and Rawls.
3 By taking into consideration the balance of harm and benefit (2.2.3). Consequences have to be taken into account only if they are decisive and after the qualitative methods (see 2.2.2) have been employed. This method has diverse versions depending on the conception of interests endorsed (material interests, non-material interests or a combination of the two).

First step: is conflict of rights possible?

I will start with a brief description of the concepts of freedom of expression and copyright. Copyright is one kind of intellectual property rights; intellectual property rights also include patents and trade marks. Copyright prevents others from copying or reproducing an author's work without his/her permission (Hart, Fazzani and Clark, 2006, p. 161). It involves defined types of cultural, informational and entertainment productions and is given to authors, playwrights, composers, artists and film directors (Cornish. and Llewelyn, 2003, p. 8). In order to be copyrighted, the work must be original,[4] recorded and created by a qualifying person (Cornish, 2006, p. 6). I will assume that copyright includes both the economic rights derived from the power attributed to the copyright owner to have control over the reproduction of her work and the moral rights derived simply from ownership of copyrighted work. Copyright is usually justified in two ways: first, in terms of the author's natural right to the economic benefits from his work; second, on the basis of its being socially beneficial, as it provides incentives for individuals to be creative.

Freedom of expression protects any kind of expressive act – strictly speaking, it does not need to be a speech. Freedom of expression consists mostly in special treatment of the value of expression:

> When there is a Free Speech Principle, a limitation of speech requires a stronger justification, or establishes a higher threshold, for limitations of speech than for limitations of other forms of conduct. This is so even if the consequences of the speech are as great as the consequences of other forms of conduct.
>
> (Shauer, 1982, p. 8)

Freedom of expression is thus not an absolute prohibition to regulate speech. Rather, it constitutes a presumption against state interference.

Freedom of expression is usually justified by three arguments. The first argument is based on the epistemic value of expression. This is the traditional Millian argument which claims that free speech allows for a free market of ideas most conducive to the truth. The second argument is based on the function freedom of expression plays in a democratic society. Free speech allows for the expression of diverse political opinions and the good functioning of democracy (Shauer, 1982, pp. 35–47). The third argument is rooted in the intrinsic value of free speech as a fundamental individual right that is constitutive of what it is to respect each individual equally (Dworkin, 1977, p. 273). Freedom of expression is here valued because it shows respects for the reasoning powers of each individual.

I will set aside the problem of the general possibility of conflict between rights. There are indeed some views that deny that rights could conflict. On a choice-based theory of rights[5] this is necessarily so, because one of the fundamental features of such a system is the compossibility of rights, that is, the mutual consistency of rights within a single system.[6] There is no conflict of rights, because rights should constitute an ordered system in which conflict is precluded. Similarly, on an interest-based theory of rights,[7] specificationists argue that there is no conflict of rights. On this specific view of the interest-based theory of rights, there might be an appearance of conflict, but it will dissolve once the situation is examined more closely. If there is an appearance of conflict, specifying/qualifying the rights will be sufficient to show that they are not in conflict (Wellman, 1995, pp. 277ff).

The rest of this chapter is based on the plausible assumption that conflicts among rights are possible. This view is compatible, however, with holding that there is no conflict between the *specific* rights of copyright and freedom of expression. I will therefore first consider three arguments to this effect.

1. The specific rights of free speech and copyright don't conflict

Freedom of expression aims at protecting the individual right to expression from illegitimate restriction. One must thus ask whether copyright law restricts freedom of expression and, if it does, whether it does so legitimately. Two accommodations have already been made by copyright law for the purpose of upholding individuals' freedom of expression. First, copyright law distinguishes between the content of the work and the form in which it is expressed.[8] It thus allows for the diffusion of the ideas that constitute the content of the work, while preventing the exact reproduction of the expression in which they have been originally conveyed (Weinreb, 1998, p. 1152–3). Second, copyright law allows for what has been called the 'fair use´ of copyrighted work, which is the reproduction of small samples of copyrighted work. Copyright law will therefore conflict with freedom of expression if and only if the following claims are true:

a) The reproduction of copyrighted work is necessary for the enjoyment of freedom of expression.
b) This reproduction constitutes a violation of copyright. This constitutes a condition on the conception of copyright employed in (a): it must be such that there is an actual conflict (and not only a *prima facie* conflict) between copyright and freedom of expression.
c) The allowances made by copyright law are not sufficient for the protection of freedom of expression.

With respect to claim (a), there is an existing literature that points to some particular cases in which the reproduction of intellectual/cultural work is necessary for the enjoyment of freedom of expression (see Griffiths and Suthersanen, 2005). The familiar examples that suggest a tension between the two rights are instances of parodies, satires and criticism.

I will now examine other instances of (a) that have not been discussed in the literature and then show that some of these are not fully covered by the accommodations already made by copyright law (c) and involve a conception a copyright in which the reproduction of a copyrighted work without permission constitutes a violation of copyright (b).

Finally, one could hold the view that freedom of expression *cannot* conflict with copyright law. This would be the case if one held that either (a), (b) or (c) would never be the case or if one held that (a), (b) and (c) would never all be true in the same instance.

1.1 Freedom of expression does not require the reproduction of copyrighted work

The first objection that could be raised against the claim that copyright and freedom of expression conflict is to argue that the reproduction of a copyrighted work is unnecessary for free expression. After all, in the case of non-intellectual property rights, such as land property, no one would make the claim that it might be necessary to violate a property right in order to enjoy freedom of expression. Let us take the case of an individual X who wants to oppose another individual Y's point of view. One way of doing this would be for X to trespass on Y's property and stand in Y's garden to protest there. But it would usually be contended that the trespassing of Y's property is not necessary as the same expressive aim might be achieved by other means. The same claim could be made in the case of a speech that uses copyrighted material. Does the speech really need the material in question for expressive purposes? Couldn't the individual use her own words?

The problem with this kind of question is that it stands against the spirit of freedom of expression, as it entails a judgement on which form a speech should take.[9] To start examining whether the form of the speech in question is legitimate is at odds with what the principle of freedom of speech is supposed to establish, that is, the total absence of restraints of speech on the basis of differences in judgement (Alexander, 2005, p. 20).

Let us imagine an individual who, for such expressive purposes, recites Sylvia Plath's poetry in the street. Our imaginary character, let us call him Ulysses, is gratuitously[10] performing in a public place the poems of another person.[11] If we were to ask Ulysses why he chose Plath's poetry, he could reply that they perfectly express what he feels. If we press him on that and ask him to express these feelings using different words, we are assuming that what he has to say can be expressed differently and that it is not perfectly expressed by these particular poems.

There are two arguments for the claim that the reproduction of copyrighted works is sometimes necessary for the enjoyment of freedom of expression. The first argument is related to the last point made about the specific expressive force of some copyrighted work: copyright is not any kind of property right, it is the property right given to the authors, composers and creators of literary, dramatic, musical and artistic works (I will refer to the authors, composers and creators as creators for short. I will refer to literary, dramatic, musical and artistic works as copyrighted work for short.) Creators fulfil a special function in society. They are talented at expressing some ideas and feelings via their art. The creator is able to convey something that others experience but cannot convey as skilfully. Individuals may thus feel that performing or reproducing an existing text, a song or an artwork is the best way of conveying their *own* feelings or ideas. Should Ulysses be charged for breach of copyright law?[12] According to current copyright law, he is breaking the law (Phillips and Firth, 2000, p. 186).

I have claimed so far that one way of arguing that the reproduction of copyrighted work is necessary for the enjoyment of freedom of expression is to invoke the special function creators have to express emotions and ideas in a way that other individuals can relate to, be inspired by, or find helpful. However, another argument is available. Instead of pointing to the special function of creators, one could point to the special function a copyrighted work can have within a cultural group. Some copyrighted works have indeed become cultural symbols and are now part of a common cultural language. They have become so imbedded in the culture of a nation that they convey a whole series of implicit references and connotations.[13] For reasons that will be fully exposed below, these copyrighted works cannot be replaced by other means without incurring a modification of their meaning. These copyrighted works belong to the community to such an extent that withdrawing them from the community would constitute a harm to its members, as they would not be able to express accurately their feelings or ideas (Gordon, 1990, p.1009).

Both these arguments could thus be used by Ulysses to explain why he cannot express himself without using Plath. Let us thus grant the fact that it might be necessary for Ulysses to use Plath's copyrighted work to fully enjoy freedom of expression. I believe so far that this could be a plausible case. Now one could still object that copyright law has made specific allowances that might seem sufficient to preserve freedom of expression. I turn now to examine this possibility.

1.2 The allowances of copyright law are enough to protect freedom of expression

Form/Content. The question here is whether the allowances of copyright law provided by the fair use principle and the form/content distinction (otherwise known as idea/expression distinction) are enough to pre-empt any conflict between freedom of expression and copyright. According to copyright law, ideas (or content) from a copyrighted work can be reproduced as long as they are conveyed in a different expression (or form). The distinction between form and content is thus crucial in respecting freedom of expression: individuals are allowed to convey ideas, they are just restricted in their use of specific expressions of these ideas. Freedom of expression does not prohibit the regulation of the formal features of expression. It looks like allowing for the reproduction of the ideas of a copyrighted work would be sufficient to protect freedom of expression.

However, let us examine more closely the belief that the ability to convey ideas contained in a copyrighted work is sufficient to preserve freedom of expression. Several objections can be formulated against the claim that the ideas present in a copyrighted work can be conveyed without the reproduction of the work in question. I will address these objections next.

(i) The translation from copyrighted work into abstract ideas is impossible

It is not clear whether it is actually possible to 'translate' an intellectual or cultural work into abstract ideas. The form might be closely intertwined with the content of the work. Often the form contributes greatly to determine the content (or meaning) and it might not be possible to identify a single definite set of ideas. As Nelson Goodman notes, it is hard to deny that

> [E]xpressing is at least as important a function of many works as is saying; and what a work expresses is often a major ingredient of its style. The differences between sardonic, sentimental, savage, and sensual writing are stylistic. Emotions, feelings, and other properties expressed in the saying are part of the way of saying; what is expressed is an aspect of how what is said is said, and as in music and abstract painting may be an aspect of style even when nothing is said.... for since expression is a function of works of art, ways of expressing as well as ways of saying must be taken into account.
>
> (Goodman, 1978, p. 29)

Goodman rejects the claim that one can actually proceed to isolate style from content in an artwork. Although style is not a synonym for form, since it conveys elements of the *content* of the artwork in question, the formal properties of an artwork constitute partly the *vehicle* of its style. If style is necessary for the understanding of the expression in question, the form itself is necessary for an appropriate interpretation of the ideas expressed in the copyrighted work. Similarly, it has been argued that the style of some philosophers' writings is crucial to understand their works.[14]

Conveying the ideas of a specific copyrighted work implies that there is one straightforward interpretation of this copyrighted work. The content of a copyrighted work might be intentionally ambiguous. Cinema critics have different interpretations of films. Moreover, some artistic creations *cannot* be transcribed into abstract ideas because they do not contain a narrative sequence of ideas. Musical pieces are a good example of non-narrative artworks.

Even if one grants the possibility of translating copyrighted work into abstract ideas, the *expressive value* of the copyrighted work might not be preserved. For instance, on the basis of the original footage of the assassination of President John F. Kennedy, one could proceed to elaborate a detailed description of his murder. This would constitute a perfect example of an attempt to convey the content of a copyrighted material without reproducing the form of this material. Although the verbal description would convey accurately the content of the original footage, the verbal description would not match its emotional force.

I believe this claim is true with respect to art; the content of artistic expression might not be translatable into another form. I believe also, however, that this argument fails because the concept of expression used in artistic circles is not the same as the concept of expression at stake in freedom of expression. The concept of expression used in artistic circles assumes subtleties in expression that could be beyond the understanding of the individual who expresses herself. Whereas an artwork can be appreciated without the artist being fully aware of the full meaning of what has to be expressed, speech protected by freedom of expression has to be self-conscious to a certain extent.

Let us take Ulysses again. Ulysses would tell us: 'I want to express myself, but I don't really know how I feel, I know I feel depressed, but I somehow believe that Sylvia Plath expresses myself.' I would find that is a justified argument for a partial reproduction of Plath's poetry. But I would certainly not argue that it justifies reproduction beyond fair use (see below). The agent has to express *himself*, and the use of copyrighted work has to be instrumental for that purpose.

(ii) The translation might be inaccurate

Second, apart from any doubt about the mere possibility of such a 'translation', the fact that this 'translation' is made by someone who is not the artist herself might distort further the original meaning of the copyrighted work. Having to do without the original artwork entails that one trusts the author of the 'translation' of the copyrighted work into abstract ideas.

I mentioned earlier that there were problems in assuming that one could have a *single* interpretation of one work. I am here questioning the accuracy of letting the translation be made by an individual other than the artist. Let us take again Ulysses as an example. If we ask him to paraphrase Plath in order to express himself, his re-creation of Plath's poetry might cause a great misunderstanding of her original work. This argument fails again because it seems to overlook the fact that the reproduction is made for the purpose of individual free expression. There might well be an inaccuracy in the translation of the work in question, but the free interpretation of copyrighted work is a crucial part of freedom of expression.

(iii) The translation is inefficient/too costly

The process of translation is time- and resource-consuming. Time and resources would be necessary for the translation, and this additional cost could be the equivalent of the copyright fee. If one wants to argue that there is a conflict between freedom of expression and copyright, one must adopt a conception of freedom in which the payment of a certain fee constitutes a restriction of freedom, as I will argue below. The supplementary cost of translating the copyrighted work would thus not be a solution to the problem but just another kind of cost. This translation is an infringement of the freedom of expression of the individual because it imposes a cost that is too high on individuals in exercising their freedom.

This argument is valid but it is difficult to think of examples in which fair use would not be sufficient. One might grant that reference and use of copyrighted work are necessary for freedom of expression, but it is less obvious to claim that an extensive use of copyrighted work is also necessary.

Fair use. The principle of fair use, which allows for restricted reproduction of a copyrighted work, is plagued with similar problems.[15] First, sampling entails a loss of complexity in the process. A play in three acts would most probably lose some of its complexity if only a section of one of the acts can be reproduced. Second, the sampling of a text is often problematic to the extent that the extraction of the sample from its context might induce a wrong interpretation of the work. The content conveyed by a part of a copyrighted work is only properly conveyed when that part is located within its whole.

This is true, once again, if one is looking at the interpretation of artworks. But in the case of freedom of expression the agent is to have some role in the expression for it to be protected speech. The reproduction of the entire work by an artist does not seem prima facie to be instrumental to the expression of the agent. The same expressive effect could have been accomplished by referring to the original work. An important exception pertains to borderline cases, that is, cases in which an individual expresses herself using copyrighted work just beyond the specified allowances. I believe that case could actually ground a conflict of rights.

I have argued so far that, in addition to the examples of parodies, criticisms and satires referred to in the literature, there could be instances, similar to Ulysses' use of Plath's poety, in which respect for freedom of expression would require violation of copyright laws. I have also indicated how the provision of fair use and the allowance made for the reproduction of content may fail to be an appropriate substitute for the full-scale reproduction of the whole copyrighted work. I have also expressed my belief that, although possible, such conflict is unlikely. I have pointed to what seems the most likely case that would trigger conflict: cases in which an individual uses copyrighted work just beyond the allowances laid down in copyright law. However, there is another reason for thinking that copyright and freedom of expression do not conflict. I will turn now to this last possibility: the conflict between the two rights is only *prima facie*.

1.3 The conflict is only prima facie

Copyright and freedom of expression might be in conflict because one has misinterpreted the demands of copyright or/and freedom of expression. The presence or absence of conflict between two rights will be directly related to the ways the rights involved are defined. I will suggest here one conception of copyright and one conception of freedom of expression that would pre-empt the possibility of conflict between the two. Let me start by suggesting one such conception of copyright.

There are two approaches that can be adopted to copyright. The first is general and focuses on a single question – whether or not a creator should have any copyright-related right attached to her work. But this seems easy enough to answer. It would indeed be hard to deny that a creator is entitled to some rights with respect to her own creation. The second approach envisages copyright as a bundle of different rights and assesses the justification for each right separately. On this latter approach, one might legitimately define copyright as a narrower set of rights, which could be entirely compatible with freedom of expression.

For instance, such a narrower conception of copyright could define it as being constituted only by moral rights of intellectual property.[16] These rights would give moral privileges of identification and integrity to the creator of a work. On most legal conceptions, copyright includes at least two moral rights: 1) the right to be identified as author or film director; and 2) the right to object to derogatory treatment of a work.[17]

These moral rights have often been treated as part of copyright law.[18] If copyright is defined as referring only to these moral rights, the reproduction of copyrighted work will not violate copyright as long as these moral rights are respected: If an individual requires the reproduction of a copyrighted work, she can do so, as long as she identifies the artist and does not damage the work in question. This conception is, however, not plausible as it does not include any economic right.[19]

Let us turn now to a minimalist conception of freedom of expression, which I will refer to as a 'libertarian' conception of liberty. A libertarian conception of liberty would characterise individuals as free as long as they are not prevented by the state from doing what they have a right to do. On this conception of liberty, having to pay a copyright fee is not tantamount to being prevented from doing what one has a right to do. The right to free speech is defined within a system of rights that limit each other. On this conception, one should be free to do only what one has a right to do *and* as long as one does not infringe the right of someone else. On that conception, it does not make sense to claim that intellectual property rights and freedom of expression conflict, as freedom of expression is constrained by property rights.[20]

I call this conception of freedom a libertarian conception because it is most vehemently defended by libertarian liberals. This label is slightly misleading however, as many non-libertarian liberals share the belief that liberties should restrain each other. Rawls (2005, p. 295) distinguishes between regulations and restrictions. Regulations are infringements that are justified by the necessity to respect another liberty, whereas restrictions are violations of rights not justified by the presence of another conflicting liberty.[21] According to Rawls: 'the priority of these liberties [the basic liberties] is not infringed when they are merely regulated, as they must be, in order to be combined into one scheme' (2001, p. 111). This regulation of the basic liberties performs *de facto* a function similar to the requirements of the libertarian conception of freedom described above; namely, allowing for the creation of a coherent system of rights and restricting the grounds on the basis of which a right could be curtailed.[22]

The libertarian conception of freedom can be objected to on two counts. First, any law restricts freedom to the extent that it imposes limits on individuals' behaviour. When libertarians claim that they maximise freedom, they are giving priority to the liberties *they* believe to be important. The question of what theory of justice is most freedom-maximising should not be resolved on the basis of a comparison of the number of laws entrenched, but on the basis of how much freedom these laws promote in the general population.[23] Second, the libertarian account becomes circular if one is free to do only what one has a right to do and this right is justified on the basis of what one is free to do (Cohen, 2001, pp. 60–1).

Let me briefly summarise the argument so far. I have claimed that there are three conditions necessary for freedom of expression to conflict with copyright.[24] I have shown that a conflict between these two rights is *conceivable*, but I would like to underline the fact that I have also claimed the *implausibility* of such a conflict. I suspect that the occurrence of such a conflict would be highly unlikely given that the three conditions need to coexist in a single instance. In particular, I have argued that it would be hard to establish that the reproduction of a copyrighted work beyond what is allowed by the copyright allowances would be needed for the enjoyment of freedom of expression. Moreover, the arguments mentioned in section 1.2 are not convincing because they use a concept of expression that is useful for artistic interpretation but might not be relevant for freedom of expression. I believe that free speech as a political right might not demand that level of subtle nuance. I pointed to one situation in which the arguments mentioned above could be satisfying: these would be cases that are presently legally borderline, cases in which someone uses a few more lines than what is warranted by fair use. I will thus proceed to examine what could be done in such cases.

2 The specific rights of copyright and freedom of expression conflict

If the three conditions are present in a single instance, there is a conflict between copyright and freedom of expression and the next step consists in trying to resolve this conflict. I shall suggest that the first question to be asked is whether the two rights have the same ranking. In order to find out what ranking each right has, one has to situate the debate within a specific theory of justice. Different theories of justice will give different weight to values and the rights that protect these values.[25]

First, a comment on theories of justice and rights. Not all theories of justice recognise individual rights, although all at least have some ranking of *values*. A fully act-utilitarian conception of justice does not necessarily attribute any weight to individual rights. Some religious conceptions of justice might not even recognise freedom of expression or property rights as individual rights.

In this chapter, I examine the conflict between copyright and freedom of expression from the perspective of a *liberal* theory of justice.[26] There is nevertheless a considerable variation among different liberal theories of justice. Although all liberal theories of justice protect individual rights, they differ in their ranking of rights. This ranking, far from being arbitrary, is underpinned by a prior judgement of the relative importance of the human interests protected by these rights. The ranking of rights reflects thus on what a conception of justice take to be the most important individual interests that need protection. There are thus two possible stands on the conflict between copyright and freedom of expression.

On the one hand, the two rights might not have the same status (see Appendix 1: 2.1). Although I am not going to discuss this possibility in this paper, let me just note that, in such a case, there are two possible ways of resolving the conflict. First, the right thing to do might be to give priority to the stronger right. This is a principled way of resolving the conflict and it is also the most likely situation (2.1.1). In such a case, the resolution of the conflict is relatively easy.[27] Let us take the example of the conflict between the right to health care and the right to private property. Let us suppose that a child falls from a tree onto a neighbouring property and hurts himself badly. The child's right to health care takes priority in this case over the respect owed to the owner's property. When the emergency services arrive, they will not wait to get the owner's agreement for them to enter his property. The right of the child takes priority over the right of the owner. Second, even when the rights hold different ranks, it can still be the case that the right thing to do is to favour the weaker right. This would occur only if there is a decisive balance of harm and benefit that would support the infringement of the stronger right (2.1.2).[28]

On the other hand, both rights might have equal status (2.2). For instance, Rawls' theory of justice (henceforth Justice-as-Fairness) would grant equal status to the rights of freedom of expression and copyright. Rawls considers both property rights and freedom of expression to be basic liberties.[29] In Justice-as-Fairness, basic liberties can be limited only when they are in conflict: 'The priority of liberty implies in practice that a basic liberty can be limited or denied solely for the sake of one or more other basic liberties, and never, as I have said, for reasons of public good or of perfectionist values' (Rawls, 2005, p. 295).

In a case such as this, we have to turn to different strategies to resolve the conflict. I suggest that the conflict could be resolved in three ways. First, it could be resolved arbitrarily, given that there is no principled way of choosing one right over the other (Appendix 2.2.1). My first objection to this is a presumption against arbitrariness in decision-making. We should strive to find rational ways of resolving the conflict with which are confronted with before giving up and opting for arbitrariness. As we shall see, there are plenty of better alternatives. My second objection is that such an arbitrary decision is grounded in the belief that, if two equally ranked rights conflict, the specific violations of the two rights are *equally bad*. However, I believe that the violation of two rights of equal status might not be equally bad. Aside from the status of rights, there are other factors that have an impact on the badness of a violation of rights. These are the significance of the specific right violation and the overall consequences of the violation of the right in question (2.2.2 and 2.2.3).

I shall focus on two more valuable strategies to resolve the conflict. One strategy is based on a non-consequentialist appeal to the values underpinning the conflicting rights (2.2.2). It represents a non-teleological way of responding to values. The other strategy considers the balance of harms and benefits (2.2.3). I am going to discuss only these two strategies and will thus ignore the arbitrary decision (2.2.1).

A qualitative analysis is used to resolve the conflict (2.2.2)

The choice of which right to privilege can also proceed on the basis of a non-consequentialist analysis of the specific rights involved. Such an analysis proceeds by applying guidelines to establish the value of upholding the rights in a particular instance. More specifically, the significance of a right claim hinges on the connection between the right claim and the value(s) it is supposed to protect.[30] This qualitative analysis gives us a template for conflict resolution when two rights conflict.

Two conditions must obtain to resolve the conflict:

1 There must be a meaningful connection between at least one of the specific right claims and the value(s) it is supposed to protect.
2 The values connected to the conflicting rights must be different and have a different ranking in the theory of justice adopted.

Condition 1 stipulates that at least one of the rights must have a meaningful connection with its underpinning value. If only one of the conflicting rights has a meaningful connection with its underpinning value, then this right should be given precedence. I assume that there is a meaningful connection when the value justifies the existence of the right in the first place and the right genuinely succeeds in protecting or expressing this justificatory value. As I briefly mentioned earlier, the right to free speech is partly justified by three arguments: an epistemic argument, a political argument and an intrinsic argument. At least one of the values involved in these arguments should be protected by the specific right claim.

I illustrate this point by pointing to a case in which the specific right claim is not protective of any of the justificatory values of freedom of expression. If we take the example of a man who shouts 'fire' in a theatre, this has no epistemic value (there is no fire; nor does he believe there is a fire), no political value and does not express the respect owed to each individual.[31] The specific right claim in shouting 'fire' does not protect any of the justificatory value that underpins freedom of expression, it is thus not entitled to the protection of freedom of speech. If only one right is connected to its underpinning value, one does not need to consider how important this value is; it is enough to demonstrate that the other right is not tied to its justificatory value.

If both rights are connected to their underpinning values, we need to turn to condition 2. Condition 2 stipulates that the underpinning values must have a different rank for the comparison to give guidance. I now describe briefly two similar procedures used by Waldron and Rawls. Waldron's procedure invokes something similar to condition 1, while Rawls' procedure is somewhat closer to condition 2.

Waldron suggests looking at what he labels 'internal connections'. These refer to the kind of link that exists between a right claim and its founding value. An internal connection exists when the right claim is faithful to the core value that justified its existence. Waldron gives the example of a race hate speech. If one does not look at the value underpinning freedom of expression, one would understand free speech as protecting any kind of speech without looking at the content of the speech in question. One would thus believe that freedom of expression protects the race hate speech. However, if one looks at internal connections, as Waldron suggests, a race hate speech contradicts in substance the value underpinning the right to free speech. It would deny free speech to some individuals on the basis of their ethnicity. If freedom of speech is valued because it is crucial in upholding the respect owed to *each* individual (the intrinsic argument for freedom of speech), any speech that does not exemplify this value should not be protected by the right to free speech.

Looking at internal connections in this way amounts to shifting the discussion from rights to values. Rights are not treated as sacrosanct entities whose value is undisputed; they have normative weight only if they have an 'internal connection' with their founding value(s).

Rawls' Justice-As-Fairness shows the same concern for distinguishing substantial from non-substantial violations of rights. I will argue here that the combination of two distinct procedures in Rawls has roughly the same function as Waldron's internal connection. These two distinct procedures are the regulation/restriction distinction and the relation of the specific right claim to the two moral powers. When Rawls applies the distinction between restriction and regulation to freedom of speech, he describes regulations as applying only to the formal characteristics of the speech act. He assumes that formal features of speech acts are the only features that would need to be regulated in order to respect other liberties. Restrictions – that is, legislations that are content-based – would not be required to respect other liberties:

> rules of order are essential for regulating free discussion. Not everyone can speak at once, or use the same public facility at the same time for different purposes.[32] Instituting the basic liberties, just like realizing different interests, requires social organization and scheduling as to time and place, and so on. The requisite regulations should not be mistaken for restrictions on the content of speech, for example, prohibitions against publicly arguing for various religious and philosophical or moral and political doctrines, or against raising questions of general and particular fact about the justice of the basic structure and its social policies.
>
> (Rawls, 2001, pp. 111–12)

However, Rawls also claims that some speech content does not deserve protection. He draws a distinction between basic liberties and other liberties. Basic liberties are those that are necessary to the full development and exercise of the two moral powers: the sense of justice and the capacity for a conception of the good.[33] Rawls refers more particularly to two fundamental cases:

a) the application of the principles of justice to the basic structure (e.g. the fundamental institutions of a society) and its social policies thanks to the citizen's capacity for a sense of justice;
b) the exercise of citizens' powers of practical reason in their pursuit of their conception of the good.

Rawls considers that freedom of speech is a basic liberty because it has an important role to play in the exercise of the two moral powers. However, he later qualifies this by pointing to specific speech acts that have no role in the exercise of the two moral powers. These kinds of speech should not be specially protected and might even be considered as offences:

> Libel and defamation of private persons (in contrast with political and other public figures) has no significance at all for the free use of public reason to judge and regulate the basic structure. In addition, those forms of speech are private wrongs. Incitements to imminent and lawless use of force, whatever the significance of the speaker's overall political views, are too disruptive of democratic political procedures to be permitted by the rules of order of public discussion.
>
> (Rawls, 2001, p. 114)

According to Rawls, speech acts that are not justified by their role in the development of public reason are not granted the special protection given by the right to free speech. This implies that he leaves room for a re-evaluation of the extent to which the right in question is connected to the reason for which freedom of expression is considered a basic liberty.

To sum up, if we combine Rawls' distinction between regulation and restriction with the justification of the right in terms of public reason, we end up having a set of procedures that perform roughly the same function as Waldron's internal connections. Both assert that specific right claims need to be interpreted in order to assess their relation to specific values. Waldron holds that these values are those that justify the right in the first place, while Rawls claims that these values are those that are fundamental for Justice-as-Fairness. Their approaches do not go all the way down to a case-by-case analysis, as they both use specific guiding principles to judge the importance of a specific right claim.

However, objections can be raised against the idea that a right is valuable only when it is protective of its *raison d'être* (or the fundamental values of a specific theory of justice). To begin with, if freedom of expression, for instance, is not protected whenever expression stands in opposition to a liberal commitment, it might give too much leeway to ad hoc personal judgements on values and, by the same token, become void.

Moreover, some expectations are built after the entrenchment of a right that are not related to the value(s) that ground(s) the right in question (or any value fundamental to the specific theory of justice). Rights are useful partly because they are rules, that is, they give specific guidance for behaviour. They establish some certainty in the interactions between individuals by attributing foreseeable rewards or punishments for adhering to or breaking the rule. This certainty is seen by Frederik Shauer as key to grounding a more solid basis for rights as such, even when they stand in opposition with the justification that once grounded them:

> Whether for reasons of expediency, or for that aspect of fairness that comes from certainty and predictability, we often choose some amount of 'ruleness' instead of instance by instance determination.... The rule itself grants rights independent of those that may be 'deserved' under the rule's justification, and thus divorcing the rule from its justification in a given instance does not even in that instance extinguish all claims of rule-based right.'
>
> (Shauer, 1987, p. 117)

Although qualitative analyses are not instance-by-instance determinations, they require interpretations that are also uncertain and unpredictable; the same objections can thus apply to them. Relying on rules is not only efficient, it is also fair. Individuals rely on the simplicity of rules to know what the legal limits to their behaviour are, so that they can adapt their behaviour to the foreseeable rewards and punishments.

Allowing for an interpretation of the rules in question would be unfair to individuals, as it would deprive them of clear guidelines. What would be the purpose of having liberties, if it was unclear what they were? The enjoyment of rights requires specific public guidelines.

Before concluding this section, I need to point to the fact that Rawls would have been led to reject the claim that freedom of expression and copyright conflict. I mentioned earlier that the application of his distinction between restriction and regulation to freedom of speech led him to conclude that it corresponded to the distinction between form and content-based legislations of speech, which is common currency in the literature on freedom of expression. According to this distinction, although freedom of expression is usually taken to prevent any kind of regulation on the content of speech, it is usually considered legitimate to regulate speech with respect to its formal features (the time, volume and place of speech can be regulated).[34] Freedom of expression is conceived, then, as protecting the content of speech but not its formal characteristics. Similarly, the idea/form distinction in copyright law allows for an expression of the content of a speech and forbids only the exact formal reproduction of the copyrighted work. Therefore, if Rawls believes that the regulations of the formal features of speech are no violation of freedom of speech, he must deny the possibility of conflict between freedom of expression and copyright. If freedom of expression protects the content of the speech but not its form, and if copyright regulates only the reproduction of the form of a particular work and not the reproduction of its content, then the two rights do not even apply to the same aspect of the copyrighted work. This leads us back to the conclusion that there is no conflict between freedom of expression and copyright (section 1.3). In order to argue that freedom of expression and copyright conflict, one has to deny the relevance of the distinction between regulations of content and regulation of form in the liberal literature on freedom of expression.

To sum up: there are two main advantages that a definite list of rights provides. First, the specification of a right into a rule prevents any contentious interpretation of principles. There is no danger of partiality on the part of the interpreter. Second, the codification of the abstract principle into the specific rule permits predictability and certainty in the system of rewards and punishment attached to rights.[35] These advantages are threatened by the adoption of a qualitative analysis of rights. There are great advantages in having a clear list of rights, but I believe that there is a remedy to the flaw of unpredictability present in the use of qualitative analysis. If some specific categories of speech were defined as falling outside the protective sphere of speech, then citizens would have enough guidance to enjoy freedom of expression. These categories would identify different types of speech. I believe that qualitative analysis is too important to be abandoned for the reason that it leaves too much uncertainty. As long as some standard interpretation is given for some categories of speech, the standards are clear enough.

Consequentialism is used to resolve the conflict (2.2.3)

The conflict between equally ranked rights can be resolved on the basis of the balance of harm and benefit (section 2.2.3). I will not have the space here to discuss the details of this approach to the conflict of rights. If both rights have a strong connection to an equally ranked value, the balance of harm and benefit could be crucial in helping us determine which right should be given priority. But even in cases where rights are of unequal status, consequentialist considerations might tilt the balance in favour of the weaker right if the balance of harm and benefit considerably favours the weaker right option over the other (2.1.2). There are three versions of this consequentialist method for decision-making. The first version interprets interests as referring only to material interests. The second version of this consequentialist approach considers only non-material interests. These would involve, in our case, the individual interest in having good conditions for the development of a social identity; access to education; and access to political involvement. The third version would consider both material and non-material interests. The problem with an analysis based on non-material interests is that, although each individual might benefit from their promotion, the extent to which they benefit is difficult to quantify. Moreover, the consequentialist consideration of interests such as the development of a social identity or access to education would lead us to argue more generally against the costs of production and distribution of copyrighted work as well as the cost incurred by the copyright fee. These consequentialist considerations on their own would thus not permit us to argue in favour of freedom of expression against copyright as such, but would ground a more general argument against any sort of property rights. There is an argument that could justify the application of consequentialist arguments specifically to the cost of copyright but it would require another paper to be developed.

Conclusion

In this chapter I have set out a taxonomy of different possible relations between copyright and freedom of expression. I have argued that there are certain forms of possible conflict between freedom of expression and copyright that have been overlooked. I have also argued that these forms of conflict are nevertheless unlikely to occur.

I acknowledged that the reproduction of copyrighted work could be required for freedom of expression because of the function creators have in society and the importance copyrighted work has for citizens in a specific cultural space. Creators are uniquely able to express feelings, ideas and opinions. Their works might become part of a cultural space and be imbued with connotations and references that are difficult to convey otherwise. I granted that this argument would open the possibility for copyright to conflict with freedom of expression in a more widespread way than so far considered.

However, I also claimed that the conflict between copyright and freedom of expression would occur only if three conditions were satisfied. I further claimed that these conditions were unlikely to occur in a single instance. I granted that the reproduction of copyrighted work could be necessary for freedom of expression, but I dismissed the idea that the allowances made by copyright law would not be generally sufficient for that purpose. I pointed nevertheless to cases in which the arguments provided would apply in a more plausible way: these are borderline cases in which the individual uses copyrighted material just in excess of what is allowed by fair use. Moreover, most of the arguments in favour of the necessity of reproducing exactly the copyrighted work rely on a concept of expression not appropriate to the political right of freedom of expression. I believe that the political right to free speech might require an awareness and an intentionality that is not required by artistic modes of expression. As a political right, freedom of speech does not require the subtlety and nuances that the best argument in favour of giving priority to free speech claimed it could have (see section 1.2).

Nevertheless, if, in these unlikely specific cases, copyright conflicts with freedom of expression, a liberal theory of justice could legitimately consider both rights to have either equal or unequal status. If a liberal theory of justice takes both rights to have equal status, this would preclude the use of a principled method to resolve the conflict. However, I described a qualitative procedure for normative assessment as providing a defensible decision-making process in these cases. This procedure is similar to qualitative methods discussed by Waldron and Rawls. I suggested that categories of speech could be used to remedy to the problems of uncertainty that afflict this procedure. I further argued that we should let consequentialist considerations decide the matter only if this kind of qualitative method fails to produce a definite answer.

Appendix 1

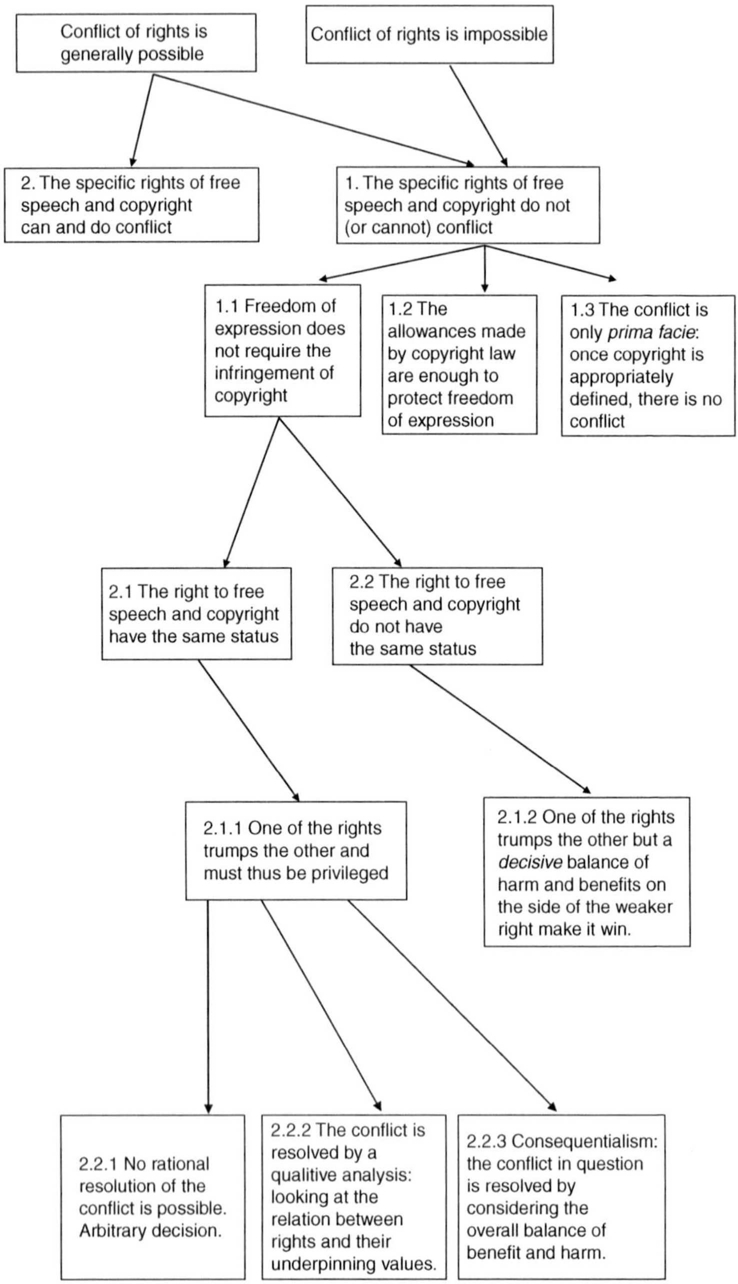
Conflict of rights is generally possible
Conflict of rights is impossible
2. The specific rights of free speech and copyright can and do conflict
1. The specific rights of free speech and copyright do not (or cannot) conflict
1.1 Freedom of expression does not require the infringement of copyright
1.2 The allowances made by copyright law are enough to protect freedom of expression
1.3 The conflict is only *prima facie*: once copyright is appropriately defined, there is no conflict
2.1 The right to free speech and copyright have the same status
2.2 The right to free speech and copyright do not have the same status
2.1.1 One of the rights trumps the other and must thus be privileged
2.1.2 One of the rights trumps the other but a *decisive* balance of harm and benefits on the side of the weaker right make it win.
2.2.1 No rational resolution of the conflict is possible. Arbitrary decision.
2.2.2 The conflict is resolved by a qualitive analysis: looking at the relation between rights and their underpinning values.
2.2.3 Consequentialism: the conflict in question is resolved by considering the overall balance of benefit and harm.

Notes

1. The free expression of artists can be guaranteed by the moral right to be attributed to the authorship of a piece of work, but does not require the economic right attached to it.
2. I believe two sets of normative issues are related to that control. First, the ownership of copyright rights by corporations might lack legitimacy because the two main justifications for copyright are based on the special relationship between the work and its author/creator. Second, there might be a limitation of autonomy entailed by the control exerted by corporations, in its selective power of determining what others would watch and listen to. The autonomy of citizens would be reduced to the extent that they would suffer from a reduction in the cultural options available to them. At least, this would be the case in Raz's conception of autonomy.
3. This issue is highly sensitive to the theory of justice endorsed.
4. The work is considered original if sufficient time, effort, technical skills and knowledge have been used (Cornish, 2006, p. 12).
5. According to a choice-based theory of rights, 'the essential feature of a duty which yields a right is that the person to whom the duty is owed is able to control the performance of that duty' (Jones, 1994, p. 32).
6. Hillel Steiner claims that the compossibility of rights (compatibility of rights with each other) is necessary for that set of rights to be possible (Steiner, 1994, p. 2).
7. On this view, an individual X has a right 'if and only if X can have rights, and other things being equal, an aspect of X's well-being (his interest) is a sufficient reason for holding some other person(s) to be under a duty' (Raz, 1986, p. 166).
8. This distinction can also be referred to as the distinction between idea and expression (see Hart, Fazzani and Clark, 2006, p. 161).
9. The question of what qualifies as speech is equally difficult to answer without violating content neutrality. However, it is crucial since what fails to qualify as speech would lose the special protection accorded by freedom of expression to the act. The liberal attitude consists typically in using a low standard for qualifying as a speech act while considering certain kinds of harm as possibly outweighing the right to free speech.
10. Note that it is indifferent whether Ulysses charges his audience or not.
11. But what criterion qualifies the street as a public place? The relevant criterion to distinguish between public and private here is the relationship between the performer and his/her audience. The character of the audience is a more important criterion than the size (Phillips and Firth 2000, p. 188).
12. Copyright protects any *materially recorded* work against the reproduction in any material form. The work can be recorded as any mode of visual or acoustic presentation and the infringement of a work's copyright could consist in a *visual* or *acoustic* performance of it (see Phillips and Firth 2000, p. 176).
13. This second argument is weaker if one takes into account the limited length of copyright (70 years). However, some artistic works might gain symbolic weight in a short span of time. The argument, if made weaker, is not entirely defeated by considering the time limitation of copyright.
14. Wittgenstein is an example of this (Kahane, Kanterian and Kuusela, 2007).

15. The owner of copyright cannot object to minor borrowings of his/her work (see Cornish and Llewelyn, 2003, pp. 440ff).
16. Economic rights can also be justified morally as the rightful desert of someone's work. By moral rights attached to copyrighted work, I refer here to some more fundamental moral rights.
17. Moreover, in the United Kingdom, two further moral rights are added: the right against fake attribution of a work and the right to privacy in private photographs and films (Cornish and Llewelyn, 2003, p. 455).
18. They clearly belong to intellectual property rights, but some have claimed that these moral rights do not belong to copyright law strictly speaking (see Cornish and Llewelyn, 2003, p. 466). I assume here that these moral rights belong entirely to copyright law, because the circumstances in which they are most likely to be threatened are cases of reproduction of copyrighted work.
19. I believe that another possible conception of copyright would also not conflict with freedom of expression. In this conception, some economic rights are not attached to the reproduction as such of the cultural product but only to its production. This conception is not market-based.
20. The libertarian strategy is thus to define freedoms, such as freedom of expression, in such a way as to pre-empt conflict between rights. One objection could be that this strategy pre-empts conflict only in a terminological sense, but amounts to giving more weight to property rights, as they are considered fundamental.
21. For another example of non-libertarian liberal using that conception, see Dworkin (1977, p. 269).
22. It has been argued somewhat similarly that the distinction between regulation and restriction is inappropriate because it grounds an absolutist division between basic liberties and all other consequentialist reasons for putting limits on the upholding of a right (Farrelly, 2007, p. 854).
23. The promotion of freedom is not necessarily maximised by the protection of libertarian rights. Taxes might limit the freedom of the individual being taxed, but they increase the freedom of those who benefit from it via social policies funded by them (see Cohen, 2001, p. 55).
24. The two claims are as follows. First, the reproduction of intellectual/cultural work is a necessary condition for the enjoyment of freedom of expression. Second, the allowances made by copyright law are not sufficient for the protection of freedom of expression.
25. I assume that rights are generally protective of values, despite the fact that in some cases the punctilious enforcement of a right might endanger the value it is supposed to protect.
26. The distinction between classical and modern liberalism is useful to bear in mind in our examination of the conflict between copyright and freedom of expression: while classical liberalism gives more weight to property right, modern liberalism is more likely to favour freedom of expression (see Ryan, 1993).
27. I mention later the possibility that the weaker right outweighs the stronger one. This could be the case only if the balance of harm and benefit favours overwhelmingly the weaker right.

28. It has to be noted that the decision should also take into account the difference in the ranking of the two rights.
29. 'Now it is essential to observe that the basic liberties are given by a list of such liberties. Important among these are political liberty (the right to vote and to hold public office) and freedom of speech and assembly; liberty of conscience and freedom of thought; freedom of the person, which includes freedom from psychological oppression and physical assault and dismemberment (integrity of the person) ; the right to hold personal property and freedom from arbitrary arrest and seizure as defined by the concept of the rule of law' (Rawls, 1999, p. 53).
30. Although I do not address that issue here, I am aware that this qualitative approach might also be legitimately applied to conflicting rights of unequal status.
31. In this case, other considerations are also at stake. Shouting 'fire' might trigger panic and the audience would attempt to flee. In this process, lives might be lost. These consequentialist considerations encourage us to wonder if the shouting of 'fire' is entitled to the protection of freedom of speech.
32. A similar remark is made by Hart: 'We have rules of order in debate so that the exchange of arguments and the pursuit of truth can be facilitated. We have these rules not so that debaters can exercise the maximum freedom to speak... but in order better to achieve the purposes of debate' (quoted in Gray, 2000, pp. 70–1).
33. 'The proposed criterion is this: the basic liberties and their priority are to guarantee equally for all citizens the social conditions essential for the adequate development and the full and informed exercise of their two moral powers in what we have referred to as the two fundamental cases. These two cases we now specify more fully:

    a) The first is connected with the capacity for a sense of justice and concerns the application of the principles of justice to the basic structure and its social policies. The equal political liberties and freedom of thought are to ensure the opportunity for the free and informed application of the principles of justice to that structure and to its policies by means of the full and effective exercise of citizens' sense of justice. All this is necessary to make possible the free use of public reason.
    b) The second is connected with the capacity for a (complete) conception of the good (normally associated with a comprehensive religious, philosophical or moral doctrine), and concerns the exercise of citizens' powers of practical reason in forming, revising and rationally pursuing such a conception over a complete life. Liberty of conscience and freedom of association are to ensure the opportunity for the free and informed exercise of this capacity and its companion powers of practical reason and judgment (Rawls, 2001, p. 113).

34. It has to be noted that, in the case of fighting words or incitements to hatred, liberals can justify content regulations (Cohen, 1993, pp. 213–14).
35. 'Particularity, in a non-ideal world, provides, among other things, certainty, predictability, uniformity, mental manageability, and insurance against misunderstanding and misapplication of general principles. If we did not believe

these values to be important, we would have no need to particularize abstract foundational rights, but could instead apply the abstraction directly to cases without the mediating force of particularized rights' (Shauer, 1987, p. 118).

References

Alexander, L. (2005) *Is there a Right of Freedom of Expression?* Cambridge: Cambridge: University Press.
Cohen, G. A. (2001) *Self-ownership, Freedom and Equality*. Cambridge: Cambridge University Press.
Cohen, J. (1993) Freedom of Expression, *Philosophy and Public Affairs*, 22(3): 207–63.
Cornish, G. P. (2006) *Copyright: Interpreting the Law for Libraries, Archives and Information Services*, 4th edition. London: Facet Publishing.
Cornish,. W. R and Llewelyn, D. (2003), *Intellectual Property: Patents, Copyright, Trade Marks and Allied Rights*, 5th edition. London: Sweet & Maxwell.
Davies, G. (2002) *Copyright and the Public Interest*. London: Sweet & Maxwell.
Dworkin, R. (1977) *Taking Rights Seriously*. London: Duckworth.
Farrelly, C. (2007) *Political Studies*, 55: 844–64.
Gewirth, A. (1981) Are There Any Absolute Rights? *The Philosophical Quarterly*, 31(122): 1–16.
Ginsburg, J. C. (2001) Copyright and Control over New Technologies of Dissemination, *Columbia Law Review*, 101(7): 1613–48.
Goodman, N. (1978) *Ways of Worldmaking*. Hassocks: Harvester Press.
Gordon, W. J. (1990) Towards a Jurisprudence of benefits: the Norms of Copyright and the Problem of Private Censorship, *University of Chicago Law Review*, 57: 1009–49.
Gray, J. (2000) *The Two Faces of Liberalism*. Cambridge: Polity.
Griffiths, J. and Suthersanen, U. (2005) *Copyright and Free Speech*. Oxford: Oxford University Press.
Hart, T., Fazzani, L.and Clark, S. (2006) *Intellectual Property Law*, 4th edition. London: Palgrave Macmillan.
Jones, P. (1994) *Rights*. London: Palgrave Macmillan.
Kahane, G., Kanterian, E. and Kuusela, O. (2007) 'Introduction', in G. Kahane, E. Kanterian and O. Kuusela (eds) *Wittgenstein and His Interpreters*. Oxford: Blackwell.
Kukathas, C. (2003), *The Liberal Archipelago*. Oxford: Oxford University Press.
Phillips,. J. and Firth, A. (2000) *Introduction to Intellectual Property Law*, 4th edition. London: Butterworths.
Rawls, J. (2001) *Justice as Fairness: a Restatement*. Cambridge, MA: Harvard University Press.
Rawls, J. (1999) *A Theory of Justice*. Oxford: Oxford University Press.
Rawls, J. (2005) *Political Liberalism*. New York: Columbia University Press.
Rawls, J. (2001) *Justice as Fairness: a Restatement*. Cambridge, MA: Harvard University Press.
Raz, J. (1986) *The Morality of Freedom*. Oxford: Clarendon Press.
Ryan, A. (1993) 'Liberalism', in R. E. Goodin and P. Pettit (eds) *Companion to Contemporary Political Philosophy*. Oxford: Blackwell.

Shauer, F. (1987) 'Rights as Rules', *Law and Philosophy*, 6(1): 115–19.
Shauer, F. (1982) *Free Speech: A Philosophical Enquiry*. Cambridge: Cambridge University Press.
Steiner, H. (1994) *An Essay on Rights*. Oxford: Blackwell.
Taylor, C. (1991) *The Ethics of Authenticity*. London: Harvard University Press.
Thompson, J. J. (1986) *Rights, Restitution and Risks*. London: Harvard University Press.
Walzer, M. (1985) *Spheres of Justice, a Defence of Pluralism and Equality*. Oxford: Blackwell.
Weinreb, L. R. (1998) Copyright for Functional Expression, *Harvard Law Review*, 111(5): 1149–1254.
Wellman, C. H. (1995) On Conflict between Rights, *Law and Philosophy*, 14: 271–95.

9

Free Software, Proprietary Software and Linguistic Justice

Gilles Falquet and François Grin[1]

In this chapter, we examine some of the distributive implications of using free or open source software (FS/OSS) as opposed to proprietary software (PS). Much of the discussion on the respective virtues of both systems has tended to focus on allocative (or 'efficiency') issues, whether in terms of the fundamental economics of the industry (Katz and Shapiro, 1998), the long-term viability of non-proprietary systems and their compatibility with market incentives (Boldrin and Levine, 2002) or more applied questions such as the balance, for users, of the benefits and costs of either system (Perens, 2005; Verprat, n.d.). By contrast, many issues related to their distributive (or 'fairness') implications have remained largely unexplored.

Our foray into this question focuses on one particular dimension of fairness, namely, the notion of linguistic justice as addressed, for example, by Pool (1991b) and van Parijs (2002). In this chapter, we shall examine whether the choice of FS/OSS over PS is likely to imply different degrees of fairness in terms of the resulting distribution of resources among different language groups. We therefore take 'linguistic justice' in its usual sense of justice among groups defined according to their linguistic attributes. However, we also explore some implications of drawing parallels between computer languages and human languages.

This chapter is organised as follows: in section 1, we identify the key features that distinguish FS/OSS from PS, stressing those that are likely to bear upon the relative fairness of using one instead of the other. In section 2, we characterise the distributive issue at hand, which requires us to move away from the usual approaches that focus on income distribution among socio-economic groups. In section 3, we introduce the concept of linguistic hegemony, explain why it can be considered unfair and show under what conditions the use of FS/OSS may improve social justice. In section 4, we discuss additional questions that may be addressed in a more detailed investigation. Our main findings are summarised in a brief conclusion.

1 Free v. proprietary software: essential definitions and distinctions

The Free Software foundation defines 'free software' as a software product that can be freely:

- executed,
- studied and adapted to the user's needs (which implies that access to the source code is granted),
- copied and redistributed to others, and
- improved and publicly released.

Although this definition does not explicitly state that FS/OSS must be available at no cost, it is a direct consequence of these 'basic freedoms' (where this expression is used in a sense distinct from its usual meaning in political philosophy). Hence, confusion sometimes arises, with FS/OSS taken to mean software obtainable without any form of compensation. In fact, much freely available software is not 'free' software in the FS/OSS sense. For example, the well-known Internet Explorer web browser, though available at no cost, is the proprietary software of Microsoft Corp. It cannot be studied or improved on by users. Other notable examples are Adobe Acrobat Reader, Real Player, Apple's iTunes or Quicktime player.

Expecting that the software can be studied, adapted and improved implies that the source code must be available. The source code of a program is a list of instructions, usually written in a high-level programming language such as C, C++, Java, Python, etc. The source code is a high-level, human-readable description of the behaviour of the program. A processor cannot directly execute the source code of a program, which must first be translated by a compiler into machine-level instructions, that is, into a binary or executable code. Since processors can only execute extremely basic instructions, each high-level instruction will yield a high number (sometimes dozens) of machine instructions. Thus, the binary code of a large and complex program, made up of hundreds of thousands or millions of high-level instructions, is an extremely complex object.

Although it is theoretically possible to study and modify the entire binary code of a program, it is generally considered practically unfeasible or unduly costly. Keeping the source code secret is thus a standard way to protect proprietary rights in the software industry. Conversely, distributing a program together with its source code amounts to providing rights to study, adapt and enhance it. Hence, the notion of 'open source software', as stated by the Open Source Initiative, is practically equivalent to the notion of 'free' software.

Free software is often released under a 'copyleft' licensing agreement, which is a mechanism to ensure that non-free software cannot be derived from free software. For instance, the GNU General Public Licence (GPL)[2] states that any software derived from the licensed (free) software must be licensed under the terms of the same licence. Hence, the GPL licence is carried over to the new versions or new software based on it. A consequence is that a GPL program may not be incorporated into a proprietary program.

The question to be addressed here is whether these specific features of FS/OSS, which are often regarded as intrinsically superior to PS in terms of democratic, decentralised access to computer technology, also make FS/OSS superior in terms of linguistic justice.

Before proceeding, a brief excursus into the issue of price is in order. All other things being equal, consumers are likely to prefer a cheaper to a more expensive product. While one might have assumed that this may speak in favour of FS/OSS, matters may be less clear-cut in practice, because the relevant signal for consumers is not the price tag (in Euros, dollars or any other currency) on a particular software (which will be positive for a PS product and zero for an FS/OSS product), but what is known as 'total cost of ownership' (TCO). TCO is a measure of how much a consumer pays every year to use the software. This includes the price of purchase where applicable, but also related costs such as personnel training, maintenance and upgrades, failure and crash recovery, system administration, hardware upgrade, etc. Once all these elements of TCO are tallied up, FS/OSS does not exhibit a clear financial advantage or disadvantage over PS. Studies yield contradictory conclusions, depending on the type of software considered, the type of organisation in which the software is installed and the actual definition of TCO. Therefore, price is unlikely to be a decisive factor in the long run; moreover, as we shall see in the following section, it is not a key aspect of the problem at hand.

Finally, the question of incentives to develop FS/OSS deserves some clarification. Developing software is extremely costly in terms of labour.

Even though the software engineering discipline has produced highly efficient tools and methodologies to analyse, specify and develop software systems, it remains a knowledge-intensive and time-consuming process. Therefore, one can legitimately ask what the incentives are to develop FS/OSS that, by essence, cannot be sold to cover the development costs.

A preliminary remark is in order when discussing FS/OSS development: it is often believed that FS/OSS is exclusively developed by computer enthusiasts who give their time and competencies free of charge. In fact, the basic FS/OSS freedoms do not forbid paying a professional programmer to develop FS/OSS software, and this is often the case. Nevertheless, a large part of FS/OSS is developed by individuals who join a 'development community'.

Rullani (2006) identifies four kinds of motivations among individual FS/OSS developers: monetary incentives (when people are paid or want to signal their capabilities to the job market); own-use (when developing a program for his/her own use and taking advantage of the collective work to improve it); learning (when the developer learns new techniques, acquires new skills by participating in a stimulating new project); and social and psychological (when he/she seeks fun, creativity or kinship through participation in a group).

In fact, these categories also apply to organisations (private companies, non-profit organisations or governmental agencies) that finance FS/OSS. The 'own-use' motivation is basically the same as in the individual case, with the addition of knowledge preservation. The aim of making the software publicly available is to stimulate the emergence of a large group of 'specialists' who will preserve technical knowledge about the software. Monetary reward may correspond to advertising (improving the company's image by providing something free of charge) or selling services that go along with the free product (packaging, documentation, books, maintenance, etc.). The socio-psychological motivation applies principally to organisations with altruistic or public policy goals such as breaking (or at least challenging) the monopoly of a particular PS vendor, providing poor countries with high-quality software or providing citizens with specific services.

2 Characterising the distributive issue

Just about every social process, whether it emerges as a result of the decentralised choices of agents operating on a free market or of targeted, centralised regulation, has distributive impacts. These processes give rise to gains and losses, and consequently some actors[3] will end up winners and others will be losers. Even in the unusual case where there are only winners, some agents stand to make considerable gains, while others will only enjoy small gains. In any case, the relative position of social actors is constantly being altered by social processes. To the extent that these changes in relative position can be formulated in terms of the amount of resources that agents have at their disposal, and since resources are a central construct in economic analysis, the identification and measurement of distributive impacts could be expected to be a major area of concern for economists (Bürgenmeier, 1994).

However, a rift regarding the handling of such issues has emerged in the social sciences. As Zajac (1995, pp. 76–7) observes, 'with the exception of a small minority who do research in economic or "distributive" justice, economists today generally do not professionally concern themselves with economic justice, beyond their concern for the advancement of Pareto optimality or "economic efficiency"'. At the most general theoretical level, matters of resource distribution have become the province of political philosophers, while the study of given manifestations of inequality, including its empirical observation, has largely been left to sociologists.[4] To some extent, this relative lack of interest may be due to the fact that two conceptually difficult questions have to be addressed at the outset.

The first is the choice of a dependent variable, namely, the nature of the resource whose distribution across individuals and groups must be examined. Most of the economic literature, because it adopts a fairly narrow notion of 'economic justice', focuses on disposable income or some related indicator of socio-economic status.[5] However, there is no reason to ignore other resources. Consequently, the distribution of commodities such as health, social prestige, power or Rawlsian 'basic liberties' is a relevant issue for studies that attempt, in line with fundamental economic theory, to identify and assess the distributive effects associated with social processes. This, however, considerably broadens the scope of economic analysis and requires handling variables that do not easily lend themselves to the sort of quantitative treatment that economic analysis enjoys (Mayer, 1993).[6]

The second issue is that of the identification of an independent variable, that is, of groups between which (re)distribution of (symbolic or material) resources occurs. The often unstated assumption in much of the social sciences, including economics as well as most normative political theory, is that the truly relevant criterion for identifying them is income group or some related indicator of socio-economic status.[7] Only a comparatively small strand of research looks into the distribution of resources across groups defined in terms of other, *non-elective* characteristics such as agents' age, health, ethnicity or mother tongue – with the notable exception of research mentioned in note 4, which provides empirical estimates of the net contribution of ethnicity or mother tongue on labour income.[8]

In this chapter, we take a broad view of distribution, by casting the net wide in our definition of dependent and independent variables. As regards the dependent variables, while retaining material resources as the main object of distribution, we are aware of the necessity of taking some symbolic elements into account. The latter are particularly meaningful for disenfranchised language communities, for whom the translation of software into their language can constitute a valuable manifestation of respect. As to the independent variables, we shall examine, in line with the literature on linguistic justice, distribution not among standard socio-economic (e.g. income-based) groups, but among language-defined groups and, more specifically, among groups of actors defined according to their mother tongue.

Contrary to some authors (e.g. van Parijs, 2004), we disagree with the notion that languages are quasi-perfect substitutes for one another, and that linguistic justice can be achieved not only through an equal treatment of all languages, but also by equipping everyone (including speakers of non-dominant languages) with skills in the dominant language. Even setting aside the simple fact that in the case of computer software, linguistic justice is easier to implement through software translation and localisation than by other means, such as the teaching and learning of a dominant language by all, there are deeper problems of fairness with this suggestion.

As shown in the following section, linguistic hegemony gives rise to massive transfers in favour of native speakers of the hegemonic language. Not only would some of these transfers resist compensation through a Hicks–Kaldor scheme[9] (even if it *were* offered, which is doubtful at best), but the actual possibility of bringing non-native speakers of the hegemonic language to a degree of competence in it that would be fully and truly equal to that of its native speakers is largely illusory (Piron, 1994).

This near-impossibility exists even in the case of a considerable increase in the resources devoted to the learning and teaching of the hegemonic language, and few are the situations where flawless competence in a second language is achieved by an entire group, unless, of course, this second language becomes their first. This usually implies what is known in sociolinguistics as language shift, and that hardly ever occurs outside of a situation of cultural and political disenfranchisement (May, 2001). For this reason giving everybody 'wide access' to the hegemonic language, far from being an avenue that guarantees fairness, is more likely to be an accessory to mental colonialism (Durand, 2001). Thus, linguistic justice is intimately bound with multilingualism – or, alternatively, if one insists on one common code, with the general adoption of a much more neutral language such as Esperanto.

3 Linguistic hegemony and computer standards

Linguistic hegemony, first introduced as a formal concept by Pool,[10] may be defined as a situation in which one natural language enjoys a strongly dominant position as the sole or main vehicle for communication between actors of different mother tongues.[11] A hegemonic language is often – though incorrectly – called a lingua franca.[12] The use of a hegemonic language gives rise to a number of asymmetries that benefit its native speakers. These asymmetries can be expressed as departures from a 'just' allocation of material and symbolic resources (Grin, 2004b). Accordingly, they may be seen as 'transfers', of which four can be readily identified:

1. The *privileged markets effect*: native speakers of the hegemonic language enjoy a dominant position in the provision of a number of goods and services, in particular translation and interpretation into this language, language teaching, the production of teaching materials and text editing.
2. The *communication savings effect*: native speakers of the hegemonic language are spared the effort to translate their messages into other languages, or to translate into the hegemonic language messages uttered by non-native speakers of the hegemonic language, because this language, owing to its dominant position, would generally be used by non-native speakers for most international communication.
3. The *language learning savings effect*: native speakers of the hegemonic language can forgo the learning of foreign languages, thereby realising a significant saving, whereas native speakers of other languages have to learn at least one foreign language very well – that is, they have to become fluent in the hegemonic language.
4. The *rhetorical and legitimacy effect*: native speakers of the hegemonic language enjoy a strong advantage over all others in negotiation and conflict taking place in their language.

The money saved – particularly as a result of the first three effects – can in turn generate an *alternative human capital investment effect*: the resources earned or saved by native speakers of the hegemonic language as a result of the preceding effects may be invested elsewhere, particularly in the development of other forms of human capital, generating additional income in subsequent periods.

Therefore, the first question that arises here is whether FS/OSS and PS differ in the extent to which they can abet linguistic hegemony. There seems to be no overwhelming empirical reason why either system should prove more or less harmful in this respect, although general analytical considerations suggest that in at least one particular context FS/OSS may be preferable. Let us examine this point in more detail.

Precisely because FS/OSS are characterised by the fact that they guarantee (at least under a 'copyleft' regime) four basic freedoms, including adapting the software and disseminating it free of charge, FS/OSS leave the door wide open to the development of linguistically differentiated (or 'localised') versions of the software.[13] As to the incentives that FS/OSS developers may have to provide differentiated versions of the software, they have been addressed at the end of section 1.

Clearly, the development of those different versions will be conducive to the maintenance of linguistic diversity and therefore impede the establishment of linguistic hegemony. By contrast, the decision to offer such linguistically differentiated versions, in a PS system, hinges on a decision by the owner of the software who typically sells licences to users. The question, therefore, is whether multiple versions of a software are more likely to emerge as a result of the voluntary work of a community of FS/OSS developers and users or of a profit-maximising decision by PS owners. This in turn depends on two factors: first, the relative position of different languages (and, in particular, whether a situation of linguistic hegemony already exists); and second, market structure in the PS sector.

Because software programs give rise to network externalities, their market can hardly be a purely competitive one, and we can therefore ignore the case of competitive markets in order to focus on some cases of imperfect competition. Let us first consider a monopoly in order to examine the way in which a situation of linguistic hegemony may affect the relative attractiveness of either system.

3.1 Monopoly

If a given natural language enjoys a hegemonic position, a PS monopolist will have little incentive to offer linguistically differentiated versions.

In this case, she will tend to offer only one version of the product – in the hegemonic language. Licence protection prevents the development of translations (or, more generally, of *localised versions* of the product), which forces software users to learn the dominant language, thereby contributing to its hegemonic status. By contrast, FS/OSS will not be subjected to this constraint and is likely to provide a more diversity-friendly environment. Consequently, an FS/OSS system is likely to be more compatible with linguistic justice than a PS system.

If, however, there is no pre-existing linguistic hegemony, a PS monopolist *may* find it profitable to offer linguistically differentiated versions of her product in order to increase sales.

Producing additional versions in other languages amounts to a form of market segmentation, through which additional sales can be achieved at a little extra cost. Since both the software itself and its translation into other languages can be considered as sunk costs, the production of additional language versions carries a low marginal cost (*mc*). Market segmentation may turn out to be particularly profitable because it may be possible to sell suitably localised versions of a software at higher prices, if consumers are willing to pay a premium for them. This yields a higher marginal revenue than the initial product.[14]

Suppose now that additional sales of the software, though made easier by the fact that it is made available in several languages, are possible *only* if the unit price goes down. The strategy may still be profitable. This case can be analysed using the standard model of a monopoly, where the monopolist faces the entire demand for the good that she produces. Consequently, increases in sales can be achieved if the price goes down not only for the additional units sold (the 'marginal' unit), but also for all the preceding units. This case is studied in the appendix, in which we derive the formal conditions for this move to be profitable.

Consequently, in the absence of pre-existing language hegemony and assuming a monopolistic market structure, there seems to be no overwhelming reason to *systematically* prefer either FS/OSS or PS systems – at least in terms of their impact on language-related distributive impacts.

3.2 Monopolistic competition

Allowing for other market structures, however, may lead us to qualify our first result, according to which FS/OSS may be superior to PS (in terms of linguistic justice) in the case of pre-existing linguistic hegemony. Even if we are not confronted with a pure monopoly, the market is likely to display the standard features of monopolistic competition.[15] In this case, a few producers serve almost the entire market; they strive to differentiate their product and to lock in their costumers with a variety of strategies in order to tip the market towards their product line (Katz and Shapiro, 1998, p. 4).

In the *absence* of linguistic hegemony, offering linguistically differentiated versions of the software is an obvious strategy to capture niche markets through product differentiation. In this case, therefore, the language-related distributive impacts will be roughly similar whether the market structure is a case of monopoly or monopolistic competition, and no systematic preference for FS/OSS or PS arises in terms of this specific distributive criterion.

If a situation of linguistic hegemony already exists, firms in monopolistic competition may also have an incentive to capture segments of the market by offering language-differentiated versions of their software. The only assumption needed for this to occur is that buyers are *not* indifferent between different language versions of the same software. In this case, sellers can try to attract users who, though capable of using the software in the hegemonic language, have a preference for working in their own language. Three elements of circumstantial evidence may be marshalled, suggesting that this situation is plausible.

First, consumers seem to have a preference, other things being equal, for language-specific products to be made available in their native language, even if they have a very good command of another language in which the product is already available.[16] Second, rough estimates of the empirical value of four of the five transfers that result from linguistic hegemony indicate that the financial amounts involved are considerable (Grin, 2005); thus, if the hegemonic language is native only to a small minority of agents, the majority has a clear interest in fostering alternative forms of international communication and, therefore, to make a conscious choice to require linguistically differentiated versions of the software. Third – and with more direct relevance – the recent development, by a PS producer like Microsoft, of minority language versions of word processing software (e.g., in Welsh and Basque, although adult speakers of Welsh and Basque are fluent in English and Spanish respectively) may be seen as evidence that even in a situation where English already enjoys a strongly dominant position worldwide, a firm engaged in monopolistic competition finds an interest in developing language-differentiated versions of its software. This willingness to provide localised, or at least translated, versions may be linked to the moderate cost of producing them (compared to the expected increase in revenue), a point to which we turn in the following section.

It is important to observe, however, that the likely superiority of FS/OSS in the 'monopoly with linguistic hegemony' case, as well as its merely possible superiority in other cases, may be questioned on the following grounds.

FS/OSS systems thrive in communities of developers who need a means to communicate efficiently. Typically, this need will encourage convergence towards a common language. Although no discipline yet offers a fully fledged theory of language dynamics, a strong case can be made that language spread is a self-reinforcing process (van Parijs, 2004). In a situation where linguistic hegemony already exists, the tendency for FS/OSS developers to use a common language may dampen whatever diversity-enhancing activity the same developers may have; in a situation without linguistic hegemony, it can contribute to its emergence.

However, since the profitability of localised versions of PS directly depends on the localisation costs and the additional market size, and considering that localisation remains a costly process (Webb Collins, 2002), it is very unlikely that specialised software will be localised for minority languages or languages used exclusively in poor regions. Our preliminary empirical results seem to confirm this (see section 4). In such a situations FS/OSS show a clear advantage in terms of linguistic justice, because their localisation can be undertaken by individuals or sponsored by governments.[17] Nevertheless, it is frequently hindered by the lack of technical resources (Souphavanh and Karoonboonyanan, 2005).

We may summarise our assessment in a two-way table as follows (Table 1), where the symbol '∼' indicates that either system may be

Table 1 A comparison of the distributive implications of FS/OSS and PS systems according to market structure and linguistic environment

Market structure in the PS sector → **Linguistic environment ↓**	**Monopoly**	**Monopolistic competition**
With pre-existing linguistic hegemony	FS/OSS preferable to PS	FS/OSS∼PS
Without pre-existing linguistic hegemony	FS/OSS∼PS	FS/OSS∼PS

preferable in terms of its impact on linguistic justice, depending on the demand and cost curves.

Therefore, pending closer examination, there seems to be no overriding argument, from the standpoint of linguistic justice, for systematically preferring FS/OSS to PS systems, or vice versa. The development and use of software is merely another terrain on which competition among different languages plays itself out, with the attendant distributive implications. This is not to deny the importance of software products in patterns of language dynamics, but such importance may be related to other aspects of the issue, which we address next.

4 Discussion

4.1 Empirical aspects of software localisation

The computer industry in general – whether it is dominated by FS/OSS or PS systems – certainly plays an important role in language dynamics, because initial development tends to take place in a dominant language. The time needed to produce and distribute localised (or at least linguistically differentiated) versions of the software creates a lag during which many users may adopt the hegemonic language version of the software. The widespread perception of English as 'the' language of science and technology hinges not only on the actual importance of companies based in English-speaking countries, but also on this time lag, since all languages are equally suited to the development of products with a significant cognitive content.[18] The time lag problem may be somewhat mitigated in FS/OSS because of the networked and distributed nature of the development teams. Even if English is often the communication language of an international development team, the cultural diversity within the team is likely to make localisation an important concern; this diversity may also prevent strong cultural biases in the software and its interface.

However, the time lag between the production of different language versions tends to diminish or even disappear for widely distributed software, like operating systems (Windows, MacOS) or office automation suites (Windows, Office, etc.) because demand is sufficiently high to make localisation immediately profitable. In addition, these very popular (and non-specialised) software products are often used by persons who would lack the foreign language skills needed to use them efficiently if they were available only in the dominant language.

This general observation supports our view, presented in section 3, that localisation is an attractive strategy even for PS owners, whether under monopoly or monopolistic competition, provided the expected increase in sales is sufficient.

If we consider more specialised but still widespread software, like Adobe's products (Photoshop or PDF-related software), we observe that they have been localised only for a few languages (from 1 to 15) while their FS/OSS counterparts (e.g. the Gimp image processing software) exist in dozens of languages. This difference is even more striking for a utility software like Winzip, which is available in four languages only while the equivalent FS/OSS (GZip) has more than 50 localised versions. This tends to prove that the demand curves for different languages are such that localisation of a PS is profitable only when the number of potential solvent customers is very high. As a consequence, such PS would rarely be translated into the languages spoken in the poorest markets. Hence FS/OSS could be preferable, in terms of linguistic diversity/justice, for specialised software. This point, however, deserves closer empirical examination, given the fact that the relative importance of language is not the same for all products, and will tend to be low, for example, for image processing software.

4.2 Computer standards as languages

Our discussion so far has focused on a comparison between FS/OSS systems on the one hand, and PS systems on the other hand, in terms of the likelihood that linguistically differentiated versions of the software are produced, under the assumption that the existence or non-existence of such versions has an impact on the emergence of linguistic hegemony. However, it is possible to envisage other conduits between the property rights characteristics of a software and the linguistic environment. A potentially important aspect is that software typically gives rises to network externalities.

According to Katz and Shapiro (1998), two types of network externalities can be identified. First, software can create fairly standard communication-based externalities, if users are able to communicate and exchange with each other *because* they use a given software. This type of externality suggests a parallel between computer standards and human languages, because human languages also operate as networks. The corresponding (language-based) network externalities are not fully explored, but several scholars have already addressed them

(Church and King, 1993; Selten and Pool, 1997). Our question then becomes whether FS/OSS on the one hand, and PS on the other, 'spread' in different ways, and if such a difference may have a bearing on linguistic hegemony and, by way of consequence, on linguistic justice.

Strong statements would be perilous. Nevertheless, precisely because of the four freedoms that FS/OSS systems guarantee, they may blossom into more varied (and initially unforeseen) applications. This process may take place in a variety of languages. Now, as we have seen in the preceding section, PS owners *also* have an incentive to offer linguistically differentiated versions of their products (except in a case where far-reaching linguistic hegemony already exists and they enjoy a monopoly situation). However, the potential superiority of FS/OSS in terms of diversity maintenance (and hence in terms of linguistic justice) hinges on the fact that even if the range of languages used in computer products is roughly the same under a PS and an FS/OSS system, the fact that the latter may engender a broader range of applications means that it will entail more varied uses of the languages concerned, first as those applications are developed, and then when they are used – what some authors (e.g. Raffestin, 1980) have called 'linguistic work'. More linguistic work contributes to the vitality of the languages in which this work takes place, and this in turn will help to counter possible drifts towards linguistic hegemony. The fact that this input into linguistic vitality operates not only through the consumption, but also through the production of software, tends to reinforce the advantage of FS/OSS over PS.

Network externalities can also arise even when agents do not actually communicate with each other using the software. In Katz and Shapiro's example, a computer system may include two components, *A* and *B*. Users may need to purchase both if, say, *A* is 'the operating system needed to make word processing programme *B* work' (Katz and Shapiro, 1998, p. 4). If more people adopt operating system *A*, a larger number of compatible applications (not only *B*, but also *C*, *D*, etc.) may become available, thereby generating a positive externality for previous users of *A*. Is FS/OSS more likely than PS to inhibit the rise of linguistic hegemony through this particular mechanism? In our view, the comparison between both systems raises the same issues as in the other case of externality. Even if the range of *languages* in which products are developed is roughly the same, whether we have a PS or an FS/OSS system, the latter will tend to favour more intense and varied linguistic work.

4.3 Linguistic justice and human-computer interface languages

Considering computer languages instead of natural languages offers another perspective on linguistic justice. Humans and computers communicate through artificial languages, whose 'alphabets' could be standard alphabetical characters, but also graphical elements such as icons, or user actions such as clicking a button, choosing a menu item, etc. For example, clicking a file icon and dragging it over the recycle bin icon means 'delete this file' in the interaction language of the Windows file explorer.

Although much simpler and less expressive than natural languages, computer interaction languages share some of their characteristics. In particular, they require a learning effort. Because of this learning cost, a user cannot freely choose an application to accomplish a given task, such as typing a letter. Rather, he/she will strongly prefer the application he/she already knows and has mastered. This eventually raises linguistic justice issues that are similar to those that arise in the case of natural languages. For instance, if a user who has learned word processor *A* receives a document that can only be processed with word processor *B*, he/she will be forced to use B and its 'foreign' interaction language. There are many similar situations where computer users must switch to another language, either at the operating system level (e.g. from MacOS to Windows) or at the application level, and pay the corresponding cost.

There is no obvious reason why FS/OSS should alleviate this type of problem. Nevertheless, we can identify at least one situation in which FS/OSS is clearly preferable. If the producer of a PS software decides, for economic reasons, to discontinue production, all the users of the product will have to switch to a new software – and learn it. This rarely happens with FS/OSS because the existence and 'survival' of such software is in the hands of its user and developer community. Thus, even if the software needs adaptations and corrections to survive, the user community, provided it is large enough, can support the corresponding development costs.

It is also worth discussing the notion of linguistic diversity among computer interaction languages. At first sight, diversity is not desirable. The world of computers would be much simpler if all word processors (or all operating systems, or all mailing applications) had the same user interface. But this would not constitute an acceptable solution in the long run, because it would prevent new innovative solutions to improve human–computer interaction. In fact, computer interaction languages differ from natural languages on one important point: they are not all equivalent in terms of communication performance.

Usability tests, which measure the time to perform a given task, the number of errors, etc., have clearly shown that some user interfaces (and hence the associated language) are better than others. Therefore, it is important to maintain the linguistic diversity of computer languages in order to explore new interfaces and make progress towards better human–computer interaction.

In this respect, FS/OSS plays an important role, because it is often the only alternative when the market is occupied by a monopolist or by oligopolists. In the current context, this is particularly true with operating systems, with only two main PS (Windows and MacOS), and office automation, with the quasi-monopoly of MS Office. In both cases, the only serious competitors are FS/OSS software, that is, the Linux operating system and the OpenOffice suite respectively. Interestingly, the complete redesign of the user interface in Microsoft Office 2007 seems to be a response to the spread of OpenOffice.

5 Conclusion

In this chapter, we have compared FS/OSS and PS systems in the specific perspective of their impact on linguistic justice, characterising the latter in terms of distance from linguistic hegemony (this latter regime being considered the least compatible with linguistic justice). Under these assumptions, we identify a number of reasons why FS/OSS systems will tend to be preferable, though not systematically so. This conclusion rests on the following results:

1. Under monopoly, and if a situation of linguistic hegemony already exists, a PS monopolist will have no incentive to develop different language versions of a software product, thereby further entrenching linguistic hegemony. By contrast, a community of developers left free to improve FS/OSS products (under a copyleft system) are likely to produce localised versions of the software.
2. Under monopoly, but in the absence of a pre-existing language hegemony, a PS monopolist may have an incentive to develop localised versions, particularly if the cost of localisation is low (see appendix). However, it is not possible to claim, pending further (and in particular, empirical) investigation, that this incentive will be strong (available evidence actually suggests the opposite), and result in greater linguistic variety than that which would result from the work of independent developers freely producing localised versions.

3 Independently of the degree of pre-existing linguistic hegemony, the same uncertainty arises under monopolistic competition, which we consider the most relevant form of oligopoly on the software market.
4 The dynamics of software development in FS/OSS contexts encourages, *ceteris paribus*, more intense and diverse 'linguistic work', both at the stage of software development and at the stage of software use; hence, any given *quantitative* effect (in terms of the number of languages in which a software is available) is likely to have higher *qualitative* effects under FS/OSS than under PS. In particular, the localisation efforts carried out in a region support the development of a local software industry.

The issue certainly needs to be examined at closer range. On the one hand, it may be useful to step back and reassess FS/OSS in the broader context of alternative modes of production in general, in which the product itself or know-how about its production is made freely available to the community at large. This can occur not only in computer software, but also in transportation (in the case of car-sharing), genetic research, file-sharing of music and texts, etc.[19] On the other hand, our understanding of the relative fairness of PS and FS/OSS would benefit from more systematic empirical estimations. Our provisional conclusion, however, is that the case in favour of FS/OSS, though not overwhelming, is plausible, particularly if other advantages, unrelated to linguistic justice, are taken into account.

Appendix

Inexpensive localisation allows the market for a product to be expanded without impacting on marginal cost (*mc*), and with only a minor effect on average cost (*AC*). In the case of a monopoly, market expansion itself is reflected in the fact that the monopolist now faces the demand curve D_2 instead of D_1. Accordingly, the marginal revenue curve shifts from mr_1 to mr_2. Whether the move is profitable or not hinges on the actual position of the demand and cost curves. The situation where this is profitable is depicted in Figure 1, where revenue increases, and therefore $\varepsilon\zeta\eta\theta > \alpha\beta\gamma\delta$. Let us note, however, that different demand and cost schedules could yield the reverse result. A formal discussion of the conditions for localisation to be profitable is provided below for a simple case with constant marginal cost and higher, but decreasing, average cost.

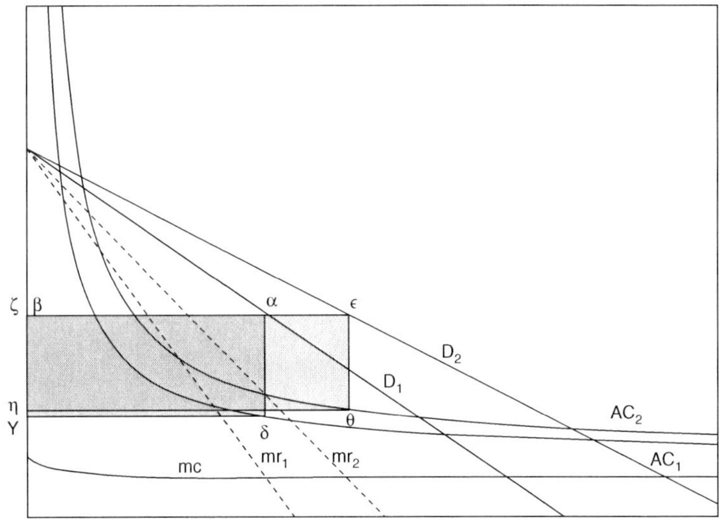

Figure 1 Increasing profits with multiple language versions of a PS

Assume a monopolist faces a demand curve given by:

$$Q = (r - sP)k$$

where quantity Q is a decreasing function of price P, k is equal to one if the software is produced in one language only, and larger than one if it is produced in an additional language. This yields the inverse demand function:

$$P = r/2 - 1/skQ$$

Marginal revenue mr is therefore given by:

$$mr = -1/skQ + P$$

A linear total cost (TC) function with constant marginal cost m and decreasing average cost will meet standard assumptions about the cost structure in the software industry. Let us therefore assume:

$$TC = \alpha + \lambda + mQ$$

where λ is the cost per localisation (in any given language), and α is the initial software development cost. Optimality implies that:

$$Q^* = (P - m)sk = k/2(r - sm)$$

If the product has been 'localised' and made available, at cost λ, in another language, we obtain total 'localised' profit $\Pi_l(Q^*)$ by subtracting $TC(Q^*)$ from total revenue, which yields:

$$\Pi_l = k[1/4s(r - ms)^2] - \alpha - \lambda$$

whereas the 'non-localised' profit Π_{nl}, is easily obtained by setting $k = 1$ and $\lambda = 0$. Therefore, under monopoly, the condition for localisation to be profitable is:

$$\Pi_l - \Pi_{nl} > 0$$

which implies:

$$k > \lambda 4s/(r - ms)^2 + 1$$

This expression can be generalised to give the marginal value of producing one additional 'localisation' of a software product already available in *j* languages, which will be positive if:

$$k_{j+1} > 4s/(r - ms)^2 \lambda_{j+1}$$

Notes

1. The authors thank François Vaillancourt for helpful comments and Patchareerat Yanaprasart for research assistance, as well as an anonymous reviewer for useful suggestions. The usual disclaimer applies.
2. The GNU General Public Licence is a type of free software license proposed by the GNU foundation. It can be found at www.gnu.org/copyleft/gpl.html. There exist several other licences that are compatible with the principle of free software.
3. Economists speak of 'agents', while practitioners of other social sciences usually speak of 'actors', making more or less specific assumptions about their behaviour. In this chapter, both terms are treated as equivalent, although we shall lean towards the economic position by assuming our actors/agents to be 'rational' in the standard sense of being (constrained) utility maximisers, irrespective of their particular social and cultural circumstances.
4. Exceptions being work on earnings differentials based *not* on a person's (acquired) human capital, but on her inborn characteristics such as ethnicity (see work reviewed in Vaillancourt, 1985a, and Grin, 1996; see also Chiswick, 1991) and gender (see e.g. classical work by Oaxaca, 1973).
5. Apart from the empirical work mentioned in note 4, textbooks, consciously or not, focus almost exclusively on the distribution of income and wealth (see e.g. Cullis and Jones, 1998; Stiglitz, 1998; Mueller, 2003).
6. In fact, this broad view of economics can be traced back to Jeremy Bentham's utilitarianism, where there are no *a priori* constraints on the sources of human welfare. It has survived the modern criticism of the elementary calculus of pleasure and pain, and remains embodied in the concept of Pareto optimality. Modern economic theory has largely endorsed the view that the

discipline is defined less by its subject matter than by its approach (Becker, 1976, p. 5).

7. Some policy analysis work also investigates (re)distribution between elective groups such as users v. non-users of public transport, homeowners v. tenants, etc.
8. Most contributions on the statistical relationship between language attributes and labour income, however, emphasise the contribution of *second* language skills, which constitute an *elective* characteristic, despite the fact that native speakers of marginalised languages may have little choice but to learn at least one majority language.
9. The reasons for this are well-known to sociolinguists (e.g. May, 2003); for an explanation formulated in a political theory perspective, see Laitin and Reich (2003).
10. The first mention is in Pool (1991), who further developed the same concept in a more recent contribution (1996) without, however, using the same label. Banking on Pool's work, Grin (2004a) discusses linguistic hegemony in the context of the 2005 enlargement of the European Union. See also Phillipson (2003).
11. The dominance of a *non*-natural language such as Esperanto is not a case of hegemony, because the absence of a community of native speakers creates a fundamentally different (that is, strictly egalitarian) structure of endowments.
12. While the term lingua franca, in everyday speech, denotes a language widely used for inter-group communication, it has a different scholarly definition. More formally, a *lingua franca* is a code that draws, in varying measure, on the native languages of different participants in linguistic exchange (Knapp and Meierkord, 2002). Therefore, it requires a specific learning effort by all. By contrast, the use of a hegemonic language requires all users to undergo the full effort of learning a *foreign* language, except, of course, native speakers of the hegemonic language, who are spared this effort.
13. 'Localisation' refers not only to the translation of text into another language, but also includes other aspects of software adaptation, such as converting units of measurement (e.g. between the imperial and the metric system or between Celsius and Fahrenheit), the positioning of roll-down menus (which will be located on the right-hand side of the screen in languages written from right to left), adapting or replacing the icons, etc.; further adaptations, going beyond user interface, may be necessary for all software that allows the creation of texts.
14. For an early discussion of the cost structure of linguistically-differentiated goods, see Hocevar (1975).
15. We ignore other forms of imperfect competition, such as oligopolies where different firms sell almost exactly the same product. Our assumption is borne out by the fact that software products, even though they are intended to perform the same task (word processing, electronic mail, etc.), *are* in fact the object of deliberate differentiation by producers.
16. Consumer surveys in Quebec (where a high proportion of French speakers have a command of English adequate for the consumption of goods labelled in English only) reveal a preference among consumers for goods to be offered and advertised in French (Vaillancourt, 1985b). Comparable results are found

for Catalonia, where just about all speakers of Catalan are also fluent in Spanish.

17. It can be argued that a government could also pay a PS producer to obtain a localised version of the software. However, this scheme would lead to a 'pay twice' situation because the localised version would still be sold, not given, to local customers.
18. If, for example, terminology is missing, it can easily be developed through language corpus planning; see Kaplan and Baldauf (1997, p. 44).
19. For a broad assessment of the 'open' mode of production, see Estermann (2006).

References

Becker, G. (1976) *The Economic Approach to Human Behavior.* Chicago: Chicago University Press.

Boldrin, M. and Levine, D. (2002) *The Case against Intellectual Property.* http://levine.sscnet.ucla.edu/papers/intellectual.pdf. Accessed 9 February 2006.

bridges.org (2005) *Comparison Study of Free/Open Source and Proprietary Software in an African Context.* Cape Town: bridges.org, http://www.bridges.org/software_comparison/SoftComp_Final_24May05.pdf.

Bürgenmeier, B. (1994) The Misperception of Walras, *American Economic Review,* 84: 342–52.

Chiswick, B. (1991) Speaking, Reading and Earnings among Low-skilled Immigrants, *Journal of Labor Economics,*9(2): 149–70.

Church, J. andKing I. (1993) Bilingualism and Network Externalities, *Canadian Journal of Economics,* 26: 337–45.

Cullis, J. and Jones, P. (1998) *Public Finance and Public Choice.* Oxford: Oxford University Press.

Durand, C. (2001) *La Mise en place des monopoles du savoir.* Paris: L'Harmattan.

Estermann, B. (2006) Le Mode de production 'ouvert'. Caractéristiques et raisons d'être, MA thesis in Management and Analysis of Public Policies (University of Geneva).

Grin, F. (1996) The Economics of Language: Survey, Assessment, and Prospects, *International Journal of the Sociology of Language,* 121: 17–44.

Grin F. (2004a) Coûts et justice linguistique dans l'Union européenne, *Panoramiques,* 69: 97–104.

Grin, F. (2004b) On the Costs of Cultural Diversity, in P. van Parijs (ed.) *Cultural Diversity versus Economic Solidarity.* Brussels: de Boeck, pp. 189–202.

Grin, F. (2005) *L'enseignement des langues étrangères comme politique publique.* Report to the French Ministry of Education [Rapport au Haut Conseil de l'évaluation de l'école, 19], cisad.adc.education.fr/hcee.

Hocevar, T. (1975) Equilibria on Linguistic Minority Markets, *Kyklos,* 28: 337–57.

Kaplan, R. and Baldauf, R. (1997) *Language Planning. From Practice to Theory.* Clevedon: Multilingual Matters.

Katz, M. and Shapiro, C. (1998) Antitrust in Software Markets. Paper presented at the Progress and Freedom Foundation Conference on Competition, Convergence and the Microsoft Monopoly, 5 February.

Knapp, K. and Meierkord, C. (eds.) (2002) *Lingua Franca Communication*. Frankfurt: Peter Lang.

Laitin, D. and Reich, R. (2003) A Liberal Democratic Approach to Linguistic Justice, in W. Kymlicka and A. Patten (eds.) *Language Rights and Political Theory*. Oxford: Oxford University Press, pp. 80–104.

May, S. (2001) *Language and Minority Rights: Ethnicity, Nationalism and the Politics of Language*. London: Pearson Education.

May, S. (2003) Misconceiving Minority Language Rights: Implications for Political Theory, in W. Kymlicka and A. Patten (eds.), *Language Rights and Political Theory*. Oxford: Oxford University Press, pp. 123–52.

Mayer T. (1993) *Truth versus Precision in Economics*. Aldershot: Edward Elgar.

Mueller, D. (2003) *Public Choice III*. Cambridge: Cambridge University Press.

Oaxaca, R. (1973) Male–Female Wage Differentials in Urban Labor Markets, *International Economic Review*, 14: 693–709.

Perens, B. (2005) The Emerging Economic Paradigm of Open Source. http://perens.com/Articles/Economic.html. Accessed 10 November 2006.

Phillipson, R. (2003) *English-Only Europe?* London: Routledge.

Piron, C. (1994) *Le défi des langues. Du gâchis au bon sens*. Paris: L'Harmattan.

Pool, J. (1991a) The Official Languages of the European Communities. Unpublished manuscript (Center for the Humanities, University of Washington: Seattle).

Pool, J. (1991b) The Official Language Problem, *American Political Science Review*, 85: 495–514.

Pool, J. (1996) Optimal Language Regimes for the European Union, *International Journal of the Sociology of Language*, 121: 159–79.

Raffestin, C. (1980) *Pour une géographie du pouvoir*. Paris: LITEC.

Rullani, F. (2006) Dragging Developers towards the Core. How the Free/Libre/OpenSource Software Community Enhances Developers' Contribution, in Free/Open source research community database, http://opensource.mit.edu.

Stiglitz, J. (1998) *Economics of the Public Sector*. New York: Norton.

Selten, R. and Pool, J. (1997) Is it Worth it to Learn Esperanto? Introduction to Game Theory', in R. Selten (ed.), *The Costs of European Linguistic non-Communication*. Rome: Esperanto Radikala Asocio, pp. 114–49.

Souphavanh, A. and Karoonboonyanan, T. (2005) *Free/Open Source Software: Localization*. New Dehli: Elsevier.

Vaillancourt, F. (1985a) Les écrits en économie de la langue: brève revue et introduction au recueil, in F. Vaillancourt (ed.) *Économie et langue*. Québec: Conseil de la langue française, pp. 13–25.

Vaillancourt, F. (1985b) Le choix de la langue de consommation, in F. Vaillancourt (ed.) *Économie et langue*. Québec: Conseil de la langue française, pp. 209–20.

van Parijs, P. (2002) Linguistic Justice, *Politics, Philosophy and Economics*, 1 : 59–74.

van Parijs, P. (2004) Europe's Linguistic Challenge, *Archives européennes de sociologie*, XLV(1): 113–54.

Verprat, M. (n.d.) *Logiciels libres: modéle technico-économique et coût total de production*. www.eikonex.net/IMG/pdf/TCO-OSS.pdf. Accessed 9 February 2006.

Webb Collins, R. (2002) Software Localization for Internet Software: Issues and Methods, *IEEE Software*, 19(2): 74–80.

Zajac, E. (1995) *Political Economy of Fairness*. Cambridge, MA: MIT Press.

10

How Efficient is the Patent System? A General Appraisal and an Application to the Pharmaceutical Sector

Paul Belleflamme

Introduction

In recent years, the legal protection of intellectual property through patents has faced substantial criticism from several quarters. Patents have been questioned regarding the *material scope of protection* (for example, the European debate about software patentability, opposing commercial software vendors and open-source advocates); the *requirements for protection* (patent offices, which are largely understaffed and overworked, are accused of granting an increasing number of 'bogus' patents, which tend to impede innovation rather than to foster it); or the *incentives for protection* (in complex industries firms accumulate patents for purely defensive reasons and not as a way to secure returns on their inventions). Criticisms become even harsher when it comes to pharmaceutical patents, which are accused of restricting access to essential drugs in both developed and developing countries, and for allowing pharmaceutical firms to make 'outrageous' profits.

Given the heat that the patent-based system has been feeling lately, a sound and rigorous economic analysis of the efficiency of this institution appears to be more necessary than ever. The objective of this chapter is to contribute to such an analysis. To this end, we start by recalling the basic economic rationale for the protection of intellectual property; we also contrast legal protection through patents with other public interventions the aim of which is to promote innovation. Then, we proceed to a review of different strands of the economic literature, both theoretical and empirical, in order to assess the efficiency of patents in general. Finally, we reconsider the theoretical arguments and empirical findings of the previous two sections in the light of the peculiarities of the pharmaceutical sector. This allows us to discuss the pros and cons of pharmaceutical patents, as well as alternative solutions put forward to promote the development of drugs for neglected diseases and to facilitate access to these drugs.

Two comments are in order before we start. First, it must be stressed that our arguments rely on partial equilibrium analyses; that is, the merits of various policy interventions are examined only in the markets that are directly affected, ignoring any effects on other industries in the economy. We use producer and consumer surplus to measure the welfare effects on participants in the relevant market. Second, our analysis is 'positive' in that we look for the most efficient policy choices. In that sense we are not primarily concerned with issues pertaining to income distribution (in fact, our partial equilibrium arguments are valid whatever the initial distribution of income). These issues are commonly thought of as normative and economists usually leave them to policy-makers, government officials or philosophers to determine. However, the positive analysis remains useful to shed light on the normative questions and to indicate the ins and outs of the policy alternatives. Hence, we will take every opportunity to complement our efficiency analysis by raising important issues pertaining to justice and income distribution.

The economics of innovation: a brief reminder

What do inventions, business methods, industrial processes, novels, songs, paintings, etc. have in common? They all result from the production of *information* (or *knowledge*). The problem with activities generating information or knowledge is that they suffer from the three generic sources of market failure: indivisibility, uncertainty and externalities. First, *indivisibilities* are present because the creation of new knowledge and new information involves large, fixed, set-up costs, requires the division of highly specialised labour and is therefore prone to economies of scale. Second, investments in research and development (R&D) involve two types of *uncertainty*: in addition to technological uncertainty (how to make new things and how to make them work), there is commercial uncertainty (how to make new things that will be adopted by the consumers); moral hazard problems ensue as it is generally impossible to attribute the failure of a project to a lack of effort or simply to bad luck.

Finally, because information and knowledge are inherently public goods, their producers generate many *externalities*. Public goods are characterised by *non-rivalness* in consumption: the consumption of the good by one person does not prevent (rival) its consumption by another person; there is thus the possibility of collective consumption. Another way to define non-rivalness is to say that a good is non-rival if, for any given level of production, the marginal cost of providing it to an additional consumer is zero. This is clearly the case for knowledge and information. Think of a new idea or of a song performed in public. Public goods are said to be 'pure' when they are also *non-excludable*, in the sense that one person cannot exclude another person from consuming that good. Whereas non-rivalness is an attribute of the good itself, excludability depends, at least in part, on the technology available for exclusion and the institutional (legal) framework that permits or facilitates such technically feasible exclusion.[1]

The three sources of market failure associated with investments in information production generate the problem of *appropriability*, which sets them apart from other investments made by firms or individuals. That is, innovators and creators face a serious risk of appropriating only incompletely the returns from their activities. As a result, there is a general presumption that markets provide too few incentives to introduce new innovations and that the production of information may well be insufficient from a social point of view. Economists therefore agree that governments ought to intervene to provide the right incentives to create and innovate.

In short, the basic problem of innovation can be seen as an incentive problem within the relationship between one principal (society) and one agent (potential innovator) in order to produce a public good (knowledge). Society will find it optimal to induce innovation when the social expected value exceeds the social expected cost. If so, the objective is to create sufficient incentives for the innovator so that the private expected compensation exceeds the private expected costs.

There are several ways to close the gap that the appropriability problem opens between social and private rates of return from innovation. The main public responses consist either in restricting the exploitation of knowledge (by instituting *intellectual property* (IP) and by protecting it, or by allowing putative competitors to form cooperative R&D ventures), or in raising the expected returns of new knowledge by lowering its production cost (through subsidisation of research and patronage of the arts). We focus here on the legal protection of intellectual property, though we shall say something about the costs and benefits of subsidisation as well.

The main objective of *IP law* is to promote innovation and aesthetic creativity. To solve the appropriability problem, IP law intends to make knowledge excludable by legal means. That is, it grants exclusive use of the protected knowledge or creative work to the creator. IP law thereby provides creators with the necessary incentives to produce new knowledge and solves the *underproduction* problem that would have resulted from the non-excludability of knowledge. However, by granting exclusive (i.e. monopoly) rights to the creator, IP law creates an *underutilisation* problem. Indeed, as the marginal cost of production is zero, any positive price creates a welfare-reducing rationing.

In order to strike a balance between these two conflicting problems, IP law grants exclusive rights only for a limited period of time and restricts the scope of exclusion. That is, IP law addresses the two problems sequentially. First, legal protection makes the good excludable: to enjoy the services, users have to pay royalties to the producer. Second, once the protection lapses, the good passes into the public domain, which means that all users may access it free of charge (i.e. at marginal cost). In other words, IP law attempts to find the best possible compromise between *dynamic efficiency considerations* (how to provide the right *incentives* to create and innovate) and *static efficiency considerations* (how to promote the *diffusion* and *use* of the results of creation and innovation).

Note that dynamic efficiency calls for the broadest and longest possible protection (to maximise the flow of new knowledge creation), whereas static efficiency calls for the absence of protection (to avoid the deadweight loss of monopoly). Therefore, the balance struck by IP law is necessarily imperfect as it is impossible to achieve both objectives simultaneously. It also raises issues in terms of justice, as it is the current consumers who finance the innovator's efforts (by paying the monopoly price), to the benefit of future consumers (who will enjoy the innovation at marginal cost).

It follows that when it comes to design the appropriate way to protect IP, the complexity is of a quantitative rather than qualitative nature: what are the level and the structure of the rent that should be left to the innovator? As we shall argue below when applying these principles to the pharmaceutical sector, designing the best incentive system for innovation becomes even more complicated when other public policy objectives, such as public health and international trade facilitation, are present. Beyond the economic issue, major issues regarding justice are also present. For instance, as we shall see, a proposed solution for the efficient provision of essential drugs in developing country is differential pricing, which amounts to setting high prices for drugs in developed countries and low prices in developing countries (and preventing parallel imports). In terms of policy objectives, this solution gives an implicit priority to public health and innovation policy over trade facilitation. More importantly, in terms of income distribution, this solution entails that consumers in developed countries subsidise consumers in developing countries (since R&D is financed through the high prices paid in the developed countries). Clearly, this type of subsidisation, which seems acceptable from a Rawlsian perspective, might be opposed in developed countries. For instance, the Pharmaceutical Research and Manufacturers Association of America argues that American consumers are unfairly bearing the burden of financing research for the rest of the world.

It is therefore important to consider alternative public intervention aimed at fostering innovation. The main alternative to IP rights consists for governments in subsidising research: they pay directly for innovations, which then pass immediately into the public domain. With respect to IP protection, this subsidisation method enhances static efficiency: as there is no need to grant exclusive rights to the innovator, the innovation is in free access and no deadweight loss ensues. However, to fund R&D, governments have to raise taxes, and this introduces distortions elsewhere in the economy and reduces static efficiency (in contrast, the patent system assigns costs to users rather than to taxpayers). Moreover, there is no guarantee that subsidies achieve dynamic efficiency. Indeed, the uncertainty surrounding the social value of an innovation might make the government over- or underestimate the amount of subsidy and, thereby, to give too much or too little incentive (in contrast, the patent system can be implemented without requiring sensible economic information that is only privately known).[2]

We now assess the efficiency of the patent system, first in general and then by focusing on the pharmaceutical sector.

The efficiency of patents in general

Although there is a wide agreement about the theoretical arguments underlying the existence of the patent regime, and about the legal protection of IP in general, there is much less consensus about how effective this institution is in practice. More than half a century ago, Penrose (1951) declared: 'If national patent laws did not exist, it would be difficult to make a conclusive case for introducing them; but the fact that they do exist shifts the burden of proof and it is equally difficult to make a really conclusive case for abolishing them.' Even though a whole new body of empirical and theoretical knowledge has emerged since then, we are still unable to revise Penrose's view. We are, however, able to refine the evaluation, as recent economic analysis has brought to light previously unsuspected costs and benefits of the patent system.

The first natural way to assess the efficiency of the patent system is to survey innovators and ask them directly whether they see patents as important. Several empirical studies have attempted to assess the relative attractiveness of the different means innovators have at their disposal to protect their inventions. In his review, Caillaud (2003) stresses that innovating firms consider trade secrets (for process innovations) and business strategies based on early-mover advantage (for product innovations) as the main means of getting returns on R&D investments and to appropriate the rents stemming from innovation. Similarly, Anand and Galetovic (2004) report survey results[3] showing that managers claim that 'lead time, learning curves, and sales or service efforts are substantially more effective in protecting IP than patents are'.

It appears thus that the appropriability problem is often better addressed through private responses (e.g. secrecy) than through public responses (e.g. patents). In particular, except for the chemical and pharmaceutical sectors (which we discuss in the next section), patent protection is generally deemed to be of little efficiency, especially for process innovations. Caillaud (2003) advances several explanations. Firms consider that: a patent can easily be 'invented around' by imitators; that a patent is costly to obtain and to enforce; and that they suffer from disclosing the information, as required by the patent.

In the light of these observations, one is tempted to ask why firms in most sectors bother to seek patent protection for their inventions. Several reasons can be advanced:[4]

(i) patents are relatively inexpensive to register (although they are generally costly to defend);
(ii) patents can serve to measure the output of a firm's R&D division and, thereby, to structure compensation and incentive schemes;
(iii) venture capitalists often demand that firms patent technology, both to block rivals and to have assets to sell in case the firm flounders;
(iv) patents can be used as a 'trading device'. The latter reason is confirmed by a number of surveys, which show that it is essentially large firms that resort to patent protection, especially in complex industries (e.g. electronics and software) where innovations overlap and where patents are then used as a 'currency' in the bargaining

process among firms (to negotiate cross-licensing agreements, for instance; we return to this argument below).

Although the previous surveys offer important elements in answer to our question, their scope remains limited. It is therefore necessary to adopt a broader perspective and examine the macroeconomic facts. The observation of the evolution of IP protection, R&D and innovation over the last three decades reveals the emergence of three basic trends: (i) IP protection has been generally strengthened and broadened; (ii) the number of patents have soared; and (iii) innovation has increased. Let us detail these in turn.

First, on the initiative of the US and Europe, *IP protection has been strengthened, broadened and harmonised internationally*. In terms of *strengthening*, in the early 1980s, legal and procedural reforms in the US provided greater protection to holders of existing patents;[5] in Europe, the European Patent Office (EPO) granted the first European patents in 1978, but a genuine European patent (superseding national patents) is still under debate. Regarding *broadening* IP, new categories of inventions have been protected, either through an extension of patent protection (software, business methods, genetic inventions) or through the creation of *sui generis* rights (e.g. for semiconductors, databases).[6] Finally, the Trade-Related Aspects of Intellectual Property Rights (TRIPS) Agreement of 1994, negotiated within the framework of the World Trade Organisation, represents a major advance step towards the *harmonisation* of IP laws. It includes a general definition of patents, which adopts US criteria, and thereby broadens the scope of patentable inventions internationally; furthermore, the US and the European Union have concluded numerous bilateral agreements with their trading partners in order to coerce them to significantly strengthen their own IP rights regimes.

Second, *the number of patent applications and grants has risen exponentially*. In the US, it more than tripled between 1980 and 2001 (it was practically stable over the previous two decades). A comparable trend is observed for European countries (although there it began later). Although nearly all technology fields experienced growth in patenting, two technology fields contributed substantially to the overall surge: biotechnology and information and communication technologies.[7]

Third, *innovation has also expanded rapidly*. An important indicator is the increase in R&D spending: in the US, R&D spending (in real terms) multiplied by 2.5 between 1971 and 2001;[8] also, as reported by the National Science Foundation, the investment in R&D by American firms employing fewer than 5,000 people more than doubled between 1987 and 1997. It must be noted, however, that R&D spending is a measure of inventive *inputs* (patents are measures of inventive *outputs*) and that some of these inputs might be wasted or never lead to a new marketable product or process. Nevertheless, the increase in R&D investment has most likely led to the discovery and commercial exploitation of a greater number of new technological leads.

This huge increase in patent counts seems to contradict what innovators claim about the relative unimportance of patents to protect their IP. The term 'patent paradox' has been coined to describe this contradictory behaviour of managers who declare that patents offer weak protection, but who nevertheless file an increasing number of them (this behaviour has been systematically documented, for instance, in the semiconductor industry).[9] The *patent portfolio theory* gives us a convincing explanation. The main idea is that, in many industries, the true value of patents lies not in their individual worth, but in their aggregation into a collection of related patents. In other words, the more patents the merrier, because patents are increasingly used as a 'trading device' or 'bargaining chip'. This trend is confirmed by a number of surveys, which reveal that it is essentially large firms that resort to patent protection, especially in complex industries (biotechnology, IT, telecommunications, electronics and software).[10]

It is because these complex industries rely heavily on *cumulative innovations* that firms have an incentive to build up patent portfolios. There are two types of cumulativeness. On the one hand, in the case of *sequential innovations*, a particular innovation leads to many second-generation innovations.[11] The main problem with sequential innovations is that a patent on the first-generation innovation confers on the patentee a hold-up right over subsequent innovations. On the other hand, in the case of *complementary innovations*, a second-generation product requires the input of a number of different first-generation innovations.[12] Here, the main problem is that the prices are higher if they are set by independent patentees rather than jointly. Indeed, if innovator A reduces the price of licence A, then the demand for licence B increases (since the two licences can only be used in combination), but this benefit is not appropriated by innovator A. Hence, both innovators have insufficient incentives to cut their prices. Moreover, the need to negotiate licences separately with the two patentees adds to transaction costs. This problem is referred to as the 'Tragedy of the Anticommons'.[13] More generally, it describes the fact that a scarce resource is prone to under-use when multiple owners each have a right to exclude others from this resource and no one has an effective privilege of use. It is the counterpart of the well-known 'Tragedy of the Commons', according to which a resource is prone to overuse when too many owners each have a privilege to use that resource and no one has a right to exclude another (as is the case with fish stocks, for example).[14]

The previous two problems are worst in industries where hundreds if not thousands of patents can potentially be applied to a given product. Shapiro (2001) describes this dense web of overlapping IP rights as a 'patent thicket', through which firms have to hack in order to bring a new product or technology to market.

Whatever the type of cumulativeness, the trade of patent rights among firms might alleviate the problems: *ex ante* licensing addresses the hold-up problem, while cross-licensing and patent pools can solve the Tragedy of the Anticommons. These private arrangements are also useful for addressing the increasing demand for interoperability and common standards that is expressed in these sectors.[15] However, this private response might be excessive. Many firms are acquiring large numbers of patents for purely defensive reasons (i.e. to keep the threats stemming from other firms' patents at bay). The global situation looks thus like a prisoner's dilemma, where the equilibrium is such that all firms file a large number of patents (following a 'balance of power' argument), but would be better off if they could commit to fewer patents.

The three basic trends observed over the last three decades raise another important question: does the strengthening of IP protection explain the huge increase in patent counts, and does this higher patenting activity explain in turn the increase in innovation? In other words, *do stronger patents induce more innovation*? The US position on IP rights (and, to a large extent, the European position as well) assumes that the answer to this is yes: it is believed that the additional innovation induced by stronger patent systems is substantial and that strengthening IP rights at home and abroad is to the good.

However, the empirical evidence to support these beliefs ranges from sketchy to nonexistent. A number of empirical studies suggest that the responsiveness to changes in patent scope is limited: stronger patents do not seem to induce more innovative effort. Sakakibara and Branstetter (2001) analysed the response to the 1988 Japanese patent reforms, which expanded the scope of the patent system there. They found no evidence of a statistically or economically significant increase in either R&D spending or innovative output that could plausibly be attributed to the reforms. Similarly, Lerner (2002) analysed the impact of major patent policy shifts in 60 nations over the past 150 years which augmented the amount of patent protection provided. An examination of 177 policy changes reveals that strengthening patent protection appears to have few positive effects on patent applications by entities in the country undertaking the policy change. Finally, Gallini (2002) surveyed recent theoretical and empirical research and concluded that the case for stronger patents as a spur to innovation is weak; however, she qualifies this conclusion by noting that evidence that stronger patents encourage disclosure and technology transfer is persuasive.

Other studies focus on understanding the impacts of isolated patent policy reforms: Kortum and Lerner (1998) and Hall and Ziedonis (2001) examined the effects of the establishment of the Court of Appeals for the Federal Circuit in the United States, Lanjouw (1998) and Scherer and Weisburst (1995) analysed how the strengthening of patent protection on pharmaceuticals affected, respectively, India and Italy. In general, these studies conclude that enhancing patent protection does not significantly spur on innovative behaviour.

Finally, empirical studies reveal that the increase in patents (innovative output) goes along with an increase in spending on R&D (innovative input). As a rule of thumb, it is often stated that technological firms file on average two patents for every $1 million they spend on R&D. Yet, in IT, the growth in the number of patents exceeds the increase in R&D expenditure, which is indicative of the patent paradox described above.[16]

The efficiency of pharmaceuticals patents

In this section, we address the topical and heavily debated question of the suitable intellectual property protection for drugs. To this end, we first review the previous theoretical arguments and empirical findings in the light of the peculiarities of the pharmaceutical sector. Our main conclusion is that the tension between dynamic and static efficiency considerations is amplified in this sector. We then examine alternatives to the patent-based system.

Let us first return to the economic analysis we developed above. The first thing to note is that the three market failures we identified are particularly acute in the pharmaceutical sector: large indivisibilities result from huge R&D fixed costs;[17] the length of the R&D process[18] and the need to get public approval for new drugs cause a lot of uncertainty;[19] finally, because knowledge is more science-based and more codified in the pharmaceutical sector than in any other sector, imitation costs are low and hence externalities (i.e. knowledge spillovers) are important. It must be added that successful pharmaceutical innovations create other powerful consumption externalities as they improve *public health*.[20] For all theses reasons, the discrepancy between social and private returns to innovation is particularly wide in the case of pharmaceuticals, and there is thus a clear need for public intervention: absent appropriate intervention, the level of pharmaceutical innovation would undoubtedly be insufficient from a social point of view.

The next question that arises is whether the patent-based system constitutes the appropriate public intervention for the pharmaceutical sector. Some first elements of an answer come from a detailed examination of the empirical findings broadly described in the previous section. Empirical studies indicate two reasons for concluding that *the patent system is relatively more efficient in the pharmaceutical sector than in other industrial sectors*. First, it appears that pharmaceutical companies rely heavily on patents to appropriate the returns from their inventions.[21] Second, macroeconomic analyses show that the pharmaceutical sector plays a leading role when looking at the patent explosion (especially in the US).[22] Note that patents are relatively efficient in the pharmaceutical sector despite the fact that the *effective patent life* (i.e. the patent time remaining at the product launch) is significantly reduced for drugs. Indeed, patents in pharmaceuticals are typically applied for early in the development process; because of the length of the regulatory approval process, marketing exclusivity occurs only after a number of years. In consequence, the US, Europe and Japan have enacted patent term restoration laws.[23] According to estimates in the US, these laws have increased the effective exclusivity period from eight to eleven years.[24]

We can conclude from this that granting patents (and extending their effective life) appropriately contributes to alleviating the underproduction problem and thereby enhances dynamic efficiency. However, the static inefficiency resulting from high monopoly prices is worse for pharmaceuticals than for most other products. We argued that static efficiency calls in general for marginal cost pricing (i.e. a price close to zero in the case of new knowledge, meaning universal access). When it comes to pharmaceuticals, static efficiency could even call for prices *below* marginal cost, because these products generate positive consumption externalities in terms of improved public health. To put it bluntly, the abstract 'deadweight loss of monopoly' takes a much more concrete and tragic form here, which can be measured, following the World Health Organisation, in *disability-adjusted life years (DALYs)* lost.[25]

It, therefore, becomes apparent why, in many developed countries, the prices of drugs are controlled and/or expenditures for drugs are covered by public or private insurance. While such interventions alleviate the static inefficiency of patents, they also distort market incentives, as potential demand levels condition research efforts. The latter consideration stresses another shortcoming of the patent-based system: as R&D priorities are decided on the basis of potential demand levels, *the system provides few incentives to develop products with relatively small economic markets*. What makes the matter worse is that those products are generally of great social need. As Ridley et al. (2006) explain it, the

> [t]hree diseases with the greatest burden are HIV/AIDS, malaria, and tuberculosis. Manufacturers do invest in R&D for HIV/AIDS, because there is a market in both developed and developing countries for these therapies. There is less incentive to invest in R&D for malaria, because more than 99 percent of disability-adjusted life years (DALYs) lost to malaria are in developing countries.

Note that the ability to pay for drugs is far from being the only condition for viable economic markets to exist: pharmaceutical markets also require 'a system of distribution, roads for efficient transportation, warehouse facilities to store inventory and trained personnel to dispense the medication' (Hammer, 2002). In many developing countries, especially in rural areas, these infrastructures are under-developed or simply nonexistent.

Although a similar problem occurs in developed countries for paediatric illnesses, preventive interventions and relatively rare diseases, we devote the rest of this section to the lack of incentives for products addressing diseases endemic in developing countries. This issue has indeed been at the centre of a widespread and bitter debate for the past several years. This debate finds its sources in the TRIPS Agreement, which requires that WTO members comply with minimum standards for IP protection. Although developing countries accepted TRIPS (mainly in return for concessions made by developed countries that would expand the developing countries' exports of agriculture and textile products), they remained fearful that patents would put drugs beyond the reach of the poor. To mitigate this risk, the 2001 Doha and 2003 Cancun declarations of the WTO affirmed the right of nations to use the exceptions of TRIPS, such as compulsory licensing and parallel imports, to meet public health concerns.[26] However, as Lanjouw (2003) rightly notes,

> [a]lthough the fight over TRIPS is proving extremely persistent and difficult to settle, it does not stem from fundamentally conflicting goals. The pharmaceutical industry wants above all to protect its major markets in the developed countries. Very secondarily it would like to see effective protection evolve in poorer countries as they grow into more attractive markets. Making profit in the poorest countries is not an industry objective. The development community and NGO activists, on the other hand, are primarily concerned with keeping prices down in the poorest countries. In substance these are not opposing objectives.

Yet, this does not mean that solutions are easy to find. As we now show, the main solutions that have been proposed may correct some of the problems of the patent-based system, but they often create problems of their own.

A first solution that is regularly put forward is *differential pricing* (which economists identify as [third-degree] price discrimination). It simply amounts to having pharmaceutical firms set different prices for the same drugs in different markets – high prices in developed countries and low prices in developing countries. Economic theory establishes the conditions under which third-degree price discrimination increases not only consumers' welfare but also firms' profits. Scherer and Watal (2002) argue that these conditions are likely to be met in the case of pharmaceuticals. However, Hammer (2002) identifies a number of complicated economic, legal and political challenges that constructing an effective regime of price discrimination raises. Among these let us just mention the necessity of preventing *arbitrage*, i.e. the activity by which the product is bought in the low-priced market and resold in the high-priced market.[27] Physical arbitrage of this sort can be prevented through national laws regulating safety and efficacy by differentiating products in terms of production, composition or packaging, and by monitoring the circulation of products (via radio-labelling or other new technology).[28]

Yet, as Hammer (2002) points out, there are also threats of informational and political arbitrage. Informational arbitrage refers to the following situation: by setting low prices in developing countries, pharmaceutical firms would reveal sensitive information about their cost structure, which large powerful purchasers in developed countries could use to obtain price concessions in negotiations. Political arbitrage follows from the reference pricing policies that an increasing number of countries employ: by forcing pharmaceutical firms to give them the lowest price they offer anywhere in the world, these policies may deter a price discount in the first place.

Other proposed solutions tend to substitute *reward mechanisms* for the patent-based system. For instance, 'a buy-out pricing system gives a cash bonus of public money to the pharmaceutical firm for the estimated profits from monopoly prices. The pharmaceutical firm would then make the drugs available to anyone in need at the marginal cost of production' (Barton and Emanuel, 2005). Alternatively, governments can purchase the pharmaceutical products and cover the R&D costs. As we indicated above, the main difficulty facing such reward methods comes from the estimation of the social value of innovation: What are the R&D costs? What is the patent's value? Which drugs should be developed? An additional limitation underlined by Barton and Emanuel (2005) is that the reduction in the number of decision-makers 'may lead to the ignoring of new research and product directions and to the politicisation of decisions. Without market constraints this may also foster inefficient R&D'.

A middle way between the property rights and rewards systems is to twist the incentives associated with patents by making private returns come closer to social returns. One such solution is the *Disease Burden Incentive System* proposed by Barton and Emanuel. This approach is 'for the government to pay for drug development, with the price reflecting the social value of its contribution to reducing global disease burden'. There are two main advantages to this method: (i) because incentives are based on disease burden rather than on market appeal, R&D efforts are shifted from the concerns of the rich to real health improvements; and (ii) this method lets pharmaceutical firms choose the best way to address a disease (they could prefer to improve sanitation rather than to develop drugs and still qualify for the reward). However, this method shares with the buy-out and government procurement systems the same problems in estimating the appropriate monetary rewards.

In the same vein, various mechanisms are proposed to reward research output within the patent-based system so as to induce pharmaceutical firms to develop therapies for neglected diseases. Kettler (2000) proposes the *transferable patent exclusivity right* system, by which a developer that licenses a product for a neglected disease would receive additional patent time for a different product, and this right could be sold on. Similarly, Ridley et al. (2006) propose a *priority review voucher*, which would be awarded to developers of improved treatments for neglected diseases, could be transferred and would entitle the bearer to priority review by the regulatory authorities for another drug. The authors estimate that priority review by the American Food and Drug Administration (FDA) 'would be worth more than $300 million for a potential blockbuster drug, because it would shorten the time the FDA takes to analyze data from an average eighteen months to about six months'. This solution would have the twofold benefit of speeding up access to blockbuster drugs in developed countries and cures for infectious diseases in developing countries.

Conclusion

We have attempted to shed light on a debate that has become quite passionate over the last few years: the efficiency of the patent-based system for the promotion of innovation. After presenting the basic economic arguments underlying the protection of intellectual property, we have extracted from the economic literature important theoretical and empirical elements allowing us to understand what it takes for patents to be socially useful and privately profitable. Finally, we have repeated the previous analysis for the special case of the pharmaceutical sector. We have argued that designing the optimal regime for the protection of intellectual property is even more complicated in this sector, because of the particularly acute tension between dynamic and static efficiency considerations, and because of the potential conflict with another, equally fundamental, policy objective, namely public health. In this light, we have compared the respective merits of various alternatives to and adjustments of the patent-based system. Our conclusion is that a middle way should be privileged, combining the positive aspects of the patent- and subsidy-based approaches, while minimising their negative aspects. The various solutions described point in that direction.

Naturally, the analysis carried out here is far from complete. We have simply proposed a number of stepping-stones in order to organise our thoughts about a complex and crucial topic. To further feed the reflection, one should discuss the relevance of public–private partnership (PPP) schemes for the fight against endemic diseases. The important contributions made by foundations like those set up by Bill and Melinda Gates and Bill Clinton (the two 'Billanthrops', as they have been nicknamed in the press)[29] to the fight against HIV/AIDS and other diseases come to mind. With the addition of Warren Buffet's donation, the Bill and Melinda Gates Foundation now equals the size of multinational companies such as Disney, Dell or Honda. Yet, whatever the sources of funding, private foundations, pharmaceutical firms and public authorities all face the same pressing question: how much should be spent in preventing and treating today's diseases, and how much should be kept to finance R&D for prevention and treatment tomorrow?

Notes

1. To understand this difference, consider TV services in most countries. A television signal is clearly non-rival since, once it is broadcast, the marginal cost of making the broadcast available to another user is zero. In order to watch terrestrial TV, all you need is a TV receiving equipment. Yet, to use such equipment, you may be required by law to pay a licence fee: those who fail to pay are legally – but not technologically – excluded from watching terrestrial broadcasts. On the other hand, cable TV broadcasts are made exclusive by encrypting the signal and charging for the device that decodes it. A similar distinction holds for knowledge: as we explain below, most countries have adopted laws instituting intellectual property and 'protecting' it; that is, IP laws allow producers of information and knowledge to prevent non-payers from using it.
2. For a thorough analysis of the relative merits of IP rights compared to a reward system, see Shavell and van Ypersele (2001).
3. Six hundred managers were surveyed by economists at Carnegie Mellon and Yale.
4. See Geroski (1995).
5. For instance, the Patent and Trademark (Bayh–Dole) Act 1980 allows universities and other non-profit organisations to patent discoveries made in their laboratories. Also, the Court of Appeals for the Federal Circuit was established in 1982 to harmonise patent law nationwide; this had the effect of strengthening patent protection.
6. See Lévêque and Ménière (2004, pp. 47–8) for a comparative analysis of US and European stances on the patentability of these inventions.
7. According to the OECD (2004), 'more than 109 609 patent applications were filed at the European Patent Office (EPO), and 179 658 patents granted by the US Patent and Trademark Office (USPTO) in 2000, compared with 60 104 and 107 039, respectively, in 1991.... Between 1991 and 2000, biotechnology and ICT patent applications to the European Patent Office (EPO) increased by 10.9% and 9.5% respectively, compared to 6.9% for all EPO patent applications.'
8. Measured in 1996 dollars, R&D spending was just below $100,000m in 1971 and just above $250,000m in 2001 (see Scotchmer, 2005, p. 272) quoting data from the National Science Board).
9. Hall and Ziedonis (2001) interviewed industry representatives and observed (in the period 1979–95) that (i) firms did not rely heavily on patents to appropriate returns to R&D, but (ii) their propensity to patent rose dramatically since the mid-1980s.
10. A survey published in *The Economist* (20 October 2005) reported the following: IBM now earns over $1 billion annually from its IP portfolio; HP's revenue from licensing has quadrupled in less than three years, to over $200 million this year; Microsoft is on course to file 3,000 patents this year, when in 1990 it received a mere five; 54 per cent of companies saw growth in

licensing of 10–50 per cent between 2000 and 2002; almost 75 per cent of executives say they expect to buy as well as sell more licences over the next two to five years, and 43 per cent expect a dramatic increase in their licensing revenue (according to a survey by McKinsey).

11. For instance, the invention of the laser led to surgical applications, spectroscopy, etc.
12. Think of firms in the electronic industry (e.g. trying to produce new peripherals to be coupled with personal computers or video game consoles) or in the biotech industry (e.g. combining patented genes to bioengineer a new crop seed).
13. See Heller and Eisenberg (1998) for more.
14. See Hardin (1968) for more. Note that Aristotle, in his comments on Plato's *Republic*, stated this theory: 'That which is common to the greatest number has the least care bestowed upon it'.
15. A recent example of a patent pool is the MPEG-2 video compression technology. Nine companies have pooled their patents to permit one-stop shopping for makers of televisions, digital video disks and players, and telecommunications equipment as well as cable, satellite and broadcast television services. Shapiro (2001) reports that broad cross-licences are the norm in markets for the design and manufacture of microprocessors.
16. This finding could be attributed to an excessive generosity by patent offices and courts towards patent filers and owners. Such an attitude can indeed encourage firms to seek IP rights for the economic power they confer, independently of their R&D efforts.
17. Grabowski (2004) reports that pharmaceutical R&D costs have been growing significantly: 'The average R&D cost of a new drug introduction for 1990s approvals is $US802 million, compared with $US316 million for the 1980s and $US138 million for the 1970s. These costs are measured in year 2000 dollars and include the costs of failed candidates and pre-clinical expenditures on discovery and lead generation.' However, Barton and Emanuel (2005) note that '[i]n some cases, significant portions of these costs, particularly those incurred early in the development process, are covered through government-supported research.'
18. According to Ceccagnoli et al. (2005), 'in Chemical and Pharmaceutical technologies only 36% of the patents involve less up to 6 man-months for the invention process and 9.63% of patents involve more than 48 months (the overall EU6 shares are respectively 52.25% and 5.40%). By contrast, in Electrical Engineering and Mechanical Engineering the share of patents requiring less than 6 months is about 60% while the share of 36 patents requiring more than 48 months are respectively 3.70% and 3.26%.'
19. Of 10,000 pharmaceutical products patented, only ten are marketed (OECD, 2000).
20. Public health is clearly a public good as it is both non-excludable (everyone benefits from the eradication of diseases) and non-rival (no one diminishes that good when benefiting from it).
21. Although industrial surveys show that patents are seen, on average, as a secondary or complementary instrument for protecting IP, Levin et al. (1987) and Cohen et al. (2000) show that patents appear to be relatively more effective in industries such as medical equipment and drugs. Other studies

support this finding. Arora et al. (2003) find that the additional payoff obtained from a patented invention relative to an unpatented invention is positive only in a few manufacturing industries, which are those where inventors patent most: drugs, biotech, medical instruments, machinery, computers and industrial chemicals. Similarly, Mansfield (1986) found that the fraction of inventions US manufacturing firms would not have developed in the absence of patents between 1981 and 1983 is the highest (60 per cent) for pharmaceuticals (compared to less than 10 per cent for firms in the majority of other sectors).

22. However, Barton and Emanuel (2005) stress that 'at least since the mid-1990s, there has been a decrease in the number of fundamentally new products, i.e., "new molecular entities"'. It is therefore not clear whether the increase in patenting activity eventually leads to more socially useful innovation.
23. See Grabowski (2002) for more.
24. See Barton and Emanuel (2005).
25. 'DALYs for a disease are the sum of the years of life lost due to premature mortality in the population and the years lost due to disability for incident cases of the health condition. The DALY is a health gap measure that extends the concept of potential years of life lost due to premature death to include equivalent years of 'healthy' life lost in states of less than full health, broadly termed disability. One DALY represents the loss of one year of equivalent full health' (WHO, www.who.int/healthinfo/boddaly/en/index.html).
26. For critical analyses of the effects of TRIPS on access to essential drugs, see, e.g., Lanjouw (1998) and Barton (2004).
27. Kaisernetwork.org reported in 2003 one incident of smuggling $18 million worth of antiretroviral agents from Senegal into Europe (quoted by Barton and Emanuel, 2005).
28. However, as Sykes (2002) notes, to determine whether a patent holder has a legal right to require nations in which it holds a valid patent to prevent parallel imports, the unsettled 'exhaustion' issue (i.e., does the initial sale by a right holder in some country 'exhausts' its rights in other countries?) should first be resolved by the WTO.
29. Billanthropy. *The Economist*, 29 June 2006.

References

Anand, B. and Galetovic, A. (2004) How Market Smarts Can Protect Property Rights, *Harvard Business Review*, December: 73–9.

Arora, A., Ceccagnoli, M. and Cohen, W. C. (2003) R&D and the Patent Premium. NBER Working Paper 9431.

Barton, J. H. (2004) TRIPS and the Global Pharmaceutical Market, *Health Affairs*, 23: 146–54.

Barton, J. H. and Emanuel, E. J. (2005) The Patents-Based Pharmaceutical Development Process: Rationale, Problems, and Potential Reforms, *Journal of the American Medical Association*, 294: 2075–82.

Caillaud, B. (2003) La propriété intellectuelle sur les logiciels, in Conseil d'Analyse Economique (ed.) *Propriété intellectuelle*. Paris: La Documentation Française.

Ceccagnoli, M. Gambardella, A. Giuri, P. Licht, G. and Mariani, M. (2005) *Study on Evaluating the Knowledge Economy – What Are Patents Actually Worth? The Value of Patents for Today's Economy and Society*. Research project ETD/2004/IM/E3/77 conducted for the European Commission, Directorate-General for Internal Market. CERM Foundation (Siena).

Cohen, W. M. Nelson, R. R. and Walsh, J. P. (2000) Protecting Their Intellectual Assets: Appropriability Conditions and Why US Manufacturing Firms Patent or Not, NBER Working Paper 7552.

Gallini, N. (2002) The Economics of Patents: Lessons from Recent U.S. Patent Reform, *Journal of Economic Perspectives*, 16: 131–54.

Geroski, P. (1995) Markets for Technology: Knowledge, Innovation and Appropriability in P. Stoneman (ed.) *Handbook of Economics of Innovation and Technological Change*. Oxford: Blackwell.

Grabowski, H. (2002) Patents, Innovation and Access to New Pharmaceuticals, *Journal of International Economic Law*, 5: 849–60.

Grabowski, H. (2004) Are the Economics of Pharmaceutical Research and Development Changing? *Pharmaeconomics*, 22: 15–24.

Hall, B. H. andZiedonis, R. (2001) The Patent Paradox Revisited: An Empirical Study of Patenting in the US Semiconductor Industry, 1979–1995, *RAND Journal of Economics*, 32: 101–28.

Hammer, P. J. (2002) Differential Pricing of Essential AIDS Drugs: Markets, Politics and Public Health, *Journal of International Economic Law*, 5: 883–912.

Hardin, G. (1968) The Tragedy of the Commons, *Science*, 162: 1243–8.

Heller, M. A. and Eisenberg, R. (1998) Can Patents Deter Innovation? The Anticommons in Biomedical Research, *Science*, 280: 698–701.

Kettler, H. (2000) *Narrowing the Gap between Provision and Need for Medicines in Developing Countries* (London: Office of Health Economics).

Kortum, S. and Lerner, J. (1998) Stronger Protection or Technological Revolution: What is Behind the Recent Surge in Patenting? *Carnegie-Rochester Conference Series on Public Policy*, 48: 247–304.

Lanjouw, J. O. (1998) The Introduction of Pharmaceutical Product Patents in India: Heartless Exploitation of the Poor and Suffering?, Working Paper 6366, National Bureau of Economic Research.

Lanjouw, J. O. (2003) A Proposed Solution yo the TRIPS Debate over Pharmaceuticals, *Technological Innovation and Intellectual Property Newsletter*.

http://www.researchoninnovation.org/tiip/archive/2003_3_c.html.

Lerner, J. (2002) Patent Protection and Innovation over 150 Years, Working Paper. 8977, National Bureau of Economic Research.

Lévêque, F. and Ménière, Y. (2004) *The Economics of Patents and Copyright*, (Berkeley, CA: Electronic Press).

Levin, R. C., Klevorick, A. K. Nelson, R. R. and Winter, S. G. (1987) Appropriating the Returns from Industrial R&D, *Brookings Papers on Economic Activity*: 783–820.

Mansfield E. (1986) Patents and Innovation: an Empirical Study, *Management Science*, 32: 173–81.

OECD (2000) Competition and Regulation Issues in the Pharmaceutical Industry. DAFFE/ CLP(2000)29.

OECD (2004) *Compendium of Patent Statistics 2004*. http://www.oecd.org/dataoecd/60/24/8208325.pdf.

Penrose. E. (1951) *The Economics of the International Patent System*. Baltimore, MD: Johns Hopkins University Press.
Ridley, D. B. Grabowski, H. G. and Moe. J. L. (2006) Developing Drugs for Developing Countries, *Health Affairs*, 25: 313–24.
Sakakibara, M. and Branstetter, L. (2001) Do Stronger Patents Induce More Innovation? Evidence from the 1988 Japanese Patent Law Reforms, *RAND Journal of Economics*, 32: 77–100.
Scherer, F. M. and Weisbrod, S. (1995) Economic Effects of Strengthening Pharmaceutical Patent Protection in Italy, *International Review of Industrial Property and Copyright Law*, 6: 1009–24.
Scherer, F. M. and Watal, J. (2002) Post-TRIPS Options for Access to Patented Medicines in Developing Nations, *Journal of International Economic Law*, 5: 913–39.
Scotchmer, S. (2004) *Innovation and Incentives*. Cambridge, MA: MIT Press.
Shapiro C. (2001) Navigating the Patent Thicket: Cross Licenses, Patent Pools, and Standard Setting, *NBER/Innovation Policy and the Economy*, 1: 119–50.
Shavell, S. and van Ypersele, T. (2001) Rewards versus Intellectual Property Rights, *Journal of Law and Economics*, 44: 525–47.
Sykes, A. O. (2002) TRIPs, *Pharmaceuticals, Developing Countries, and the Doha Solution* , University of Chicago Law & Economics, Olin Working Paper 140.

11

Patents on Drugs – the Wrong Prescription?

*Peter Dietsch**

Introduction

Theories of justice and intellectual property are vast topics in their own right. The contributions to this volume examine how they relate. How do our justifications for protecting intellectual property fare from an ethical perspective? Any attempt to tackle this question in a relatively short chapter like this one will have to be restricted in scope. My claims are limited in four ways. First, I concentrate on one kind of intellectual property protection, namely patents. Second, the claims of justice put forward concentrate on one context of justice, namely the distribution of health goods. Third, the discussion of distributive issues concerning health is limited further in that I single out the distribution of drugs rather than, for instance, access to doctors or hospital services. Finally, I adopt a cosmopolitan perspective, emphasising inequalities in the access to drugs at the international rather than at the national level.

At the heart of the chapter lies a conflict between patent protection in the pharmaceutical sector and the principle of justice that the distribution of health goods should depend on medical need rather than on the ability to pay. I call this the *needs principle*. Current institutional arrangements in the pharmaceutical industry, of which patent protection forms an integral part, violate the needs principle in two ways. First, the industry's research and development efforts are skewed in favour of developing drugs for the diseases of the rich. Consider the fact that malaria, pneumonia, diarrhoea and tuberculosis, which make up 21 per cent of the global disease burden, receive 0.31 per cent of all public and private spending on health research (GFHR, 2004, p. 122). Second, even when the drugs produced reflect medical needs, patent protection allows pharmaceutical companies to sell them at prices that poor patients cannot afford. Most of these patients live in the developing world. We can label these two kinds of violations of the needs principle *production failure* and *access failure* respectively.[1]

Critics of patents on drugs often base their case on access failure. Remedies to this problem include price subsidies in countries with socialised medicine or compulsory licensing agreements for developing countries. This chapter suggests that production failure poses at least as significant a threat to the justification of drug patents. To see why and how the needs principle trumps the case for patents in this sense, it is useful to start with a brief overview of how the patent system is justified. Then, I defend the needs principle as our criterion of justice in the health sector and spell out the implications of accepting this principle for justifying patents on drugs. Finally, I evaluate a series of policy options to promote the needs principle in practice.

Patents as rewards and incentives

A patent provides exclusivity rights to the use and exploitation of inventions.[2] To be awarded a patent, an invention has to satisfy a number of criteria. The US Patent Office requires novelty, non-evidence and usefulness of the invention, whereas the Europeans put the emphasis on novelty, the presence of an inventive step and potential for industrial application. Patent duration has recently been harmonised to 20 years by the TRIPS (Trade-Related Aspects in Intellectual Property Rights) Agreement signed under the auspices of the World Trade Organisation. The effective protection of a marketable product may be considerably shorter, given that patents are frequently filed when much of the R&D is still to be done. Other forms of intellectual property rights feature copyrights to protect various kinds of artistic work, trade marks to cover brands, and trade secrets for business practices to be kept confidential. Although these other forms of intellectual property rights also have distributive consequences that should be subject to normative scrutiny,[3] in this chapter I concentrate on patents.

Today, the patent system forms a well-established, economically significant and rarely questioned part of the institutional landscape in industrialised countries. The first thing an inventor does is take his brainchild to the patent office; the US Patent Office issued in excess of 150,000 patents in 2004, its Japanese and European counterparts tallied up over 100,000 and over 50,000 respectively. Corporate revenues from licensing technologies to other companies is estimated at an annual $100 billion worldwide and growing fast.[4]

Contrary to what their central role in today's marketplace might suggest, the initial introduction as well as the justification of the patent system were highly controversial. As Fritz Machlup and Edith Penrose (1950, pp. 28–9) document in an exemplary piece of economic history, the academic controversy surrounding patents was never resolved. Rather, the decisive argument that led to the institution of patent systems in most industrialised countries by the end of the nineteenth century was political. In an increasingly protectionist international climate, patents were seen as a safeguard against foreign competition – a line of argument that, despite or perhaps precisely because of the phenomenon of globalisation, is frequently invoked again today.

In a normative context, we have to reconsider the justification of patents. What exactly makes it a good idea for a society to have a patent system of the sort briefly described above? Only with a response to this question in hand will we be able to arbitrate conflicts with other norms, like the needs principle.

There are two kinds of justifications for the patent system that can be viewed as complementary. The first is based on considerations of justice, the second appeals to the beneficial consequences of the patent system. Both come in several versions.[5]

Justice-based arguments for patents

Inventors make a useful and valuable contribution to society. They should be protected against free riders who bring applications of the invention to market without having invested the same amount of time and money. On one view, they should at least be able to recoup their investment. Note the special status this argument assigns inventions in a market economy. Whereas for standard enterprises being copied is simply part of the business risk they take, the special social contribution of inventors justifies shielding them from this risk.

Note that the justice-based argument for patents does not automatically justify the patent system as we know it. The ideal patent from this perspective would expire once the investment costs have been recovered. Obviously, such a fine-grained patent system is not practicable. Critics of the justice-based argument for patents have also pointed to the possibility of alternative rewards, including prizes, awards or government funding of research projects (Machlup and Penrose, 1950, p. 19; Langinier and Moschini, 2002, p.18). Economists frequently highlight the fact that even in the absence of patent protection, new product developments based on inventions are likely to be profitable in the short term thanks to the first mover advantage of the inventor (Machlup and Penrose, 1950, p. 18). Some have considered this advantage, whose value is inversely related to the level of competition in the industry, as an appropriate and sufficient reward for the inventor's contribution.

A second, more controversial version of the justice-based argument holds that inventors have a natural property right to their ideas. This position is premised on a libertarian theory of property. I will bracket it here.[6]

Consequence-based arguments for patents

Unless the profits of inventors are protected for a certain period of time, the incentive to develop new, socially desirable products will be significantly reduced. Who would even think about pouring millions of dollars into the development of a new drug, for instance, if they had no guarantee of being able to reap the benefits from their investment? This argument to shore up the incentives of inventors represents probably the most plausible justification of the patent system.

There are three issues at stake here. First, does the basic claim hold? Does the patent system increase the level of socially desirable research? Second, is the patent system the most effective means to promote research and development? Alternative incentive schemes based on prizes and awards, or on publicly funded research, may prove more effective in promoting socially desirable inventions. Third, do the benefits of the patent system outweigh its costs? These include legal fees spent on patent disputes,[7] the costs in economic efficiency – the so-called deadweight loss – associated with granting temporary monopoly power to firms, and the loss to society that occurs through the temporary limitation on the use of newly developed ideas and technologies.

It is not the purpose of this chapter to sift through the substantial amounts of data necessary to answer these empirical questions.[8] Though the evidence in all three cases seems sketchy, I will, for the sake of argument, assume that the premises of the consequence-based argument for patents are sound in most economic contexts. However, I will in a later section present reasons to believe that the pharmaceutical sector represents an exception to this rule.

A second, less persuasive kind of consequence-based argument for the patent system suggests that it encourages the disclosure of trade secrets.[9] I will bracket this argument here.

As we shall see, both the justice-based and the consequence-based justification of patents are trumped by the needs principle when it comes to patents on drugs, albeit for different reasons.

Distributive justice and health goods

Bernard Williams considered it a 'necessary truth' that 'the proper ground for the distribution of medical care is ill health' (1962, p. 121). This is one possible formulation of the needs principle that I put forward as the appropriate distributive norm to govern the distribution of health goods. Whether one calls it a necessary truth or a fundamental distributive principle, there cannot be an ultimate justification for it. All one can hope for is to make it more plausible to those who do not already accept it. This is the primary aim of the present section. In addition, I shall comment on a potential critique of the needs principle, on its scope and on its relation with the market mechanism.

Even those who consider distributive inequalities due to individual choices, talents or even luck as legitimate and fair tend to acknowledge that equality has its place in certain contexts. This intuition has been captured well by what the economist James Tobin calls specific egalitarianism. 'This is the view that certain specific scarce commodities should be distributed less unequally than the ability to pay for them' (Tobin, 1970, p. 264). Health goods are a primary example of this kind of good.

The rationale for considering health goods a special case appeals to the nature of the needs they cater to. Health needs can be distinguished from ordinary preferences in two important ways. First, ordinary preferences, like my wish to have an ice cream, are chosen, whereas health needs are typically not a matter of choice.[10] Second, health is objectively important to carry out a rational plan for life. Whereas other characteristics may be specific to particular life plans – as manual dexterity is to a career as a concert pianist – health is of strategic importance for any life plan. That said, some health issues, like the prevention and cure of potentially fatal illnesses, are more important than others, like the treatment of the common cold.[11] These considerations explain why we think that the distribution of health goods should track health needs rather than the ability to pay.

Despite its intuitive appeal, the needs principle is not immune to criticism. Suppose a doctor has to choose between minimally enhancing the life of a gravely ill patient by performing a very expensive operation on the one hand, and using the same money to cure ten less gravely ill patients on the other. It is not clear whether the more pressing health need of the one patient is sufficient to trump the potential benefits to the others. A whole literature on the cost-effectiveness of the allocation of medical resources has sprung up over the last decades, attempting to solve this kind of dilemma.[12] It may well be that these considerations require us to modify the needs principle and make it sensitive to the costs of catering to the health needs in question. However, this possibility is of little relevance to the present focus on patent protection, and I will therefore bracket it here.

A caveat should also be added with respect to the scope of the needs principle. Whose need should feature in our considerations of allocating medical resources? Do the obligations of any particular country's taxpayers to come up with medical resources merely extend to the health needs of its residents? Or should the needs principle be applied internationally? In other words, are we talking about domestic or global justice in the distribution of health goods? These are tricky questions, to which reasonable people can give different answers. Here, I will limit myself to the following observation. Defenders of a domestic justice approach seem to have a relatively strong case when it comes to health goods financed through national taxation, as is the case for hospitals in most countries.[13] On the other hand, a cosmopolitan or global approach to justice in health seems plausible where international structures are already in place. This is the case for the pharmaceutical industry, which is dominated by multinational companies. Since the structures of producing drugs are global, it seems appropriate to evaluate these structures using a cosmopolitan perspective.

I am aware that this is far from a defence of a cosmopolitanism. Yet, I cannot provide such a defence here.[14] Instead, my objective is to argue that from such a perspective, the case for patents on drugs is unconvincing.

Finally, anticipating the argument below, it may be helpful to explicate the relation between the needs principle and the market mechanism. Does respecting the needs principle entail costs in terms of allocative efficiency? To answer this question, it is essential to realise the inherently instrumental character of efficiency.[15] Efficiency is not a value in itself, but it is a measure of how well we are doing in promoting other, primary values. For example, some economic models assume that this primary value is growth. However, in the context of health goods, as I have argued, the primary value is the satisfaction of the needs principle. From this perspective, the idea of a conflict or tradeoff between the needs principle and allocative efficiency is nonsensical.

An efficient allocation in this context is precisely one that respects the needs principle.

In the words of Amartya Sen, the moral standing of the market hinges on its consequences. According to Sen, it is implausible to think that 'the value of the market can be divorced from the value of its results and achievements' (Sen, 1985, p. 7). The performance of the market for pharmaceuticals is tainted by two kinds of failure. First, the market fails to *produce* drugs for those who cannot back their medical needs with the necessary ability to pay. Second, even allowing for a cost-reducing insurance system, poor people often do not have *access* to existing drugs due to their high prices. This second problem is exacerbated by patent protection, which enables producers to charge higher prices than they would be able to in the presence of competition.

The needs principle and patents on drugs

Suppose we accept that the production and allocation of drugs should satisfy the needs principle. What follows from this acceptance for the justification of patents in the pharmaceutical industry? In this section, I will argue that the needs principle trumps both the justice-based and the consequence-based justifications of patents. In the final section, I will then assess the implications of this insight for tackling production and access failure at a policy level.

As a preliminary remark, note one feature that the needs principle and the patent system have in common. They both represent attempts to correct for what is considered to be a failure of the market mechanism to deliver on certain social objectives. We decide to grant patents to inventors because we consider either that the market does not provide them with a just reward or because we believe patents boost socially useful inventions, or both. Similarly, in some economic contexts, we deem the distributive principle of the market, that is 'to each according to his or her productive capacities', unacceptable. An institutional structure built on the needs principle is one alternative to the market structure. One way to phrase the question of the present section is to ask which of these corrections for market failure should take priority.

First, I will examine the relation between the needs principle and the justice-based justification of patents. Recall that patents, independently of their justification, perpetuate the production failure of the market for drugs, and they exacerbate its access failure by allowing pharmaceutical companies to charge higher prices. These factors contribute to the fact that the distribution of drugs worldwide does not satisfy the needs principle. What can we say about this conflict?

Both the needs principle and the justice-based justification of patents advance claims of justice. The former focuses on the necessity to cater to people's health needs, whereas the latter centres on an appropriate reward for inventors. Which of these considerations should carry the day? I presume it is uncontroversial that catering to health needs is of more fundamental importance both to individual human beings and to the functioning of a society than appropriate rewards for inventors. Faced with this trade-off, I believe we should give absolute priority to the needs principle. In other words, we should abolish patents if and when they prove to be an obstacle to satisfying the needs principle. Having said that, we are here faced with a question whose answer admits degrees. Someone may propose a compromise that tries to address both people's health needs and rewards to inventors to some extent. In any case, we can conclude that the needs principle and the justice-based justification of patents can, and have to be, weighed against each other.

The relation between the needs principle and the consequence-based justification of patents is of a different kind. In this context, my remarks at the end of the last section on the moral standing of the market become relevant. Here is the short version of the argument. Patents boost socially useful inventions. The standard of usefulness in most economic contexts is the development and production of goods for which there will be demand on the market. However, not so in the context of health goods. Here, so the argument runs, the standard of usefulness of the market is replaced by the needs principle. This undermines the consequence-based justification for patents on drugs.

Since the consequence-based justification of patents is often regarded as the dominant one, it is important to look at this argument in more detail. My claim is not that granting patents to pharmaceutical companies does not generate drugs that cater to people's health needs. Of course they do, and the industry is adamant in emphasising that it would not be able to play this role without patent protection.[16] Instead, the point is that the way the pharmaceutical industry develops and brings to market drugs does not satisfy the needs principle. To repeat, there are two violations of the needs principle. First, there is a production failure in that the development of drugs against the diseases of the poor, which make up a significant part of the global disease burden, is relatively under-funded. Second, there is an access failure in the sense that pharmaceutical companies charge prices that poor patients cannot afford.

In sum, the consequences of granting patents on drugs fall far short of the social objectives we have in the production and distribution of drugs. However, one has to be careful not to throw the baby out with the bathwater. The fact that the patenting of drugs does not produce the desired results does not in itself imply that the practice is unjustified. To make this stronger argument, one needs to come up with a better institutional alternative. Before we can say that drugs on patents are the wrong prescription, we need to identify a different, or at least a complementary one. In the final section I will discuss several candidate policies to address the violations of the needs principle under the present institutional structure.

I suggested earlier that the needs principle trumps the two justifications for patents on drugs. The discussion of the last few paragraphs allows me to refine this formulation somewhat. With respect to the justice-based justification of patents on drugs, my argument has been that the justice claim of the needs principle weighs more heavily than the justice claim of rewarding inventors.

The case of the consequence-based justification of patents on drugs is more complex. Accepting the needs principle implies that inventing certain drugs, namely those resulting in a maximal reduction of the global disease burden, is more important than inventing others. On this criterion, patents on drugs deliver poor results. Is there an institutional arrangement that would serve this aim more effectively?

Policy options

What can be done to move closer to satisfying the needs principle in the production and distribution of drugs internationally? There is no lack of proposals of what to do. Which of these actually work is to a large extent an empirical question. Under these circumstances, I think it would be misleading to suggest that there is a panacea for the problems identified in this chapter. Even the strongest proposal will have a number of drawbacks. Nor do I intend to add any fundamentally new suggestion to the list. Instead, my goal is to assess how some of the existing suggestions are likely to fare according to two criteria. This discussion will I hope allow us to impose some much needed structure on the public debate around the issue of drugs and distributive justice. The two criteria are these:

1 How can we expect any particular solution to fare in addressing production failure and access failure respectively? Many of the political fixes under consideration address only one of these dimensions.

2 The lack of progress is due to two kinds of shortcomings of existing policy suggestions. They often pose problems of motivational feasibility or political feasibility, or both.[17] Though I by no means intend to play down political feasibility, I believe motivational feasibility poses a more serious problem still. In discussing reform proposals, I therefore want to classify them according to the kind of feasibility constraint they are subject to.

Before turning to the discussion of individual policy measures, let me define what I mean by motivational and political feasibility respectively. I will take a policy to be motivationally unfeasible if it requires economic agents to act against their self-interest under conditions of information asymmetry. A policy that requires me to engage in a counter-prefential action X while it is hard or impossible for the state to verify whether I really did X is likely to be unsuccessful. Constraints of motivational feasibility are of course contingent, in the sense that they depend on individual preferences. However, change in these preferences tends to be slow.

By contrast, I will take a policy to be politically unfeasible if certain political institutions or current political majorities stand in the way of implementing it. Nowadays, two examples for important obstacles in the path of reforming the patent system for drugs are the lobbying power of the pharmaceutical industry and the absence of an international structure to effectively tax multinational companies.

The distinction between the two categories is far from clear-cut. For instance, one could redescribe the political feasibility constraint imposed by lobbying practices as a motivational feasibility constraint on the political actors in question. Nonetheless, the distinction can be useful, as the following discussion should demonstrate.

I will now evaluate a number of reform policies according to the two criteria introduced. They will be organised into two groups. Members of the first group (A) run into constraints of motivational feasibility, whereas members of the second group (B) face 'merely' constraints of political feasibility. Within both groups, I will start with the policies that address production and access failures to a lesser degree.

A1) An international code for the pharmaceutical industry[18]

Why impose external regulation when internal regulation can do? Some commentators believe that rather than imposing a reform from the outside, what is needed is a self-imposed code of ethics ensuring that the pharmaceutical industry lives up to its social responsibility in producing and distributing drugs according to the needs principle. How one views this kind of proposal depends on one's confidence in the notion of corporate social responsibility. I belong to those who think that it does not come naturally to companies to internalise social objectives that run counter to their business interest. Therefore, I believe that this kind of self-regulating will either not take reform very far or falter on grounds of motivational infeasibility, or both.

However, suppose for a moment that members of the pharmaceutical industry were indeed willing to subscribe to the cause of the most pressing medical needs. Could a code of ethics resolve the problems of production and access failure? On the plausible assumption that R&D on drugs for 'poor diseases' is not profitable, I think at least production failure would persist to some degree. At the same time, given the enormous profits of the pharmaceutical industry,[19] an ambitious piece of self-regulation could in principle go a long way towards addressing both production failure by investing profits in drugs for 'poor diseases' and access failure by cross-subsidising drugs for the poor.

A2) Alternative incentive schemes for producing essential medicines

If the market logic fails to produce satisfactory results, perhaps the incentives structure for pharmaceutical companies should be changed more fundamentally. Thomas Pogge (2005) has put forward a proposal that involves rewarding companies according to an indicator measuring the number of lives saved and improved by their drugs. In principle, such a scheme has the potential to address the failure in both the production of and access to what Pogge calls essential medicines, that is ones that can save or drastically improve lives.

However, once again a serious problem of motivational feasibility looms. Companies would have every incentive to overstate the amount of good their drugs are doing. Given the serious measurement problems involved – imagine assessing how many lives of AIDS patients a particular drug has saved in the course of one year in South Africa, say – foolproofing such a system against abuse looks difficult indeed.

B1) Various changes to patent regulation

Ideas in this category include shortening the length of patent protection, enforcing the condition of 'novelty', no longer awarding patents to 'me-too' drugs, and modifying the TRIPS Agreement to keep open the possibility of compulsory licensing for developing countries.[20] Moreover, in the United States, the voices calling for a reversal of several administrative changes that made the process of obtaining and legally defending patents much easier in the 1980s and 1990s are becoming louder (see Jaffe and Lerner, 2006).

Most of these reforms are likely to dent pharmaceutical profits to various degrees, and are therefore heavily opposed by the industry's lobby. Despite facing this hurdle of political feasibility, they are motivationally feasible in the sense that, once in place, they would be enforceable and the industry would have little choice but to play by the new rules.

Administrative changes to the patent system have the potential to go a long way towards addressing access failure under the status quo. Compulsory licensing, for example, is an effective means to make essential medicines more accessible to the poor. On the other hand, the prospects for addressing production failure are not as good. None of these changes will shore up the incentives of pharmaceutical companies to invest into R&D on 'poor diseases'.

B2) Public research and development of drugs

One classic response to market failure is for the state to take over. Faced by current production and access failures, one might consider abolishing patents on drugs altogether, and financing their R&D through public money instead. This approach has a better chance of addressing the production failure than the policies discussed so far, since it could specifically promote the development of drugs for 'poor diseases' that private companies consider unprofitable. However, the extent to which production and access failures could be addressed ultimately depends on the amount of public money made available.

I would like to make three comments on this suggestion. First, despite the fact in some countries public provision works well with respect to providing other health-related goods and services like hospitals and medical services, one cannot take for granted that public provision of drugs would do better than private provision. The public choice literature reminds us that government fixes for market failure might just make matters worse.

In fact, in the case of R&D on drugs, there are two reasons to think that publicly funded research would make matters worse. These underlie my other two comments: Second, contrary to national spending decisions on hospitals, doctors and the like, there is no international institutional structure in place that could administer this research. Any intergovernmental approach, on the other hand, is likely to be crippled by high decision costs concerning the contribution key to the scheme as well as its spending priorities.

Third, though a lot of research on essential medicines is done in universities and other parts of the public sector already,[21] shutting private sector R&D on drugs down altogether would result in an immense loss of know-how. This may be a path-dependent, but still significant argument in this context.

B3) Tax and transfer approaches

One way to avoid any loss of private sector know-how is to make the pharmaceutical industry work in the name of the needs principle through the setting of tax incentives. In effect, this amounts to public subsidies to render previously unprofitable drugs financially interesting to the pharmaceutical industry. The tax and transfer approach on its own addresses production failure only. However, it can easily be combined with policies targeting access failure, as for instance compulsory licensing agreements.

At the national level, this kind of policy has already been tried in the United States in form of the Orphan Drug Act. Under this Act, tax incentives as well as patents granting seven-year exclusivity reduce the break-even point for many drugs. Though not flawless, the Act has generally been regarded a success.[22] An alternative to structuring the policy as a subsidy would be to tax pharmaceutical companies more heavily (and those who do no research on neglected diseases heaviest) and spend the proceeds on public research on drugs.

The biggest barrier in terms of political feasibility of any such measure at the international level is the reluctance of national governments to cede any fiscal authority. Consensus to raise tax rates on pharmaceutical companies globally, even with the noble aim of funding essential medical research, is far off.

Conclusion

When asking the question ‘Are patents on drugs just?’ one has to keep in mind two things. First, provided one accepts that the production and distribution of drugs should be governed by the needs principle, neither a justice-based nor a consequence-based approach is able to provide a convincing justification of patents at all in this context. Second, though patent protection no doubt promotes R&D on drugs for which there is a demand, it does not help to address the problems of production and access failure. In the case of access failure, it arguably even makes things worse.

Despite this fairly negative record of patents on drugs, the practical conclusions are far from clear-cut. Whether or not we should get rid of patents on drugs depends on the institutional alternatives. The discussion of several policy options has illustrated that the tension between patents and the needs principle can potentially be reduced by combining patents with complementary policies.

Acknowledgements

* I would like to thank Vincent Bourdeau, Axel Gosseries, Mira Johri, David Lametti, Alain Strowel and two anonymous referees for their feedback on previous drafts of this chapter. I have also benefited from comments when presenting its content at the Léger Robic Richard seminar series in intellectual property at McGill University, as well as at the Centre de Recherche en Éthique de l'Université de Montréal (CREUM).

Notes

1. I borrow this distinction from De George (2005), who uses it to argue that pharmaceutical companies have a moral obligation to address these failures through self-regulation.
2. I would like to thank one of the anonymous referees for providing me with this concise definition of patents.
3. Cf. for example what Frank and Cook (1996) have called the winner-takes-all phenomenon, which is closely linked to the definition of copyrights in music.
4. *The Economist*, 'A Survey of Patents and Technology', 22 October 2005.
5. For a more detailed discussion, let me refer to De George (2005), Machlup and Penrose (1950), Hettinger (1989), as well as Langinier and Moschini (2002). Kitch's (1977) distinction between reward theory and prospect theory to justify patents parallels tracks the distinction between justice-based and consequence-based arguments for patents. Svatos (1996) presents a case against the latter.
6. For an insightful discussion of this argument, see Hettinger (1989).
7. To give an example, Microsoft 'is currently involved in 32 patent disputes, and spends close to $100m a year in legal costs' (*The Economist*, 'A Survey of Patents and Technology', 22 October 2005).
8. See Belleflamme (2006) for an empirical assessment of whether the patent system actually results in more inventions. Jaffe and Lerner (2006) suggest that a series of changes to the US patent system in the 1980s and 1990s have caused the costs of the patent system to increase dramatically.
9. For a critique of this argument, see Machlup and Penrose (1950, p. 26).

10. Though some health needs can arise as a consequence from certain choices an agent has made – for instance the choice to smoke.
11. For a more detailed discussion of the issues addressed in this paragraph, see Daniels (1981).
12. See Murray (1994), Brock (2004) and Anand and Hanson (2004) for critical discussions of both QALYs (quality-adjusted life years) and DALYs (disability-adjusted life years).
13. Note, however, that this argument is contingent on fiscal boundaries tracking national boundaries.
14. For a useful review of the cosmopolitan perspective as well as its critics, see Caney (2002).
15. For a lucid discussion on this point, see LeGrand (1990).
16. See De George (2005, pp. 551–2) and Angell (2004) for accounts of how much pharmaceutical companies make of this argument.
17. An earlier draft of this chapter did not contain this distinction concerning feasibility arguments. I thank one of the anonymous referees for pushing me to say more on this point.
18. This approach is championed by De George (2005).
19. See Angell (2004) for figures documenting the fact that big pharma has consistently been among the most profitable industries worldwide.
20. Compulsory licensing agreements allow for the production of generic drugs in exchange for a royalty paid to the patent holder. Although TRIPS reserves any country the right to impose compulsory licensing agreements under conditions of a public health emergency, some commentators have argued that developing countries will find it increasingly difficult to invoke this clause (see Sterckx, 2004, p. 61).
21. According to the [National Institute of Health], 55% of the research projects leading to the discovery of the 5 best-selling drugs in 1995 was performed by researchers whose work had been financed with taxpayers' money' (NIH administrative document cited in Sterckx, 2004, p. 65).
22. See www.fda.gov/orphan/oda.htm for the amended Orphan Drug Act, as well as De George (2005, p.12) for a brief discussion.

References

Anand, S. and Hanson, K. (2004) Disability-Adjusted Life Years: A Critical Review, in S. Anand, F. Peter and A. Sen (eds.) *Public Health, Ethics, and Equity*. Oxford: Oxford University Press.

Angell, M. (2004) *The Truth about the Drug Companies*. New York: Random House.

Belleflamme, P. (n.d.) Patents and Incentives to Innovate: Some Empirical Evidence. Unpublished manuscript.

Brock, D. W. (2004) Ethical Issues in the Use of Cost Effectiveness Analysis for the Prioritisation of Health Care Resources, in S. Anand, F. Peter and A. Sen (eds.) *Public Health, Ethics, and Equity*. Oxford: Oxford University Press.

Caney, S. (2001) Review Article: International Distributive Justice, *Political Studies*, 49(5): 974–97.

Daniels, N. (1981) Health Care Needs and Distributive Justice, *Philosophy & Public Affairs*, 10(2): 146–79.

The Economist (2005) A Market for Ideas – a Survey of Patents and Technology, 22 October.
De George, R. T. (2005) Intellectual Property and Pharmaceutical Drugs: An Ethical Analysis, *Business Ethics Quarterly*, 15(4): 549–75.
Frank, R. H. and Cook, P. J. (1995) *The Winner-Take-All Society*. New York: Free Press.
Global Forum for Health Research (2007) *The 10/90 Report on Health Research 2003–2004*. Geneva: GFHR). www.globalforumhealth.org. Accessed 6 April 2007.
Hettinger, E. C. (1989) Justifying Intellectual Property, *Philosophy and Public Affairs*, 18(1): 31–52.
Jaffe, A. B. and Lerner, J. (2006) *Innovation and its Discontents*. Princeton. NJ: Princeton University Press.
Kitch, E. W. (1997) The Nature and Function of the Patent System, *The Journal of Law and Economics*, 20: 265–90.
Langinier, C. and Moschini, G. (2002) The Economics of Patents: an Overview. Working paper 02-WP 293. Center for Agricultural and Rural Development, Iowa State University. ideas.repec.org/p/isu/genres/2061.html. Accessed 6 April 2007.
LeGrand, J. (1990) Equity versus Efficiency: the Elusive Trade-off, *Ethics*, 100(3): 554–68.
Machlup, F. and Penrose, E. (1950) The Patent Controversy in the Nineteenth Century, *The Journal of Economic History*, 10(1): 129.
Murray, C. J. L. (1994) Quantifying the Burden of Disease: the Technical Basis for Disability-Adjusted Life Years, *Bulletin of the World Health Organisation*, 72: 429–45.
The Orphan Drug Act, www.fda.gov/orphan/oda.htm. Accessed 6 April 2007.
Pogge, T. W. (2005) Human Rights and Global Health: a Research Program, *Metaphilosophy*, 36(1 & 2): 182–209.
Sen, A. (1985) The Moral Standing of the Market, *Social Philosophy & Policy*, 2(2): 1–19.
Sterckx, S. (2004) Patents and Access to Drugs in Developing Countries: an Ethical Analysis, *Developing World Bioethics*, 4(1): 58–75.
Svatos, M. (1996) Biotechnology and the Utilitarian Argument for Patents, *Social Philosophy & Policy*, 13(2): 113–44.
Williams, B. (1962) The Idea of Equality, in P. Laslett and W. G. Runciman (eds.) *Philosophy, Politics, and Society*, 2nd series (Oxford: Blackwell).

12
Is It Ethical To Patent Human Genes?

*Annabelle Lever**

Human gene patents are patents on genes that have been removed from human bodies and scientifically isolated and manipulated in a laboratory. The US Patent and Trademark Office (USPTO) has issued thousands of patents on such genes, and patents have also been granted by the European Patent Office (EPO).[1] Legal and moral justification, however, are not identical, and it is possible for a legal decision to be immoral even though it complies with legal precedent and procedure. So, it is surprising to learn that some people believe that the legal justification of human gene patents can remove the most serious moral objections to them.[2] Yet, those who are well versed in patent law often believe that confusion over some quite basic legal and scientific facts accounts for moral objections to such patents[3] and, in particular, for the belief that they justify the ownership of one person by another.[4] Once these confusions are removed, they contend, we will see that there is nothing especially alarming about patents on human genes and no reason to believe them to be immoral.[5]

Such claims seem especially surprising because the morality of an invention is generally supposed to have little role in the decision about whether or not the invention deserves a patent under US law. Although article 53 of the European Patent Convention prohibits patenting inventions, the publication or exploitation of which would be contrary to public order or morality, it turns out that this clause rarely justifies withholding a patent from an invention that otherwise meets legal criteria. Thus, although more than 320,000 patents have been granted by the EPO since its creation, this clause has never been used successfully to strike down a claim for a patent. As Ulrich Schatz explains, 'Poisons, explosives, extremely dangerous chemical substances, devices used in nuclear power stations, agro-chemicals, pesticides and many other things which can threaten human life or damage the environment have been patented, despite the existence of the public order and morality bar' in almost all European countries.

Indeed, this chapter shows, while ethical objections to human gene patents are often controversial, they need not be unreasonable, nor need they depend on mistaken assumptions about patent law. Rather, they may reflect familiar ethical concerns about the dominance of commercial imperatives in modern societies; the disparities in power and wealth among individuals and countries; and the lack of public discussion, transparency and accountability surrounding significant changes in people's rights, status and opportunities. Hence, I conclude, ethical concerns cannot be easily dismissed and, indeed, point to the need to think harder about the nature and justification of patent law itself.

Legal facts about human gene patents

Human genes can only be patented in the US (or anywhere else) if they can be distinguished from genes as they naturally occur in human bodies. To be patentable in the US an object or process must count as an invention, not a discovery, in addition to meeting legal tests such as those for novelty, non-obviousness and usefulness. It is, therefore, a legal fact about patents that they do not apply to naturally occurring objects, unless these have been sufficiently altered by human effort so as to count as 'made by man' for legal purposes. Thus, human genes can only pass the threshold test, which marks them as legally patentable, if they have been altered sufficiently to be legally distinguishable from naturally occurring genes, which cannot be patented.

Though the genes in your body are not patentable, the degree of manipulation and alteration required to isolate and identify a human gene scientifically means that genes so altered and manipulated can merit a legal patent. This is hardly surprising, for human genes that are patentable have scientific and commercial properties that distinguish them from naturally occurring genes. For example, while there are several methods of sequencing DNA, all of them require at least some of the following: isolating DNA, purifying DNA, removing a small segment of the DNA from its place in the genome and connecting it to bacterial DNA, chemically unwinding DNA and constructing radioactive or florescent copies of the genomic DNA fragment.[6] As Ossorio explains, 'When a patent claims a particular DNA sequence, it must teach others how to "make" that sequence – the patent must give enough information that another investigator can synthesize the sequence *de novo* or clone the sequence herself.'[7]

In *Diamond v. Chakrabarty*,[8] the US Supreme Court upheld a patent on oil-eating bacteria, arguing that such a patent was consistent with legal objections to patenting natural objects that have not been significantly altered by human endeavor. In *Parke-Davis and Co. v. H. K. Mulford and Co.*,[9] a lower court held that purified human adrenaline was patentable because, through purification, it became 'for every practical purpose a new thing commercially and therapeutically'. Hence, given the work that goes into scientifically isolating and identifying a gene, and the changes in the properties of the gene that this involves, treating human genes as patentable inventions does not, in and of itself, threaten the bodily integrity of human beings.

Moreover, critics claim, the difficulty with the main moral objections to human gene patents is not simply that they confuse legally patentable genes with naturally occurring genes; they also confuse patenting with owning. Thus, they fail to see that whatever the complexity involved in legal ownership, a patent simply does not confer legal ownership of anything. One can have a legal patent on a bicycle without owning a bicycle. Indeed, one can have a legal patent on an invention, but lack any legal rights to use that invention, let alone to license others to use or manufacture it. This is because the only legal right conferred by a patent is the right to prevent others from using or possessing one's invention: 'patents do not grant rights of use or possession, only rights to exclude'.[10] Hence, Ossorio concludes, a human gene patent cannot be identified with legal ownership of human bodies, not simply because human gene patents confer no rights over naturally occurring genes, but because patent rights confer none of the positive rights to possess and use in which ownership typically consists.

Attention to the legal facts about human gene patents, then, does remove some serious doubts about their morality. We may be sceptical that these patents are necessary to promote research and investment in biotechnology, or in the prevention and cure of human suffering.[11] Nevertheless, doubts on this score hardly imply that human gene patents are intrinsically immoral, as they would be if they prevented people from using their genes to live or to reproduce. Moreover, while these legal features of human gene patents do not alleviate the concern that patenting may exacerbate existing inequalities between rich and poor countries, or between rich and poor people in the same country,[12] they suggest that there is nothing about a legal patent that precludes government regulation of licensing agreements with these worries in mind. For example, governments might require patent holders to license the use and manufacture of human genes for medical purposes (thereby implying that the right to exclude is not absolute),[13] prohibit their use for others and limit how much they can charge for their use or manufacture by poor countries or poor people.[14] In these ways any morally objectionable consequences of human gene patents could be met, and even pre-empted, while acknowledging their legality. Yet this, too, would be impossible, were human gene patents the moral equivalent of slavery.

Patenting vs. owning

However, if we can lay to rest the worry that human gene patents literally threaten our self-ownership, the moral significance of the legal distinction between patenting and owning is less conclusive than one might suppose. The right to exclude is, in itself, a very powerful property right, and the patent system typically implies that someone – if not the patent holder – is entitled to use, license or sell a patented invention.[15] Thus, the differences between patenting and owning are probably less significance for ethical controversy over gene patents than the differences between absolute and non-absolute property rights, or between patent systems that allow compulsory licensing and those that forbid it.

For example, the difference between patenting and owning – conceptually, morally and politically – depends on one's background assumptions about people's rights, liberties and powers. Hence, the right to exclude can be a very significant and controversial right, and may be sufficient to transform what previously would have been collective property into private property. Likewise, it might be sufficient to turn what had previously been unowned into the exclusive property of one person or corporation. So, if one assumes that human genes were unowned and unownable prior to patenting, one might rather be struck by the fact that patenting creates a right to prevent others from using or possessing a gene – as would private ownership – and less by the thought that it creates only one of the many rights in which private ownership consists. Hence, the ethical significance of the distinction between patenting and owning depends fundamentally on the background assumptions about people's rights and duties that we use to interpret it.

Moreover, some experts in patent law define patent rights so as to include the positive right to use associated with ownership. Thus, Gerrtrui Van Overwalle refers to a patent as a 'legal title granting its holder the exclusive right to exploit' an invention. [16] This is understandable, because it is implicit in any patenting system that *someone*, if not the patent holder, is usually entitled to exploit an invention for commercial purposes.[17] In fact, patents typically grant a limited monopoly to patent holders in order to reward inventors for putting the details of their invention into the public domain. Even if the patent holder does not own the patented invention, it is typically the case that someone else is entitled to do so and is thus in a position to use, sell, profit from and, even, give away or destroy the patented invention. Consequently, patenting either presupposes that the necessary ownership rights are available or that they will be forthcoming, so that inventing will be profitable not simply for the inventor, but for others as well.

In short, patents put quite significant powers in the hands of a patent holder, and are designed to do so. Typically, they amount to a monopoly right to license, exploit and profit from an invention; less typically they simply grant a right to exclude others from using or profiting from it. Absent compulsory licensing schemes and other limitations on the rights of patent holders, then, patents can seriously constrain commercial and non-commercial uses of human genes. Indeed, the Nuffield Council on bioethics made its concerns in this area quite explicit, and highlighted the difficulty of 'designing around' genes as a reason to suppose that compulsory licensing might be justified in the case of human gene patents, even if it were not in the case of other inventions.[18]

Human gene patents can threaten people's jobs and careers, as well as their health and well-being. They can bring research to a standstill and inhibit the development of medical tests and products.[19] Gene patents, therefore, raise concerns about the power that that they grant their holders over the lives, employment, hopes and prospects of large numbers of people. After all, the point about gene patents is that they promise to help us to understand and cure some particularly cruel and devastating diseases. Thus, it seems unlikely that ethical objections to human gene patents will be resolved by recognising the differences between patenting and owning. Rather, what is most likely to matter are the constraints on patenting that governments feel entitled and able to make. Here, it is the *similarities*, and not the *differences*, between patenting and owning that are likely to prove decisive.

Ethical objections to monopoly powers and rights

Critics of human gene patents are often accused of being ungrateful or of being unwilling to reward those who have advanced scientific and medical knowledge. Or they are thought to have overlooked the fact that patented inventions are not spontaneous natural occurrences, but require human effort and skill. These seem to be standard responses to critics of gene patents.[20] However, it is not self-evident that people lack rights to use or possess something, such as land or medicine, that they did not create, or that they cannot be harmed or unjustly treated if they are denied such rights by law. Indeed, the thought that this is a real possibility underpins objections to libertarian views about people's rights from a wide variety of philosophical perspectives.[21]

Perhaps one has no right to the creation of a gene that can be scientifically manipulated and commercially manufactured in ways that are useful and medically beneficial. However, it does not follow that one therefore lacks rights to those genes once they have been invented. Indeed, if patenting rights are assumed to be absolute (as they might be on libertarian views of rights), so that patent holding can prevent the use or commercial development of inventions, however useful and desirable, there might be very strong moral objections to the idea that human genes are legally patentable.

Generally, one assumes, those who hold patents on human genes will try to avoid behaving in ways that generate negative publicity, and so will be careful about denying patents to people if this would prove embarrassing. The key point, however, is that if the rights created by a patent are understood to be monopoly rights, a patent holder might be legally entitled to behave in ways that would seem obnoxious or arbitrary to most people. Indeed, inventors might feel *morally entitled* to behave in such ways, whether or not they are legally entitled to do so. Thus, they may suppose that if they are legally entitled to keep an invention to themselves rather than sharing it with others, they should have broad rights to do as they see fit with their invention, no matter what other people think. Likewise, they may reason, they should be legally entitled to refuse to license it, because they could have withheld their invention altogether. So, it is easy to see why inventors might resist compulsory licensing agreements, ceilings on licensing fees and efforts to exempt research from licensing requirements altogether.

Inventors have an interest in patenting, not merely because it enables them to gain publicity and renown from their inventions, as well as any commercial benefits, but also because it protects them from the difficulties of trying to develop and profit from their ideas while keeping them secret.[22] We are accustomed to the idea that the public owes a debt of gratitude to inventors, which patenting reifies in the form of a temporary monopoly. But if debts of gratitude are not all one-way, it is unclear that people must be ungrateful or mean-spirited in order to reject monopolies on patented genes; or, indeed, to assert that, like other property rights, it is unethical to treat patents as absolute. Such a response is reinforced when one considers that patents are often held by companies rather than by solitary inventors,[23] and that monopoly rights to exclude or exploit have no automatic relationship to gratitude. After all, discoveries get no special protection however useful and beneficial they may be. So, while constraints on the monopoly created by patents will require justification, they need not imply ingratitude, an unwillingness to support inventions and inventors by other means, or the belief that people are always entitled to share in the creative efforts of others.

Patents and human dignity

Ethical concerns with the patenting of genes, however, are not limited to worries that people may be unable to buy, lease or sell services that they ought to be able to buy, lease or sell. On the contrary: many people object to the patenting of genes because they deny that genes should be thought of as property at all. Some of these objections reflect explicitly religious premises and others appear to have an implicitly religious character, even though they have no overt theological content.[24] The belief that genes should never be treated as property certainly depends on a particular conception of moral value, and one that we might reasonably reject. Nonetheless, as I shall show, it need not be unreasonable and need reflect no confusions about legal and scientific facts. In particular, it need not exaggerate the differences between humans and other animals, or the ethical significance of the human genome.

What might motivate objections to the commercialisation of genes? Quite plausibly, it is the thought that human capacities for invention, and for reflective thought and action, cannot readily be separated from our genetic endowment. Those troubled by the commercialisation of human genes, for example, may believe that the reasons to condemn the ownership of one person by another tell against treating human genes as though they were cars, which are patentable, or as great pieces of art, which are not. They may be willing to say that some reasons for patenting genes are better than others. Nonetheless, they may think that all patents in human genes, and all efforts to turn human genes into property, confuse human beings and their potential with that of objects – however lovely, useful and valuable.

Such objections need not imply that all biotechnology research is immoral. Nor, importantly, need they depend on any confusion about scientific facts about genes. Those who believe that it is immoral to patent human genes may be well aware that the human genome is very like the genome of worms, not to mention that of animals with whom we identify more closely. Just because humans do not differ greatly from other animals, it does not follow that we should be indifferent to the moral significance of whatever differences that there are. Indeed, they might think, it would be as wrong to ignore the significance of these differences as to focus on them at the cost of appreciating the moral significance of the similarities among living things.

An implication of this view might be that some patents on animal genes are immoral, just as some uses of animals are immoral. This, indeed, is Munzer's position: 'other things being equal', he concludes, 'the arguments tend to justify genetically related property rights in bacteria more readily than in plants, in plants more readily than in animals, in animals more readily than in chimeras, and in chimeras more readily than in humans'.[25] But whether this objection to patenting human genes extends to other biotechnology patents – or, indeed, to other patents generally – it need no more exaggerate the genetic differences between humans and other animals than objections to rape or justifications for marriage exaggerate those between one person and another.

Racist assumptions may underpin objections to rape or to marriage, but they need not.[26] Likewise, some arguments against patenting human genes may exaggerate the genetic and non-genetic differences between humans and other animals. But there is no compelling reason to suppose that this must be so.[27] Hence, one does not have to be a genetic fundamentalist in order to worry that human gene patents are immoral. Given the current state of our knowledge, one might simply suppose that our genetic endowment constitutes an important part of the reason why humans have the morally significant capacities that they have, including the capacity for conscious reflection on the moral significance of their genetic attributes.[28]

For people who think this way, and so suppose that there is something morally wrong with treating genes as property, their concerns about the way that people see and treat their genes may extend to the way that people treat their natural and social environment.[29] Some people tend to think that our genetic endowment is more closely connected to our sense of ourselves as moral agents than is our environment. Others disagree. Rather, they think that our natural, political and social environment is at least as significant as our genes for our ability to recognise, develop and exercise our moral capcity.[30] Consequently, their objections to patenting human genes may reflect their concerns about the destruction of some human habitats and ways of life, and to the ways that other human habitats and ways of life are fostered and insulated from criticism and change.

We can therefore object to patents on human genes without mistakenly supposing that commercial objects are incapable of having non-commercial meaning or value for people. Wedding rings, for instance, can be intimately bound up with our identities even though they are commercial objects, and their emotional value to us may not reflect their commercial value at all.[31] But this does not show that *genes* cannot be devalued by commercialisation. The fact that wedding rings are expensive is increasingly a reason why they have emotional value. Even where this is not the case, rings have been commercial objects for so long that their commercial status does not generally constitute a threat to their emotional value. This is not so with genes which, until recently, were not commercial objects. Even now, they are rarely conceived of as industrial objects. So it is quite possible that genes can be devalued by being turned into property, even though we often value objects we buy and sell quite highly.

It would be a mistake, therefore, to suppose that objections to the commercialisation of genes must imply a lofty disdain for commercial objects or society; or some particular animus against the modern world. Instead, those who object to the commercialisation of genes may simply wish to draw a line between commercial and non-commercial values in one place rather than another, not because commerce itself threatens human dignity, but because the commercialisation of human *genes* would do so. Indeed Munzer claims that 'it could offend human dignity to sell or license for cloning genes that relate to, say, the shape of one's face, key features of one's temperament, or salient aspects of one's intelligence', although he wants to leave open the possibility that some human gene patents might be ethically justified.[32]

Ossorio supposes that such are views absurd, because she can see no reason why we should be diminished 'if one person can make, use, or sell copies of another's extracorporeal, non-particularized body parts' (p. 414) However, the morality of copying human genes – with or without a patent – is likely to depend in part on what is done with the copies. Were genes used to make a new type of toy, for instance, or a new type of food, even Ossorio might feel less sanguine about copying human body parts.[33] It is true that people do not always pay much attention to the fate of their discarded body parts – be it hair, nails or organs. But that does not prevent them from being shocked or perturbed by the results of their carelessness.[34] Such reactions may be irrational. But before reaching such a conclusion, it seems desirable to investigate further how the commercialisation of cloned genes might threaten respect for the human body, for human attributes or for human feelings.

In short, I do not believe that one needs to draw untenable lines between nature and nurture, genes and environment, individual and society or one species and another to believe that patenting human genes is immoral. Though one may have to make some controversial assumptions or reach some controversial conclusions if one believes that human gene patents are intrinsically immoral, neither the assumptions nor the conclusions need be unreasonable, even if they are not the only reasonable ones that one might reach. So, while some ethical objections to the patenting of human genes collapse when confronted with legal facts, I do not see that they all must do so.

The justification for patenting

Indeed, it is not clear that objections to patenting, however interpreted, must be any less reasonable or any more speculative, controversial and sectarian than justifications for these particular patents, or for a patenting system in general. Once one considers that most justifications for patents on human genes depend heavily on the thought that patenting in general is justified, it becomes clear how speculative, controversial and morally problematic are most arguments for these particular patents.[35]

The justification for a system of patent rights reflects two different considerations. On the one hand, there is the thought that patents are a solution to the problem of motivating people to invest their time, energy and money in the creation and development of socially useful knowledge and products. On the other, there is the thought that patents are a solution to the problem of rewarding people who successfully contribute to the public good, given that all of us have incentives to try to enjoy these benefits without acknowledging and rewarding those who made them. Neither reason by itself singles out patents as opposed to other ways of rewarding and motivating people.[36] Taken together, however, patents appear to have attractive features that other ways of motivating and rewarding people lack. For example, patents ensure the publication of useful knowledge, and not merely its creation. They establish rules that are relatively automatic and capable of being fairly applied to the problem of deciding what counts as knowledge deserving of recognition and reward. They tailor the size and costs of rewards to inventors based on the preferences, beliefs and interests of people in the invention, and so on. In short, patents seem to combine concerns for efficiency, reciprocity, freedom and equality in an attractive way.

But appearances are, to some extent, deceptive here, as in other matters. Like other private property rights, it is unclear that patent rights actually reward merit, and they certainly do not seem to reward effort *per se*.[37] The relationship between benefit and reward created by patent rights may be very loose, as is the relationship to the common good or public interest.[38] Once we recognise this, it is hard to know how well patents motivate the creation or publication of knowledge that otherwise would not be produced or publicised. And it is very hard to know how far the legal, economic and political benefits conferred by patent rights tailor reward to merit or proportion it to benefits conferred. In short, the justification for a system of patent rights rests largely on speculation about human motivations, needs and interests.

There is a further difficulty with patents, as compared to other ways of rewarding and motivating people, which moral objections to human gene patents highlight, even though they rarely raise them explicitly.[39] If patents look democratic when compared to the granting of titles of nobility, to inheritable personal powers to tax, and so on, they do not look especially democratic when contrasted with tax breaks, election to public office or to public honours.[40] If, from a democratic perspective, patenting is attractive because it involves specifying public criteria for rights, and then providing a relatively automatic procedure through which people can determine whether they are entitled to those rights, it also has considerable disadvantages. For the public may have no idea about the significance of the inventions that provide the claim to a patent or about the adequacy of the criteria used to confer these rights.[41] This casts doubt on the idea that the benefits created by patentable inventions are sufficiently general or public to merit special reward. It also means that very significant changes in people's rights, expectations and beliefs may occur without ever being publicly acknowledged, discussed or chosen. In a democracy, this should cause some concern.

Legislators can pay attention to the sorts of things are being patented and why.[42] Moreover, in any system that gives private individuals the power to alter their legal relationship to each other, as will bodies of private law, many changes in people's rights, powers and expectations, for good and bad, are likely to occur without public knowledge, representation and control. Still, the moral objections to patenting point to the need to think more carefully about the place, content and justification of a patenting system in a democratic society, and in particular, its implications for democratic forms of accountability, choice and participation. For some of the bitterness, mutual distrust and incomprehension evidenced by debates on genetic patenting reflects the lack of open public debate on the issue, and the assumption that ordinary people have little knowledge about or control over legal rights, public policies and scientific developments that may fundamentally affect their lives.[43]

Thus, proponents of patenting suppose that the public is unlikely to know even quite basic and straightforward facts about patent rights, such as their justification, the sorts of things to which they apply or the way that they differ from other rights. Likewise, critics of patenting, especially in the US, clearly suppose that most people do not know that plants, animals and human genes can all be patented. This contrasts with the situation in Europe where efforts by groups like the Greens and Greenpeace to publicise these issues mean that people have been subjected to questionnaires, as well as a great deal of publicity about recent developments in the law and biotechnology. Yet it is evident that in the US, too, there is a public interest in, and demand to know more about, recent advances in biotechnology and their legal, scientific, moral and political implications for people's lives. Thus, one can find articles about genetic testing and its moral and medical implications in local, as well as national, newspapers; public interest in, and public sources of information on, the science of the genome project, as well as more sensational developments like the cloning of sheep. By contrast, it is rare to find discussions of the ethics or the economics of patenting human genes outside relatively specialised and obscure journals and book presses.

Of course, given what one might consider to be the disastrous consequences of the politicisation of abortion in the US, it would be foolish to assume that democratic discussion of patents on human genes – whatever that might mean or involve – would preclude confusion, mutual suspicion or promote the speedy and principled resolution of complex questions of ethics and public policy. But it would, at least, give people the chance to learn about, and to participate in, decisions that can fundamentally shape their life prospects and those of future generations, even if it failed to promote other desirable things.

If, as seems likely, the patenting system has made such discussion and decision-making significantly less likely, despite considerable public interest in biotechnology and its consequences, there is reason to incorporate concerns for democratic participation and accountability into one's evaluation of human gene patents. This is partly because concerns about the justification for patents in general can quite properly affect our judgement about the merits of any particular patent. More fundamentally, though, it is likely that ethical objections to patenting human genes reflect doubts about the democratic credentials of the motivations, procedures and criteria that have led to this development.

Conclusion

Ethical disputes about human gene patents are not over the meanings of words alone, but over the justification of public policies and legally binding rights, powers and obligations. They require us to consider not only the justification of past practices and institutions, and of present actions and decisions, but of the terms on which, in future, people will have access to the knowledge, powers and liberties that they need to live and flourish. What those terms will be is still largely open to influence from a variety of quarters, but probably not for long. As we have seen, remarkably little is settled legally, morally and politically by treating human genes as legally patentable. However, what is possible conceptually can become practically unthinkable. This chapter highlights the costs of such a transformation for moral and political judgment.

Acknowledgement

* I would like to thank the Program in Ethics and the Professions, Harvard's Kennedy School of Government, for a Senior Fellowship which enabled me to do the research for this chapter, and especially to Dennis Thompson and Arthur Applbaum. Thanks also to Tanya Aplin, Julian Cockbain, Graham Dutfield, Jan Mertens, Axel Gosseries and Alain Strowel for their help in updating and revising this chapter. I am also grateful to Jason Borenstein, editor of the *Journal of Philosophy, Science and Law*, who published the original version in the inaugural issue of *PSL*, and has allowed the revised version to be published here.

Notes

1. For a useful discussion of the patent system, including the differences between US and European patent law, see The Nuffield Council on Bioethics (2002), ch. 2) available at www.nuffieldbioethics.org.
2. For the main critical positions, see Annas (1998 pp. 21–2); Rifkin (1998, ch. 2); and Meister et al. (1997 pp. 185–201). The volume is based on

the proceedings of the International Workshop on Biotechnology, Patents and Morality: Towards a Consensus, Department of Philosophy and Moral Science and the Centre for Environmental Philosophy and Bio-Ethics, University of Ghent, January 1996. It consists in a series of relatively short presentations by legal experts, representatives of various environmental groups, and so on, and provides a helpful introduction and concluding summary of the proceedings and debate.

3. Ossorio (2002 pp. 408–19). Ossorio was the director for the genetics section of the American Medical Association's Institute for Ethics when she wrote this article.
4. It is hard to find a published source for this belief, but it occurs frequently enough in general discussions about patenting to merit attention (see Crespi, 1997, pp. 219–23 and especially p. 225; also Ossorio, 2002, p. 411). However, Jeremy Rifkin claims that 'genetically altered human embryos and fetuses as well as human genes, cell lines, tissues, and organs are potentially patentable, leaving open the possibility of patenting all of the separate parts, if not the whole, of a human being' (1998, pp. 44–5).
5. See Schatz (1997, pp. 159–60, and, more generally, pp. 160–6). Shatz is the former principal director, International Affairs, EPO, Munich. Just to prove his point, the onco-mouse was originally refused a patent by the EPO, but this was reversed in 1992. 'In the overall balance the Examining Division concludes that the present invention cannot be considered immoral', the EPO maintained (Munzer, 2002, p. 447). Munzer makes plain his disagreement with the EPO's conclusion at p. 452.
6. Ossorio (2002, p. 412)
7. Ibid.
8. *Diamond v. Chakrabarty*, 447 US (1980). For a more sceptical view of this decision, see Sagoff (2002 pp. 420–37, especially pp. 434–6).
9. *Parke-Davis and Co. v. H. K. Mulford and Co.*, 189 F. 95 (SDNY 1911), affd 196 F. 496 (Second Cir. 1912), p.102. Quoted in Ossorio (2002, p. 413).
10. Ossorio (2002, p. 411).
11. Ibid., p. 409. See also Heller and Eisenberg (1998, p. 5364; www.Sciencemag.org). This is a response to Doll (1998). Doll maintains that 'A strong US patent system is critical for the continued development and dissemination to the public of information on DNA sequence elements', and that 'It is only with the patenting of DNA technology that some companies, particularly small ones, can raise sufficient venture capital to bring beneficial products to the marketplace or fund further research'.
12. For such concerns, see Dronamraju (1998, especially chs. 13 and 15); and McNally and Wheale (1998, ch. 18). For a sceptical view, see Crespi (1997, pp. 229–35).
13. However, as Shulman notes, 'Compulsory licensing is anathema to many participants in the US patent system' (1995, p. 7; available at www.usis.usemb.se/sft).
14. See Ossorio (2002, p. 418). The Nuffield Council's discussion paper notes that 'in the case of patents that have been granted for diagnostic tests based on genes, compulsory licensing may be required to ensure reasonable licensing terms are available to enable alternative tests to be developed' (Executive Summary, p. xi; and ch. 5, sections 5.25–29, pp. 54–6).

15. As Ossorio says, 'patents are intended to encourage not just the pursuit of knowledge, but the practical application of that knowledge in marketable form' (2002, p. 416).
16. Van Overwalle (1997, pp. 139–48). The quotation comes from p.139.
17. Hence the significance of the denial of any positive rights by the EPO in the case of the onco-mouse. See Munzer (2002, p. 447), who notes that the EPO stressed that all it was granting was the right to exclude others, rather than a 'positive right to use the invention'.
18. Nuffield Council on Bioethics (ch. 5.12–13, p. 50).
19. The Nuffield Council discussion paper notes that 'one study in the US indicates that research on genetic testing has been inhibited by patents on DNA sequences: almost half of the research laboratories which were surveyed have ceased to pursue such research because of existing patents. Another US study found that as many as 30% of laboratories have discontinued or not developed genetic testing for haemochromatosis because of exclusive licensing of patents' (ch. 5.15, pp. 50–1). Dutfield and Suthersanen report David Porteous' complaint that patent-related legal problems have affected the ability of scientists in Scotland to conduct gene-based diagnostic tests for breast cancer, 'despite the fact that geneticists do not even need to read Myriad's patent specifications since all the knowledge required to conduct the test is already in the public domain' (2005, p. 15). David Porteous is head of Medical Genetics, Edinburgh University. The article discusses the worry that companies are increasingly turning to copyright and trade secrets as ways to protect their investments, *in addition to* using patents.
20. For example, Ossorio notes that critics of patenting 'must engage the question of why people who actually generate…knowledge do not deserve some compensation for their efforts and contribution; [and why] having a common interest in the genome does not necessarily mean that we can appropriate the fruit of other people's labor' (2002, p. 418).
21. For a helpful discussion, see Kymlicka (1990, especially ch. 4).
22. For the difficulties involved and, therefore, the significance of patent rights as opposed to trade secrets, see Munzer (2002, p. 439). Importantly, patents are 'usually a more robust set of property rights than a trade secret, for the patentee can exclude others from making or selling the patent invention or discovery, even if these others arrived at the invention or discovery independently'. In the US, apparently, there is no federal provision for protecting trade secrets, so this is a matter for state law. See also Dutfield and Suthersanen (2005, pp. 16–19).
23. In fact, Dutfield and Suthersanen (2005, p. 13) remark that patents have become 'a form of currency in inter-firm transactions', and quote Fowler's observation that 'For many companies, the patent becomes the product', with the result that research decisions in many companies now depend on the advice of patent lawyers at least as much, and possibly more than, the opinions of scientists (1994, p. 173).
24. Warren (2002, pp. 147– 7, especially p. 152).
25. Munzer (2002, p. 452). He concludes: 'There should be a limited public-interest exception to patent suppression. Very few expressed sequence tags should be patentable; for most ESTs a weaker form of intellectual property rights is in order. Some genetically engineered bacteria and plants should be

patentable...The suffering of genetically engineered mice should cast doubt on their patentability under the European Patent Convention...'. Munzer does not suppose that all human gene patents are unjustified; but it is clear that, even so, he supposes that there is a variety of ethical distinctions that need to be made. There is no reason to suppose that these are any more difficult to make if one believes that human gene patents are never justified than if one allows that some are.

26. See *Loving v. Virginia*, 388 US 1 (1967), in which the Supreme Court finally struck down anti-miscegenation laws.
27. Wilkie (1998, p. 12).
28. Apparently, 'even the "gene" is beginning to look like a rather fuzzy concept' as a result of recent advances in molecular biology, according to Dutfield and Suthersanen (2005, p. 11). 'The sheer complexity, subtlety and context-dependence of DNA....cast[s] a sceptical light on the view that genes should be treated as a text in four letters containing instructional information'. Instead, genetic messages, apparently, seem more like poetry, in their complexity and ambiguity than like instruction manuals (ibid., p. 10). Dutfield and Suthersanen even quote a Swedish scientist who is reported to have said, 'we tend not to talk about "genes" anymore; we just refer to any segment that is transcribed [to RNA] as a "transcriptional unit"' (ibid., p. 11). This suggests that references to genes might better be replaced with 'genetic materials', in order to catch the increasing ambiguity of the concept.
29. Mertens (in Sterckx, 1997, p. 190) implies that this is, indeed, the case for the Greens; and Meister implies that it is also true for Greenpeace (ibid., p. 185). Hence I do not see the clear differences that Ossorio does amongst ownership, human dignity and commodification objections to human gene patenting, even though it can be helpful to distinguish them.
30. See, for example, Dworkin (2002, especially ch. 6).Consequently, I think Warren overstates the objections to what she calls 'the Sanctification of Genes' (2002, pp. 153–5).
31. Ossorio (2002, p. 415).
32. Munzer (2002, pp. 49–50).
33. Ibid., pp. 49–50. In fact, Ventria Bioscience, an American company, is conducting field trials of rice that has been combined with human genes to make it produce beneficial human proteins, including lactoferrin, which is found in human breast milk. The hope is that these antibacterial proteins will help treat children with diarrhoea, which is a major cause of infant death in the developing world. But imagine that the point was simply to make food visually more appealing, or cheaper, rather than to produce medicine as inexpensively and safely as possible. See Adam (2007 pp. 6–9, section G2).
34. For an example of the problem, see *Moore v. Regents of the University of California* (793 P.2d 479 9cal.1990), concerning the fate of John Moore's spleen.
35. See Ossorio (2002, p. 409): 'An underlying assumption of the patent system is that other, non-market incentives will not lead to as good or as much development of new and useful knowledge and products' and 'The assumption is that without patents the biotechnology industry could not compete effectively for private capital against other industries, such as the computer industry'. Neither of these assumptions, of course, is self-evidently correct.

Moreover, as Ossorio notes, while 'patent law can be described as serving a positivist, functionalist strategy: we choose the rule governing patentability to accomplish the goal of getting new and useful knowledge disseminated, and the rules are justified according to whether or not they accomplish this goal.' Her conclusion is that 'In practice, this is an empirical determination which is quite difficult to make with any confidence' (ibid., p. 408).

36. Hence, Resnik is wrong to suppose that a purely utilitarian justification of patents is possible, even if we suppose that such a justification would operate against a background of moral and legal rights precluding such things as theft and forced labour. See Resnik, 1997, p. 4, online).
37. Concerning effort, see Ossorio (2002, p.408), and Resnik (1997, p. 4): 'the law seems to reward results, not contributions and efforts'.
38. See Ossorio (2002, p. 409) concerning what may be a substantial difference between the socially optimal rate of invention and the maximal rate of invention.
39. Exceptions are Mertens (1997, pp. 189–90), Van Overwalle (1997 p. 147) and Emmott, (1997, pp. 192 and 194).
40. Grants are understood as an alternative to patents, not as an addition to them. Hence, they do not raise the concerns about 'double-dipping' usefully described by Ossorio (2002, p. 409).
41. Shulman (1995, p. 2) notes of the USPTO that 'despite its size, age and pedigree, the agency must surely rank as one of the least-known agencies of the US government', he also expresses doubts about the ability of the USPTO to interpret its criteria for awarding patents, and gives the example of the patenting of Kirchoff's law, first expounded in 1845.
42. Resnik (1997, p. 1)notes that 'In 1996 the US Congress considered a measure, the Ganske-Wyden Bill (Hr1137) that would have prevented the PTO from awarding patents that do not involve a new machine or compound'. This, so it seems, would have met some of the concerns about patents raised by Gleick (2000, pp. 44–9). However, this would have no obvious effect on the 'capture' of the PTO by companies pursuing patents, on which the PTO frequently depends both for expertise and for revenues. Gleick notes: 'In 1991, the patent office was cut off from general tax revenues and required to subsist entirely on fees from its operating budget. The political argument was that customers should pay for government services. Thus, officials think of their fee-paying applicants as their customers: *the more the better*' (ibid., p. 41; emphasis in the original). Gleick says, 'It is virtually forgotten that government's customers also include the rest of the nation, the citizenry at large, whose fortunes depend on the agency's judgments and policies'.
43. Martens (1997, pp. 198–90).

References

Annas, G. J. (1998) Life Forms, the Law and Profits, The Hastings Center Report.

Crespi, S. (1997) The Morality of Patenting, in S. Sterckx (ed.) *Biotechnology, Patents and Morality*. Aldershot: Ashgate, pp. 219–23.

Doll, J. (1998) The Patenting of DNA, *Science*: 280.
Dronamaraju, K. R. (1998) *Biological and Social Issues in Biotechnology Sharing*. Aldershot: Ashgate.
Dutfield, G.and Suthersanen, U. (2005) DNA Music: Intellectual Property and the Law of Unintended Consequences, *Science Studies*, 18(1): 5–29.
Dworkin, R. (2002) *Sovereign Virtue*. Cambridge, MA: Harvard University Press.
Fowler, C. (1994) *Unnatural Selection: Technology, Politics and Plant Evolution*. Yverdon: Gordon and Breach.
Heller, M. A. and Eisenberg, R. S. (1998) Can Patents Deter Innovation? The Anticommons in Biomedical Research, *Science*: 280.
Kymlicka, W. (1990) *Contemporary Political Philosophy: An Introduction*. Oxford: Clarendon Press.
McNally R. andWheale P. (1998) The Consequences of Modern Genetic Engineering: Patents, 'Nomads' and the 'Bio-Industrial Compex', in Wheale, von Schomberg and Glasner (eds.) *The Social Management of Genetic Engineering*. Aldershot; Ashgate, ch. 18.
Meister, I., Mertens, J., Emmot, S. and Alexander,. (1997) The Case for and against the Patenting of Biotchnological Inventions', in S. Sterckx (ed.) *Biotechnology, Patents and Morality*. Aldershot: Ashgate, pp. 185–201.
Munzer, S. R. (2002) in J. Burley and J. Harris (eds) *A Companion to Genethics: Philosophy and the Genetic Revolution*. (Oxford: Blackwell, pp. 438–54.
Ossorio, P. (2002) Legal and Ethical Issues in Patenting Human DNA, in J. Burley and J. Harris (eds.) *A Companion to Genethics: Philosophy and the Genetic Revolution*. Oxford: Blackwell, pp. 408–19.
Resnick, D. (1997) The Morality of Human Gene Patents, *Kennedy Institute of Ethics Journal*, 7(1).
Rifkin, J. (1998) *The Biotech Century: Harnessing the Gene and Remaking the World*. New York: Putnam, ch. 2.
Sagoff, M. ((2002) Are Genes Inventions? in J. Burley and J. Harris (eds.) *A Companion to Genethics: Philosophy and the Genetic Revolution*. Oxford: Blackwell, pp. 420–37.
Schatz, U. (1997) Patents and Morality, in S. Sterckx (ed.) *Biotechnology, Patents and Morality*. Aldershot: Ashgate, pp. 160–6.
Shulman, S. (1995) Patent Medicine, *Technology Review*:.7
Van Overwalle, G. (1997) Biotechnology Patents in Europe: From Law to Ethics, in S. Sterckx (ed.) *Biotechnology, Patents and Morality*. Aldershot: Ashgate, pp. 139–48.
Warren, M. A. (2002) The Moral Status of the Gene, in J. Burley and J. Harris (eds.) *A Companion to Genethics: Philosophy and the Genetic Revolution*. Oxford: Blackwell.

Legal cases

Diamond v. Chakrabaty, 447 US (1980)
Loving v. Virginia, 338 US (1967)
Moore v. Regents of the University of California, 793 P.2.d 479 9Cal. (1990)
Parke-Davis and Co. v. H. K. Mulford and Co., 189 f. 95 (SDNY 1911)

Discussion papers

The Nuffield Council of Bioethics (2002) *The Ethics of Patenting DNA: A Discussion Paper*, www.nuffieldbioethics.org.

Newpapers and magazines

Adam, D. (2007) Down by the Pharm, *The Guardian*, 30 April section G2, pp. 6–9.

Glecik, J. (2002) Patently Absurd, *The New York Times Magazine*, 12 March, section 6, pp. 44–9.

Wilkie, T. (1998) The Lords of Creation, *Prospect Magazine*, July, 32, p. 12.

Index